READING TECHNICAL BOOKS

ANNE EISENBERG

New York City Community College

READING TECHNICAL BOOKS

HOW TO GET THE MOST
OUT OF YOUR READINGS IN

General physics and chemistry

Automotive, electrical,
and mechanical technology

Civil and
construction technology

Metallurgy

Industrial arts

Data processing

Technical courses

Engineering technology courses

PRENTICE-HALL, INC.,
ENGLEWOOD CLIFFS, NEW JERSEY 07632

Library of Congress Cataloging in Publication Data

Eisenberg, Anne (date)
    Reading technical books.

    Bibliography: p.
    1. Technology—Study and teaching.
2. Technical literature.   3. Reading comprehension.   I.   Title.
T65.3.E37   607'.36   78-672
ISBN 0-13-762138-8

Printed in the United States of America

10   9   8

PRENTICE-HALL INTERNATIONAL, INC., *London*
PRENTICE-HALL OF AUSTRALIA PTY. LIMITED, *Sydney*
PRENTICE-HALL OF CANADA, LTD., *Toronto*
PRENTICE HALL OF INDIA PRIVATE LIMITED, *New Delhi*
PRENTICE-HALL OF JAPAN, INC., *Tokyo*
PRENTICE HALL OF SOUTHEAST ASIA PTE. LTD., *Singapore*
WHITEHALL BOOKS LIMITED, *Wellington, New Zealand*

CONTENTS

**II
USING A TECHNICAL BOOK**

INTRODUCTION

Books in technical fields are difficult to read.

1. There is a whole new vocabulary
2. Familiar, everyday words have entirely different, technical meanings.
3. The reader has to switch from words to equations and back again.
4. The illustrations are often highly specialized.
5. Most of all, technical books are "saturated" with ideas. Technical and scientific writing is dense, presenting one idea after another, relieved only by a few everyday examples.

This book is concerned with these special features of technical books that make them difficult to read. The content is drawn from technical courses, introductory science courses, and engineering technology courses. All the examples include fundamental ideas in physics and chemistry, which are basic to applications in electrical, electromechanical, mechanical, automotive, civil, construction, materials, and industrial arts technology as well as many other technical fields.

The book starts with the basic ingredient in technical books—definitions of terms—and builds from there. It shows you how to use examples, classification, contrast, cause-effect diagraming, block diagrams, charts, graphs, line drawings, and tables to understand and remember technical information. It gives a method for underlining and taking notes on your textbooks. Toward the end it offers extra information on vocabulary development, taking notes on technical lectures, and general study techniques. It is a step-by-step program that you can do by yourself, or in a classroom.

The book builds chapter by chapter a pair of basic skills: how to shake all the information you will need out of a technical textbook and how to organize it so you'll remember it—during exams and during your career. For this purpose it provides a system for improving your reading in technical subjects.

Each chapter has the same pattern of organization. An introduction explains the reading technique covered in that chapter. Then there are practice exercises, the first of which are short and the succeeding ones become longer. The last exercises in each chapter are taken from actual textbooks. They give you a chance to apply what you are learning in a "real-life" situation.

This book is designed mainly for students in community and junior college technical and industrial programs and for students entering beginning science courses; it should also be useful for students in technical institutes, for high school students in vocational technology and career education programs who want to sharpen their reading abilities, and for those in general career training programs in which efficient, accurate reading is a goal.

Before you begin this book—or any book—look it over; explore its resources. When most people read a book, they open it to page 1, read the page, turn to page 2, read that, and repeat the process until it's time to stop. Instead, spend a few minutes on the table of contents. It will give you an idea of where you're going and how you're going to get there. Leaf through the chapters, getting a general notion of their contents. Look for appendixes or a glossary of terms in the back.

If you take these preliminary steps in reading the book you're now holding, you'll discover that Chapters 1–6 provide the basics of technical reading, Chapters 7–10 show how to apply the basics in taking study notes, and Chapters 11–12 give ways to develop vocabulary and general skills on your own.

The author would like to thank Mina Shaughnessy and the staff of the Instructional Resource Center of City University of New York for their support and encouragement; Dr. John K. Hawes, coordinator of the Reading Unit at New York City Community College, for his attentiveness during the time this book was written and tested; Dr. Josephine Piekarz Ives of the graduate reading program at New York University for her encouragement; and Gary Benenson, physicist and electrical engineer, for going through the text for appropriateness of science content.

I

BASICS OF TECHNICAL READING

1

DEFINITIONS OF TERMS

Definitions of terms are the building blocks of all technical writing. They are basic. If you don't understand the terms, you won't be able to understand the theories based on them. It would be like trying to put up a building on top of a sand dune. Without a foundation—a clear and precise understanding of the technical terminology used by an author— you won't really understand technical information.

The use of language in science is special and particular. Each term has a very *precise* meaning. This is entirely different from the way language is used in everyday life.

For instance, you might describe someone you know as "nice." But what do you mean when you use this word? Your definition of "nice" is probably not the same as the next person's. Each person means something slightly different when using this term. In contrast, the word "elasticity" has a technical meaning which does not change from person to person—or even from language to language. Elasticity is *the ability of a solid to regain its shape after a deforming force has been applied*—and it means this whether you are in Brooklyn or Boston, in France or the United States.

In your scientific and technical books and manuals, each term will have a definition that is as fixed as though it were engraved on a piece of stone. Even ordinary words like "fundamental" and "specific," which come up constantly in the laboratory and in texts, are not used in the ordinary sense. They have highly precise meanings, agreed upon by scientists and rigidly adhered to.

HOW TO DEAL WITH TECHNICAL TERMS

There are three kinds of terms that are particularly important:

1. *Terms that have entirely different meanings than they do in everyday life.* Words such as "work," "power," and "force" have entirely new meanings when they are used in their scientific or technical sense. For instance, you probably think you've done some work if you sit down and study for an examination. But although you may sit and study for hours, unless you exert force through a distance, a physicist would say you hadn't done any work at all. In a physics book, work is defined as *the effect that is accomplished when a force is exerted upon some object and moves it a certain distance.* Work has nothing to do with sitting in a chair and reading a book!

2. *Terms that are used with more precision than they are in everyday life.* Words like "fundamental," "specific," and "modulus" are terms with extremely precise definitions. You may have heard of spelling demons— words that are often misspelled. To be a good reader of scientific and technical English, you'll have to be aware of "meaning demons"— words that demand due respect for their exact meanings. Here is a list of some of these terms.

Meaning demons

absolute	fundamental	rate
conservation of energy	intensity	relative
critical	inversely	specific
derive	modulus	spontaneous
dissolve	phenomenon	uniform
empirical	physical principle	

3. *Terms that are frequently confused.* Do you know the difference between mass and weight? energy and force? force and pressure? These terms are often interchanged in everyday usage. However, when they are used technically, their meanings are entirely different. There are many such terms in scientific and technical writing.

Sometimes students are in such a hurry to do the homework problems in their science books that they never actually give the book a careful reading. Instead, they skim the text quickly, turn to the problems, and then flip back to the text only when they need to find the equation that solves the problem. Don't be this kind of reader! If you use a textbook only to solve the problems, you will never learn what the book is about, and you probably won't even solve many of the problems correctly.

The text is the mainstay of any course. Learn the terms in the text and you'll be on your way to learning the theories that are built from the terms.

This chapter will explain many ways to identify terms and then give exercises and problems for practice in using definitions to understand and remember technical information.

IDENTIFYING DEFINITIONS

Usually the author will define each new term as it is introduced.

EXAMPLE   This chapter is concerned with *matter*. Matter is defined as *anything that occupies space and has weight.*

Term   **Definition**

Matter   That which occupies space and has weight

Usually the term will be stated first; then the definition will be given. Sometimes, however, the definition comes before the term.

EXAMPLE   Another general property of matter is that it occupies space. This is referred to as volume.

Term   **Definition**

Volume   Property of occupying space

A definition may be signaled by such words as "is defined as," "means," or "refers to."

EXAMPLES   Weight *is defined as* the force of earth's gravity on an object. By weight we *mean* the force of earth's gravity on an object. Inertia *refers to* the property of matter that resists any change in its motion.

A definition may simply be a phrase set off by commas.

EXAMPLE   Matter has certain general properties: mass, the quantity of matter; volume, the amount of space occupied by matter; weight, the force of the earth's gravity on matter; and inertia, the tendency of matter at rest to remain at rest, and matter in motion to remain in motion, unless acted upon by an external force.

Terms   **Definitions**

Mass   Quantity of matter
Volume   Amount of space occupied by matter
Weight   Force of earth's gravity on matter
Inertia   Tendency of matter at rest to remain at rest, and of matter in motion to remain in motion, unless acted upon by an external force

An author may give a list of characteristics to serve as a definition. Here are some examples where terms are defined by listing their characteristics.

EXAMPLES   A solid has a definite volume and a definite shape.

A liquid has a definite volume but not a definite shape; instead, it takes on the shape of the container.

A gas has neither a definite volume nor a definite shape.

Terms	Definitions
Solid	Something having definite volume and definite shape
Liquid	Something having definite volume but no definite shape
Gas	Something having no definite volume and no definite shape

EXAMPLE   What is a solid? A solid has a definite volume and a definite shape. It resists any force trying to deform its shape. Solids have many properties, such as tenacity, ductility, and malleability.

Term	Definition
Solid	Something that has definite volume and definite shape, resists deforming force, and has properties of tenacity, ductility, and malleability

DEFINITION VS. EXAMPLE

A definition is not the same as an example. Here is a paragraph giving the definitions we have discussed. After each definition there are examples.

EXAMPLE   A solid has a definite volume and a definite shape. Glass, bricks, and ice are solids. A liquid has a definite volume but not a definite shape. Water is a liquid. A gas has neither a definite volume nor a definite shape. Air and steam are gases.

Terms	Definitions	Examples
Solid	Something having a definite volume, definite shape	Glass, bricks, ice
Liquid	Something having a definite volume, no definite shape	Water
Gas	Something having no definite volume, no definite shape	Air, steam

Often a definition will be accompanied by both examples and other kinds of information.

EXAMPLE   A solid has a definite volume and a definite shape. Ice is an example of a solid. The word "solid" is derived from the Greek *holos*, meaning *entire*. A liquid has a definite volume but not a definite shape. Water is an example of a liquid. The word "liquid" is derived from the Latin *liquere*, meaning *fluid*.

Terms	Definitions	Examples	Other general information
Solid	Something having a definite volume, definite shape	ice	Derived from *holos,* entire
Liquid	Something having a definite volume, no definite shape	water	Derived from *liquere,* fluid

LOOKING AHEAD The exercises that follow will sharpen your ability to identify and remember definitions. The exercises start short, and gradually lengthen out. Excerpts from technical textbooks are at the end of the chapter.

Refer back to these pages as you do the exercises.

By the time you finish the chapter you should be able to do the following things:

1. Distinguish between definitions and statements that are not definitions.
2. Locate definitions of terms in longer selections, underline them, and use the information to answer questions.
3. Note how entire chapters may be based on definitions of terms.
4. Use your ability to identify terms to help remember textbook information.

SUMMARY

1. In technical books, one of the author's main concerns is to define new terms.
2. Read for definitions: identify them, underline them, and pause to think about their meaning. This will help you recall information long after you have finished reading it.
3. Definitions vary in length. A term may be defined in a single phrase set off by commas, or it may be defined by a long list of characteristics written out in several paragraphs.

EXERCISE 1.1

DIRECTIONS Each of the following lists has three sentences. Only one of these sentences is a definition of a term. Underline the one sentence in each group that defines a term.

1a. Water is a liquid.
  b. A liquid is a fluid that has a definite volume but not a definite shape.
  c. The word liquid is derived from a Latin word meaning "to flow."
2a. Air is a gas.
  b. A gas is a fluid that has neither a definite volume nor a definite shape.
  c. Liquids and gases have different properties.

3a. A solid is an object with a definite volume and a definite shape.
  b. A grain of salt is an example of a solid.
  c. Liquids, solids, and gases vary in their properties.
4a. Moving water possesses kinetic energy.
  b. Kinetic energy and potential energy are different terms.
  c. Kinetic energy is the energy that moving bodies possess.

EXERCISE 1.2

DIRECTIONS   In each of the following paragraphs a term is defined. Read
the paragraphs and answer the questions that follow.

What is matter? Scientists have defined matter as anything that occupies
space and has weight. Bricks are an example of matter. Water is an
example of matter. Air, too, is an example of matter, because it occupies
space and has weight.

1. The term that the author is defining in this paragraph is
   (a) water
   (b) bricks
   (c) matter
   (d) air
2. Underline the entire definition used in the above paragraph.

But how shall we define energy? The water pouring down from a waterfall has the energy to turn the blades of a waterwheel. The lumberjack
wielding his ax is using energy. The wind that lifts a kite has energy.
There is a common definition of energy that is useful here: energy is
the ability to do work.

3. The term that the author is defining in this paragraph is
   (a) the operation of a waterwheel
   (b) the operation of a waterfall
   (c) energy
   (d) the uses of an ax
4. Underline the definition given in the paragraph.
5. Write out the definition given in the paragraph.

EXERCISE 1.3

DIRECTIONS   After each of the following items are three choices. Only one
choice is a definition. Underline the correct choice so that the
completed sentence is a definition of a term.

1. **Matter**
   a. is of fundamental importance in the composition of the universe.
   b. and energy are the two fundamental factors in the composition of the universe.
   c. is anything that occupies space and has weight.

2. **Pressure**
   a. is force per unit area.
   b. is exerted by all liquids on the containers that hold them.
   c. is exerted differently in gases than in liquids.

3. **Cohesion**
   a. is greater in solids than in liquids.
   b. is different from adhesion.
   c. refers to the force of attraction between molecules.

4. **Kinetic energy**
   a. may be converted from potential energy.
   b. is clearly demonstrated when the blades of a waterwheel are turned by a waterfall.
   c. is the energy that an object has because of its motion.

EXERCISE 1.4

DIRECTIONS   (1) Underline the definition of the term; (2) circle the term that is being defined.

EXAMPLE   The mechanics of liquids is called hydrodynamics.

1. In this chapter, we shall begin with the study of linear motion. This is motion along a straight line.

2. The mechanics of liquids is called hydrodynamics; the mechanics of gases is called pneumatics.

3. If a body is placed within a fluid, the fluid exerts an upward force on the body. This upward force is termed buoyancy.

4. One's weight is different on a high mountain than in a low valley. In fact, one weighs slightly less on a mountain top. This is because on the mountain top the force of gravity is less than in the valley, as one is farther from the earth's center. Weight is actually the force with which a body is attracted toward the earth. What would you weigh 20 miles up in space?

5. What is pressure? It is helpful to imagine a large cinderblock with one jagged edge. How would you hold it on your palm? The block weighs the same whether you place your palm under its smooth side or try to balance the block on its tip. The only difference is that one of these two ways might hurt your hand. Why? The force per unit area is very great when the block is placed tip down. The area of the tip, where all the force is exerted, is small. Pressure is force per unit area.

DIRECTIONS   After you read the following passage, underline all definitions of terms. Then answer the questions that follow the passage.

GENERAL PROPERTIES OF SOLIDS

The molecules of solids are close to each other, and they vibrate in a fixed position. There is a strong force of attraction between molecules in a solid. Because of the strong attraction between molecules, solids have certain properties. These properties, which are defined below, are tenacity, hardness, malleability, and ductility.

Tenacity is a measure of a solid's resistance to being pulled apart. Steel has a high tensile strength; concrete has a much lower tensile strength. That is why concrete is reinforced with steel.

Hardness is a measure of a substance's ability to scratch another substance. The diamond is the hardest solid, as a diamond is able to scratch all other substances.

Malleability refers to a solid's ability to be hammered or rolled into thin sheets. Gold is famous for its malleability. Copper, tin, and aluminum are other examples of malleable materials.

Ductility is the ability to be drawn out in the form of wires. Copper and gold, for instance, can be drawn through a die to make wire.

QUESTIONS

1. What are four basic properties of solids? _____
2. Define the terms "hardness," "tenacity," "malleability," and "ductility."

_____

_____

DIRECTIONS   After you read the following passage, underline all definitions of terms. Then answer the questions that follow that passage.

TWO PROPERTIES OF LIQUIDS

If you place a paper clip gently on the surface of water, the paper clip will float. Why does the water support the weight of the paper clip?

In a sense, the surface of water behaves like a stretched membrane. This behavior has to do with the phenomenon of *surface tension*. Surface tension refers to a liquid's ability to resist penetration. It occurs because of the strong cohesiveness of molecules at the liquid's surface. When the paper clip is placed on the water, the surface of the water resists being penetrated by the paper clip.

Viscosity is another property of liquids. If you've ever taken a bottle of ketchup, chocolate syrup, or honey from the refrigerator and tried to pour it, you have noticed that these liquids flow more slowly when cold than when they are at room temperature. Internal resistance to flow is called viscosity. Viscosity depends on both the constitution and the temperature of a liquid.

QUESTIONS

1. Define the term "surface tension." _____

2. Define the term "viscosity." _____

EXERCISE 1.7

DIRECTIONS   After you read each of the following paragraphs, underline all definitions of terms. Then write out the terms, definitions, and examples beneath the paragraphs. (See the introductory text for examples.)

1. Energy is usually defined as the ability to do work. Wind possesses energy. This energy can be used to turn the blades of a windmill.

Term   **Definition**   **Example**

_____   _____

2. Types of energy may be distinguished. Kinetic energy is the energy possessed by moving bodies. Potential energy is energy that is stored and may be released as kinetic energy. For example, water above a dam has potential energy, which is released when the water thunders over the spillway.

Terms   **Definitions**   **Examples**

_____   _____

_____   _____

3. Time is not important in the definition of work. It is fundamental, however, in the definition of power. When you measure how quickly a certain amount of work is done, you are measuring power. Power is the rate of doing work. Another way to say this is that power is work per unit time.

$$\text{Power} = \frac{\text{work}}{\text{time}}$$

Term	Definition
_____	_____

4. The kinetic energy of water flowing over a dam can be used to turn the blades of a turbine. The energy of a machine in motion, such as the energy of the turbine, is referred to as mechanical energy.

Term	Definition	Example
_____	_____	_____

EXERCISE 1.8

DIRECTIONS   Read the following textbook selection. Underline all terms and their definitions. Then write out the terms and definitions below.

PROPERTIES OF SOLIDS

Solids, as previously noted, are composed of molecules. Sometimes these molecules attract each other and sometimes they repel each other. For instance, take a rubber ball and try to pull it apart. You notice that the ball stretches out of shape. However, when you release the pulling force, the ball returns to its original shape. We can see that when molecules are slightly pulled out of position, they attract each other. When they are pressed too close together, they repel each other.

This combination of attraction and repulson is called elasticity. Elasticity is the ability of a solid to regain its shape after a deforming force has been applied. Most solids have the property of elasticity; however, some are only slightly elastic. For example, wood and styrofoam are two solids whose elasticity is small.

Not every elastic object returns to its original shape. If too large a deforming force is applied, it will become permanently deformed. Take a door spring and pull it apart as far as you can. When you let go, it will probably not return to its exact original shape. When a solid is deformed in this way, it is said to have been deformed past its elastic limit. If the deforming force is great enough, the body breaks apart.[1]

Terms	Definitions	Examples
_____	_____	_____
_____	_____	_____

EXERCISE 1.9

DIRECTIONS   Here is a section taken directly from a physics book. This will give you an opportunity to practice your ability to identify terms in a real-life situation. As you read, notice how important the definitions are; they are the skeleton of this chapter. All the other information is supported by these definitions. (1) Underline all terms and definitions as they occur in the text. (2) Answer the questions that follow the exercise.

MECHANICAL ENERGY

A quantity more basic to the understanding of physical phenomena than either force or motion is energy. This quantity is rather difficult to define, but most of us have a concept of what it is. We are aware that our very existence depends upon the energy we receive from the sun. Energy is stored in the food we eat, in the coal, oil, and gas we burn to keep us warm, and in the fuel our motors consume to furnish us with transportation. We harness the wind and waterfalls to run our machines and to generate electrical energy, which we use to light our homes and operate our many electrical appliances. What is this thing called energy, which varies so much but which is so essential to each of us? At first glance, these so-called energies seem to have nothing in common, but on further study we realize that they are all capable of doing work. Hence, we define energy (Gr. *en ergon,* in work) as the ability to do work.

Work   In everyday usage the word work is used to refer to almost any kind of useful activity. In mechanics, it is understood in a more restricted sense. Here it means the effect that is accomplished when a force is exerted upon some object and moves it a certain distance. If there is no motion, no work has been done. A boy who sits down quietly with a book to study, and without moving a muscle continues to read and think, does no work. A less studious boy who goes out with bat and ball, finds playmates, and has a lively game, does work. The first boy may have accomplished a much more useful result. He may have conceived a new and prolific idea that will bring him wealth or fame or benefit mankind, but he has exerted no mechanical force. He has done no work. The other boy has probably accomplished something useful, too, in terms of health and development, but that in itself does not constitute work. The essential difference is that he has exerted forces and overcome mechanical resistances. He has exerted forces upon the bat and the ball and upon his own body, and he has made them move. He has therefore done work.

The amount of work done depends in part upon the magnitude of the force exerted and in part upon the distance the object moves in the direction of the applied force. The amount of work can be found simply by multiplying the force exerted by the distance through which resistance is overcome.

$$\text{Work} = \text{force} \times \text{distance force acts}$$

The amount of work done when a 1-lb force acts through a distance of 1 ft is called 1 ft-lb (foot-pound). . . .

Power   A certain amount of work might be done in a second, in a week, or in a month. How fast the work is done is very important. This is particularly true in this age of automation, when machines are used to run factories, to drive dynamos, to power automobiles, trains, and airplanes, and to do countless other jobs. The value of a machine depends on how much work it can do per hour, or per second. A diesel engine must be able to exert a large force on a long train and move it at a high speed. A large force acting over a relatively large distance each second means that many foot-pounds of work per second are being done. . . . The rate at which work is done is called power.

$$Power = \frac{work}{time}$$

Potential energy   To raise a heavy object off the ground requires work, and the amount done is equal to the product of the weight of the object and the distance it is raised. As a result, the object can do work when it falls back to the ground. While held stationary at a certain height, no mechanical work is being done, but the object definitely possesses the ability to do some work. This ability to do work is called potential energy. A brick resting on the top of a building has stored up energy equal to the work done to carry it up there. The brick may remain on the roof for a year or more, and during that time it will continue to possess the same amount of energy. If a 7-lb brick were carried to the top of a 50-ft building, it would possess 350 ft-lb of energy.

$$Energy = 7 \text{ lb} \times 50 \text{ ft} = 350 \text{ ft-lb}$$

Whenever this brick is allowed to fall to the ground, it will do 350 ft-lb of work upon whatever it strikes, an amount equal to its potential energy. Hence,

$$Potential \text{ } energy = weight \times height = wh$$

. . . Dammed-up water also has the ability to do work. It may flow down a flume and strike a water wheel or a turbine, causing it to rotate. The water wheel or turbine could drive other machinery, perhaps a dynamo. The higher the level of the dammed-up water, the more energy it possesses. The energy due to elevation is called gravitational potential energy.

Instead of an elevated object, we may have a bent spring or a stretched rubber band. Each of these exerts a force of reaction in opposition to the bending or stretching force. If released, both the spring and the rubber will fly back. Each has a capacity for doing work, that is, has energy. In both of these cases this energy may be utilized. The spring, for example, may be that of a clock, which keeps the wheels and hands in motion until the spring is unwound, until the clock has run down. The stretched rubber may be that of a boy's slingshot used to shoot pebbles.

Kinetic energy   An object in motion also possesses the ability to do work on whatever it strikes. We swing a hammer in order to drive a nail into a plank. The heavier the hammer or the faster it moves, the farther it drives the nail into the wood. The energy a moving object possesses is called kinetic energy.

Other forms of energy In addition to those mentioned, there are many other kinds of energy of which most common is heat energy. Steam, diesel, and gasoline engines demonstrate that heat is capable of doing work. The kind of energy stored in coal and other fossil fuels is chemical energy. In a beam of sunlight or radio waves, transmitted by a broadcasting station, is a form of energy called radiant or electromagnetic energy. An electric current, flowing in a wire, possesses electrical energy, for it has the ability to run motors and do work. An atomic reactor gets its energy from a loss in mass during the nuclear reaction; hence, we consider mass to be a form of energy. We will study most of these energies in detail, later.[2]

QUESTIONS

1. Define the term *energy*. _____

2. In the vocabulary of science, words have very specific meanings, which may be completely different from their everyday meanings. Define *work* using a scientific definition, rather than the everyday definition.

   _____

3. *Work* can be defined in words. It can also be defined in the form of an equation. What is the equation used to measure amount of work?

   _____

4. Define the term *power* in words. _____

5. Define the term *potential energy* in words. _____

6. Define the term *kinetic energy* in words. _____

SPRINGBOARD 1

This book is designed to be a springboard into your regular reading.

Try out what you have learned about definitions of terms in the textbooks you are reading now. If you are using a general science, chemistry, or physics book—or any book in a technical area—you can put this skill to work immediately. It will also work for textbooks in the social sciences.

Choose one chapter from your reading this week.

1. Underline all definitions of terms in the chapter.
2. Pause to think about the meaning of each definition.
3. Write each definition down on a 3 × 5 card. Write the *term* on the front. Write the *definition* on the back.

4. Review the terms by saying the definition to yourself. Check the back of each card to see if you're right.

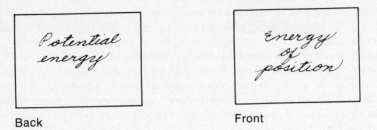

Back   Front

1. Dale Ewen, et al., *Physics for Career Education.* Englewood Cliffs, N.J.: Prentice-Hall, Inc., 1974, p. 185.
2. E. J. Cabel, et al., *The Physical Sciences*, 5th ed. Englewood Cliffs, N.J.: Prentice-Hall, Inc., 1969, pp. 36–40.

2
USE OF EXAMPLES

Examples are important parts of technical books. They are one of the main tools a reader can use to understand the ideas an author is presenting.

For instance, here are two passages on energy. Which gives you a clearer idea of what the terms "energy" and "kinetic energy" mean?

Passage A

Energy refers to the ability to do work. There are many forms of energy: one form is kinetic energy, the energy of motion.

Passage B

The word "energy" is in common use—there are high-energy light bulbs and high-energy breakfast foods. Yet do you know what the word "energy" actually means? *Energy refers to the ability to do work.* The wind, for instance, has energy, because it can do the work of turning a windmill. Falling water also has energy, because it can be used to turn the blades of a water-wheel.

There are many forms of energy. One form is the *energy of motion,* called *kinetic energy.* For example, the falling water that turns the blades of the waterwheel, and the wind that turns the windmill, are both examples of *kinetic energy.*

The second passage gives a clearer idea of the meaning of the terms "energy" and "kinetic energy" because there are examples of both these terms.

The ideas presented in science books are often very complicated, and examples are a mainstay when you are trying to grasp complicated ideas. Unfortunately, there are not that many examples in most technical and scientific books. Authors of scientific books generally place a great value on expressing their ideas briefly. The language of science is known for its economy or briefness of expression. Science books are rarely wordy or "chatty"; their style is trimmed down. This means that one important point may follow another, with very few examples or stories from everyday life to separate successive ideas. Because scientific writing is "saturated" in this way with difficult ideas, the examples the author gives become particularly important to you, the reader.

Many people who are interested in science find that they cannot understand or remember much of their textbooks. Part of this may be because the ideas themselves are new, and sometimes they are hard to grasp. But a lot of the difficulty has to do with the way that science books are written. One way to cope with the "density" of the style is to learn to use the author's examples. They will bring the ideas that they illustrate home to you. When you begin thinking about examples, you may also find that there are examples from the laboratory or from class that are also most useful in illustrating the ideas in the text.

This chapter will explain the purpose of examples, and suggest ways to use them to understand and remember technical information.

IDEAS VS. EXAMPLES

An idea, and an example of an idea, are two different things. For instance, read the following statement:

> Potential energy may be defined as the energy of position. A stretched rubber band has potential energy. Water stored behind a dam has potential energy.

Idea	Examples of idea
Potential energy is the energy of position	Stretched rubber band Water stored in dam

Note the difference between the idea and the examples of the idea. The "stretched rubber band" and the "stored water" are closer to our everyday experience than the more abstract words "energy of position."

The author uses examples to illustrate particular ideas. Authors deliberately use *concrete* examples from our everyday lives—examples such as rubber bands—to make *abstract* ideas clearer. Examples are a bridge from the concrete to the abstract.

Usually the author states the idea and then gives the example.

> A liquid has no shape, but it does possess definite volume. Water is a liquid.

Idea	**Example**
Liquids have definite volume, but not a definite shape	Water

> Matter that has its origin in organisms that were once alive is referred to as organic. Oil, coal, the foods we eat—all these are examples of organic materials. All members of the plant kingdom are composed of organic matter, as are all members of the animal kingdom.

Idea	**Examples**
Organic matter is matter that was once alive	Oil, coal, plants, animals, food

A paragraph may state more than one idea; each idea may have its own examples.

> Matter that has its origin in organisms that were once alive is referred to as *organic*. Oil, coal, fruits, meats, and vegetables—all these are examples of organic materials. All members of the plant kingdom are composed of organic matter, as are all members of the animal kingdom. Matter that is *inorganic* did not originate in living organisms. Pure water, granite, glass, and minerals are examples of inorganic material.

Ideas	**Examples**
Organic matter—matter that was once living	Oil, coal, plants, animals, food
Inorganic matter—matter that was never alive	Pure water, granite, glass, minerals

Usually the author will state the idea first, then give examples to clarify the idea. However, at times the examples will come before the idea:

> Water that is pure, granite, glass, and minerals are a few examples of inorganic materials. Inorganic materials are those that do not originate in once-living organisms.

Idea	**Examples**
Inorganic materials—do not originate in once-living organisms	Pure water, granite, glass, minerals

19

Examples are often easier to understand than the ideas they illustrate. One reason is that examples are more concrete than the ideas they illustrate. Another reason is that the ideas may be stated so briefly, or in such complicated language, that they are not easy to understand.

Consider the following paragraph. Can you understand the definition without "thinking through" the examples?

> What is a self-fulfilling prophecy? *A self-fulfilling prophecy is an expectation that an individual has that then gives rise to behavior consonant with the expectation.* For example, a young man may worry so much about saying "the wrong thing" at a job interview that he ends up doing just that at the job interview. Another young man may worry so much in advance about failing his driving test that, when the time comes, he actually fails—even though he knows the material!

In this paragraph the definition of a self-fulfilling prophecy may be difficult to understand. It is put very briefly, and you may not be familiar with all of the words. However, the examples are fairly clear. By using them, you can arrive at some understanding of what the author means by the term "self-fulfilling prophecy."

> *LOOKING AHEAD* The exercises that follow are designed to sharpen your ability to identify examples and use them to understand and remember technical information.
>
> Refer back to these pages as you do the exercises. By the time you finish the chapter, you should be able to
>
> 1. Distinguish between ideas and examples of ideas.
> 2. Locate ideas and examples of ideas in longer selections.
> 3. Answer questions based on your ability to think through supporting examples.

SUMMARY

1. An idea, and the example of an idea, are two different things.

2. The author uses examples to clarify ideas. Examples function as a bridge from the concrete to the abstract.

3. Examples occur in single sentences, in paragraphs, or as the underlying structure for entire selections. Any one paragraph may state more than one idea, and each idea may have its own set of supporting examples.

4. Think through examples. They will help you master the ideas that they illustrate. These ideas are the backbone of your textbook.

EXERCISE 2.1

DIRECTIONS   Each of the following lists has three sentences. Only one of these sentences is an example. Underline the one sentence in each group that is an example.

1 a. Matter is defined as anything that occupies space and has weight.
  b. Matter may occur in three states: liquid, solid, or gaseous.
  c. Air, water, and bricks are all types of matter.

2 a. Water stored behind a dam has potential energy, which will be released when the water thunders over the spillway.
  b. Energy is the ability to do work.
  c. Potential energy is the energy of position; kinetic energy is the energy that moving bodies possess.

3 a. A body at rest tends to remain at rest and will move only when acted upon by an external force.
  b. This property of tending to remain at rest is called *inertia.*
  c. If one puts a box on the shelf, one expects it to remain there.

4 a. Once a body is in motion, it tends to continue in motion unless acted upon by an external force.
  b. This property of moving bodies to remain in motion unless interfered with is called *inertia.*
  c. A ball rolling along a smooth surface can be expected to continue rolling along uniformly unless acted upon by an outside force.

5 a. The law of inertia is demonstrated when you brake your car sharply, and your body continues going in the car's original direction even after the car has stopped.
  b. The law of inertia refers to the tendency of bodies at rest to remain at rest, and for bodies in motion to continue in motion, unless interfered with by an outside force.
  c. Newton's first law of motion is often referred to as the *law of inertia.*

EXERCISE 2.2

DIRECTIONS   In each of the following paragraphs, an idea and supporting examples are given. Read each paragraph, then answer the questions.

A body at rest tends to remain at rest and will move only when acted upon by an external force. Obviously this is true from one's own experience—if one puts a box on the shelf, one expects it to remain there. This property of tending to remain at rest is called *inertia.*

1. The example the author uses is _____

2. The idea the author presents is that _____

_____

Once a body is in motion, it tends to continue in motion unless it is acted upon by an external force. This property of moving bodies to remain in motion unless interfered with is called *inertia*. For instance, a ball rolling along a smooth surface can be expected to continue rolling along uniformly unless acted upon by an outside force. The force that would eventually slow the ball is friction.

3. The example the author uses to illustrate the idea is that _____

_____

4. The idea the example illustrates is that _____

_____

Newton's first law of motion is often referred to as the *law of inertia*. The law of inertia refers to the tendency of bodies at rest to remain at rest, and for bodies in motion to continue in motion unless interfered with by an outside force.

5. The idea the author presents in this paragraph is that _____

_____

6. The example the author uses to illustrate the idea is:
    (a) the law of inertia
    (b) the tendency of bodies at rest to remain at rest
    (c) the tendency of bodies in motion to remain in motion
    (d) the author does not give an example

7. Write your own example of the idea expressed in the above paragraph.

_____

EXERCISE 2.3

DIRECTIONS   Here are five paragraphs. (1) Write out the important idea in each paragraph. (2) Name the examples that illustrate the idea.

SAMPLE   A gas is a fluid that has neither a definite volume nor a definite shape. Air is an example of a gas.

Idea: *Gas — fluid with neither definite volume nor definite shape.*

Example: *Air.*

1   The law of conservation of energy states that energy can be neither created nor destroyed. However, energy can be converted from one form to another. Electrical energy, for instance, can be converted into heat energy — that is what happens when you turn on your toaster.

Idea: _____

_____

Example(s): _____

2   One's weight is different on a high mountain than in a low valley. In fact, one weighs slightly less on a mountain top. This is because on the mountain top one is further from the earth's center. The force of gravity becomes less as one goes further from the center of the earth. Weight is actually the force with which a body is attracted toward the earth.

Idea: _____

Example(s): _____

3   Once a body is in motion, it tends to continue unless it is acted upon by an external force. This property of moving bodies to remain in motion unless interfered with is called *inertia*. For instance, a hockey puck skimming along smooth ice can be expected to continue skimming unless acted upon by another force.

Idea: _____

_____

Example(s): _____

4   What is pressure? It is helpful to imagine a large cinderblock with one jagged edge. How would you hold it on your palm? The block weighs the same whether you place your palm under its smooth side or try to balance the block on its tip. The only difference is that one of these two ways might hurt your hand. Why? The force per unit area is very great when the block is placed tip down. The area of the tip, where all the force is located, is small. Pressure is force per unit area.

Idea: _____

Example(s): _____

5   If you are riding along in a car, and suddenly you have to jam on the brakes, who stops first—you or the car?

Suppose you don't get a seat on the subway and, just as the train starts, you are in the process of opening your newspaper. Why do you have to brace yourself? It is as if, when the train starts moving, your body does not want to go along. However, once the train is in constant motion, you no longer have to brace yourself. You only have to support yourself again when the brakes are applied. If you think about this situation, it will help you with the notion of *inertia*.

Inertia is the property of matter that resists any change in its motion. In the example of our subway rider, the body tended to maintain its state of motion and to resist any change in that state. The law of inertia may be stated as follows: every object remains in a state of rest or in uniform motion along a straight line unless an outside force causes it to change this state.

Idea: _____

_____

Example(s): _____

EXERCISE 2.4

DIRECTIONS Read the following paragraphs. Afterward, state the important idea(s) and any examples.

GRAVITY

1 Our atmosphere is held around the earth by the force of gravity. The moon is held in orbit by the earth's gravity. When we throw objects up in the air, we expect them to return to the earth, drawn by the force of gravity. Gravity is defined as the force that the earth exerts on objects.

Idea: _____

Examples: _____

NEWTON'S THIRD LAW OF MOTION

2 To apply a force on one object, we must be able to push against some other object. To walk, the foot pushes back against the floor, which exerts a forward force on the foot and, through the foot, to the body to propel it forward. To start a car moving, the rear tires push backward on the road, as evidenced by the direction in which the tires throw dirt, and the road reacts with a forward force upon the wheels, as indicated by the motion of the car. While a person is sitting in a chair, he pushes down on the chair with a force equal to his weight, and the chair pushes upward on the person with an equal force. If he pushes on his forehead with a finger, he can feel both forces; the one on the forehead produced by the finger, and the other on the finger produced by the forehead. The harder the push, the greater these forces become, but they are always equal and opposite. Newton observed that forces always came in pairs, and he stated his third law as: *For every force of action there is an equal and opposite force of reaction.* This means that whenever one object

exerts force upon another object, the second object exerts an equal and opposite force on the first object.[1]

Idea: _____

_____

Examples: _____

CENTRIPETAL AND CENTRIFUGAL FORCE

3   In the case of a car turning a corner, the road must exert a frictional force on the car toward the center of the curved path while the car, due to its tendency to travel in a straight line, exerts an outward force on the road. These two forces are equal and opposite. The inward force on the car is the centripetal force, whereas the outward force on the road is called the *centrifugal force*. Note that the centripetal force is the only force acting upon the moving object. If a stone is whirled at the end of a string, the string pulls inward on the moving stone to keep it on a circular path, and the stone, due to its tendency to fly off tangentially, exerts an outward force on the string, which is felt by the hand whirling the stone. These two forces do not act upon the same object; the centripetal force is on the stone while the centrifugal force is on the hand. From these two examples we see that the *centripetal force is always on the moving object, while the centrifugal force is on the object producing the circular motion.* According to Newton's third law, these forces are exactly equal in magnitude but opposite in direction.[2]

Ideas: **a.** _____

  b. _____

_____

Examples: _____

EXERCISE 2.5

DIRECTIONS   Read the following passage. Underline the important idea. In this case the important idea is a term and its definition. Then write out the term, the definition, and the supporting examples.

From the days of childhood we are aware of the distinction between an object and the substance of which it is made. A beaker and a rod can both be made of glass. A chair and a table can both be made of wood. The chair can be broken to pieces, but the pieces are still made of wood. When we begin to analyze the properties of objects, we find that some depend on the size, others on the shape. A lead brick is heavy, but a bit of lead filing is lighter than a drop of water. An iron pipe is rigid, but a thin iron wire can easily be bent. On the other hand, there are properties of an object that depend only on the substance from which it is made. An iron nail rusts; so does an iron frying pan. Water freezes whether there is a bucket of it or just a spoonful.

In this chapter we shall begin our study of properties of substances that are independent of the size or shape of the sample being investigated. We shall refer to such properties as characteristic properties.[3]

Term	Definition	Examples

EXERCISE 2.6

DIRECTIONS   In the following passage, the author *defines* two terms, and gives *examples* of the terms. (1) Read to define the terms "gravity" and "weight." (2) Use the author's *examples* of "weight" to help you understand the *definition* of weight.

MASS AND WEIGHT

. . . In its usual meaning, weight is a measure of the pull of the earth on an object. We all know that this pull exists—in fact, we depend on it to hold us down to the earth. We call it *gravity*. (Again the name does not help us understand it.) To measure this pull it is necessary to devise an experimental procedure and to define a standard pull which will establish the units in which to express the measurement. The usual experiment for determining the weight, or the pull of the earth on an object, is to measure the amount of stretch (or sometimes the compression) produced on a calibrated spring when the object is hung (or placed) on the spring. The standard unit most familiar to you is the *pound*. Typical calibrated springs that you will recognize are the grocer's scale and the bathroom scale.

. . . Why then does it make any difference whether we talk about weight or mass if there seems to be such a close relationship between them? Here is the important point: for any given object, the weight (as indicated by the reading on a spring balance) depends on the location of the spring balance. For example, an object having a mass of 100 kg has the weight of 220.4 pounds in Boston, Massachusetts. If we take the same object and the same spring balance to the Panama Canal, we measure a weight of 219.9 pounds; at Stockholm, Sweden, we read 220.7 pounds. Even worse, on the moon we would measure only 37.3 pounds; on Mars, 88.3 pounds; and on Jupiter, 591 pounds—all with the same object and the same balance. Surely, then, the weight of an object is not a property belonging to the object itself. Instead, it is a description of the interaction between the object and the earth.[4]

QUESTIONS

1. Define the term "weight." _____

2. What is the most familiar measurement of weight? _____

3. The author gives many examples in the second paragraph. In each example an object's weight is given. What idea do these examples illustrate?

_____

_____

EXERCISE 2.7

DIRECTIONS   In the following passage, the author states the law of inertia, and then gives two examples of the law. Read to understand the author's statement of the law of inertia. The examples will help you. Then answer the questions that follow.

LAW OF INERTIA

We now want to examine the relationship between forces and motion. There are three relationships or laws which were discovered by Isaac Newton during the late seventeenth century. The three laws are often called Newton's laws. The first of these is the law of inertia: a body which is in motion continues in motion with the same velocity (at a constant speed and in a straight line), and a body at rest continues at rest unless an unbalanced force acts upon it.

Inertia is the property of a body which causes it to remain at rest if it is at rest or to continue moving with a constant velocity unless an unbalanced force acts upon it.

When the accelerating force of an automobile engine is no longer applied to a moving car, it will slow down. This is not a violation of the law of inertia because there are forces being applied to the car through air resistance, friction in the bearings, and the rolling resistance of the tires. If these forces could be removed, the auto would continue moving with a constant velocity.

Anyone who has tried to stop quickly on ice knows the effect of the law of inertia when frictional forces are small.[5]

QUESTIONS

1. What examples does the author give to illustrate the law of inertia?
   a. A moving automobile in which the engine is suddenly cut off.
   b. Newton's three laws.
   c. A moving automobile in which the engine is suddenly cut off; someone trying to stop quickly on ice.

d. A moving automobile in which the engine is suddenly cut off; someone trying to stop quickly on ice; Newton's three laws.

2. Why is it more difficult to brake a car on an icy surface than on a regular road?
   a. There is less air resistance and friction on the bearings.
   b. The law of inertia is sometimes violated.
   c. The frictional forces are smaller and, therefore, the car tends to continue moving.
   d. None of the above.

3. What slows an automobile down when the force of the engine is

   suddenly stopped? _____

EXERCISE 2.8

DIRECTIONS   Here is a selection on force and motion taken directly from a physics book. In it, the author *defines* the terms "inertia," "air resistance," "centrifugal force," and "centripetal force," and gives *examples* of each term. The examples are designed to make these difficult ideas clearer to you, the reader. (1) Read to understand the terms "inertia," "inertial mass," "centripetal force," and "centrifugal force." (2) Use the author's *examples* to help you understand the law of inertia. Then answer the questions that follow the selection.

FORCE AND MOTION

Whenever we see an object suddenly begin to move, we assume at once that something has acted, or is acting, upon it to produce the change. If the object is a sled, we infer either that someone is pulling or pushing on it or that it is on a slope steep enough to cause it to slide under its own weight. If the object is an automobile, we assume that its engine is moving it or that the car is on a gentle incline with the brakes released. If branches or leaves begin to sway, we say the wind is blowing. If earth and rocks suddenly fly into the air in all directions, even a deaf man will come to the conclusion that there must have been an explosion. Experience has taught us that objects at rest will always remain in that condition unless they have been acted upon by outside forces.

When we see a hard-hit baseball leaving the bat, clearly headed for some place outside the ball park, we do not expect it to continue forever. A golf ball, no matter how hard or how well hit, soon comes to rest. An automobile is provided with brakes for making it stop quickly, but no one doubts that it would finally stop, without this mechanism or any other visible interference, even if traveling at a high speed on the best of our straight highways. We are predisposed to say that objects do not tend to continue in motion, and we feel that their natural condition is one of rest.

Certain facts, however, urge us to hesitate in adopting this conclusion. If the ball field is hard and bare or the grass of the golf course short and dry, the ball travels much farther than it would under the usual conditions. It would go still farther if struck over a stretch of smooth ice. Even ice and air, however, offer some resistance to motion. If this resistance could be completely eliminated, should we see the ball travel on indefinitely?

Galileo's experiment on motion   Galileo undertook to solve this problem about three and a half centuries ago. Using two planes, as shown in Fig. 1, he allowed a ball to roll down plane *A*. It rolled up plane *B* to about the same level from which it started. When the plane was lowered to position *C*, the distance the ball traveled was greater, and again it rose to approximately the original level. This was also true for smaller angles of the plane. Galileo then wondered what would happen if the plane were lowered to a horizontal position. He reasoned that if the ball were unopposed by friction, it would move on indefinitely, trying to find its original height, which, of course, it could never accomplish.

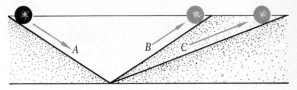

Figure 1.
An early experiment on
the laws of motion

Galileo's conclusion can be applied to the baseball and golf ball. They ultimately stopped, not because rest was their natural condition, but because of the opposing forces of the ground and air. In the absence of frictional forces, they would have traveled on forever.

Air resistance   Air is lightweight and moves rather freely; nevertheless any object moving through it experiences an opposition or a drag, which is called *air resistance*. To show that air has an appreciable amount of resisting force, hold a sheet of paper or a palm leaf at arm's length, and swing it broadside. The paper bends backwards, or the fan veers. You have undoubtedly held your arm out an open car window and felt the resisting force. At slow speeds it is relatively small, but at high speeds it is very large. The air resistance on an automobile is one of the reasons why fuel consumption per mile is greater at higher speeds. This resistance can be decreased by streamlining the automobile. Falling objects, such as hailstones, raindrops, and parachutes, do not increase in speed indefinitely as they descend. Each reaches a certain constant speed, called its *terminal speed*. At this speed the resistance offered by the air is just about equal to the weight of the object. The greater speed of airplanes at high altitudes is largely due to lessened air resistance.

Inertia It may be stated, then, that an object at rest will continue at rest and that an object in motion will continue in motion without changing its speed unless it is acted upon by an outside force. This property of matter to resist any change in its motion is called *inertia*.

Inertia is utilized in many of our most useful devices. In driving a nail, the hammer has so great a tendency to continue its motion that it pushes the nail before it. A pile driver acts in the same way. An ax or hatchet is effective by reason of the inertia of the entire tool.

It is because of their inertia that balls of all kinds continue their motion when thrown or struck, that long, heavily loaded trains and great ocean liners require so much time in starting and stopping, and that heavy and high-speed projectiles are able to have such great destructive power.

The question immediately arises as to how we can determine the amount of inertia an object possesses. This is done by measuring the quantity of material in it as evidenced by its inertia. This quantity is called its *mass* and can be determined by comparing the weight of an object with that of a standard mass. The larger the mass, the greater the tendency an object has to resist any change in its motion. A sledge hammer is more massive than a tack hammer and therefore has a greater tendency to keep moving.

Motion in a curve It is also a matter of common observation that objects in motion tend to move in straight lines. Sparks fly off tangentially to a rapidly turning emery wheel, and mud flies off car wheels. Passengers in the car find themselves lurching toward the outside of the curve as the car rounds a turn, their bodies tending to continue traveling in straight lines. If the curve is too sharp or the speed too great, the car may not be able to round the corner and will leave the road along a tangent to the curve. The car is more likely to fail to make the turn if the pavement is wet or icy because the front wheels cannot get enough tractional force to turn the car. Instances like these convince us that any moving object tends to travel in a straight line and will follow a curved path only if a transverse force is applied. Such a force is directed toward the center of curvature of the path which the object is to follow and is called *centripetal force*. The force needed to hold a moving object on a circular path is larger for a heavy object than for a light one. It increases rapidly as the speed of the object increases and is greater for sharp turns than for longer ones.

While an object is moving around a curve, it is continually trying to travel in a straight line, thus producing an outward pull on whatever is constraining its motion. This outward pull is called the *centrifugal force*. When a stone is whirled at the end of a string, the string pulls inward on the stone to keep it on the circular path, and the stone exerts an outward force on the string, which we feel on our hand. Note that these two forces do not act on the same object; the centripetal force is on the stone, while the centrifugal force is on the string (Fig. 2). These two forces, however, are exactly equal in their magnitudes but they are opposite in their directions.

Centripetal forces, or lack of them, are employed in many household and industrial devices. For example, in some washing machines the

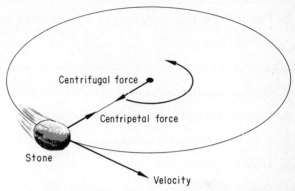

Figure 2. Centripetal and centrifugal forces.

water is removed from the fabric by rotating the clothes in a cylindrical metal basket. The adhesive force between the water and the clothes is not sufficient to keep the water on the circular path, which the clothes are forced to follow. The water flies off at a tangent through the holes in the basket.

Newton's first law of motion We learned from the previous discussion that an object tends to resist any change in its speed or in the direction of its motion. In order to vary either of these, an external force is required. This phenomenon was completely described by Isaac Newton, an English physicist and mathematician, and is known as his first law of motion. It may be stated as follows: "Every object continues in its state of rest or of uniform motion along a straight line unless it is compelled by an outside, unbalanced force to change that state."[6]

QUESTIONS

1. What examples does the author use in the first paragraph?

2. What idea do these examples illustrate?

3. Note the examples of the baseball and golf ball used in paragraphs 2, 3, and 4. Why do the golf ball and baseball eventually come to to rest?

4. Cite at least three examples of air resistance.

_____

5. Cite at least three examples of inertia.

_____

6. Cite at least four instances of the tendency of objects to move in a

straight line. _____

_____

7. Give an example of centrifugal force. _____

8. Give an example of centripetal force. _____

9. Define _air resistance:_ _____

10. Define _terminal speed:_ _____

11. Define _inertia:_ _____

SPRINGBOARD 2

This book can be a springboard into your regular reading.

Try out what you have learned about examples in the textbooks you are reading now. If you are using a general science, chemistry, or physics book—or any book in a technical area—you can put this skill to work immediately. It will also work for textbooks in the social sciences.

Choose one chapter from your reading this week.

1. Underline all definitions and then write them down on 3×5 cards.

2. Write the _term_ on the front; write the _definition_ on the back.

3. Beneath the definition, write down one or two _examples_ of each term.

4. Review the terms by saying the definitions and examples to yourself. Check the back of each card to see if you are right.

Potential energy	Energy of position a-Stretched rubber band B-Water behind a dam
Front	Back

1. Willard J. Poppy and Leland L. Wilson, *Exploring the Physical Sciences,* 2nd ed. Englewood Cliffs, N.J.: Prentice-Hall, Inc., 1973, p. 154.
2. Poppy and Wilson, *Exploring the Physical Sciences,* p. 155.
3. *College Introductory Physical Science.* Newton, Mass.: Education Development Center, Inc., 1969, p. 33.
4. *College Introductory Physical Science,* p. 16.
5. Ewen et al., *Physics for Career Education,* p. 55.
6. Cable et al., *The Physical Sciences,* pp. 18–21.

3

CLASSIFICATION AND LISTING

Can you memorize the items in this group in 60 seconds?

coulombs	atomic particles	electrons
spur	volts	types of gears
watts	worm	electrical units
bevel	neutrons	protons

How about the items in this group? Can you memorize them in 60 seconds?

Electrical units	Atomic particles	Types of gears
coulombs	neutrons	spur
watts	electrons	bevel
volts	protons	worm

The second group is much easier to remember than the first. This is because it is much better organized. This kind of organization has a name. When you take a subject, such as the group of items in the first example, and break it down into parts, such as electrical units, atomic particles, and types of gears, you are *classifying*. Classification is placing things in categories.

Technical and scientific writers have many different ways of expressing their ideas, but one of the most common patterns they use is *classification*. Sometimes they may also add *lists* of items that they tick off under each classification.

If you took all the information in an article on electrical conductors, for instance, and stripped it down to essentials, you might find that it was organized as follows:

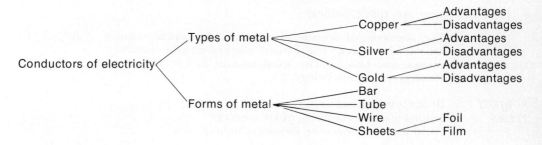

If you can recognize the ways an author uses classification to divide information, you can increase your ability to understand and remember the information. It is possible to read a pamphlet, manual, or textbook and remember very little of it—if you don't know what the "shape" or "structure" is. Practice in classification will give you an eye for this kind of structure.

Most important of all, classification is a stepping stone to a very important skill—the ability to take clear study notes. People who want to understand and remember the information in technical lectures and books have discovered that it is impossible to remember such information just from listening, or from reading "once over lightly." The best way to nail down the information is to take notes—and classification is the core of all note-taking systems.

This chapter will provide many exercises designed to develop your ability to read for classification patterns, and use these patterns to take notes. By putting together your understanding of definition, example, and classification, you will have the beginnings of a system to read, notate, and remember scientific and technical information.

EXAMPLES OF CLASSIFICATION

Here is a sentence that classifies:

Matter may occur in three forms: solid, liquid, or gas.

Even though this classification is only one sentence long, there is a very clear distinction between the *subject* and the *items*.

The subject is the topic about which something is written. The items are the subtopics or subcategories. They are the divisions the author makes in the main topic.

In this case, the information in the sentence might be expressed as follows:

SUBJECT   Forms of matter
ITEMS   Solid, liquid, gas

Here is a paragraph that classifies:

> The observational sciences are divided into natural sciences and social sciences. The natural sciences include chemistry, physics, and biology. The social sciences include economics, sociology, and anthropology.

SUBJECT   Divisions in observational sciences
ITEMS   Natural sciences: chemistry, physics, biology
              Social sciences: economics, sociology, anthropology

SIGNAL WORDS

There are words that signal classification and listing: *as follows, furthermore, moreover, also, and-and, either-or, neither-nor, in addition, first-second, next, many, the other, various, another point, what is more.*
Here are some examples of classification with signal words italicized:

1. There are *two types* of fluids. *First,* there are liquids. These are substances with definite volume, but no definite shape. Instead, they take the shape of their container. *The other type* of fluid is gas. Gas is a substance with neither a definite volume nor a definite shape.
2. Liquids take on the shape of their container. *In addition,* they are very sensitive to the force of gravity.

Signal words are helpful when you are first learning how to use this pattern. However, after a while you will be able to identify classification or listing whether the author actually uses signal words or not.

PUNCTUATION

Punctuation is important in classification-listing. The colon (:) is used to stand for words "as follows." It is often followed by a list.

EXAMPLES   Matter may occur in three forms: solid, liquid or gas.
               The observational sciences are divided into two areas: natural sciences and social sciences.

The semicolon (;) and the comma are often used to separate items in a list.

EXAMPLES   The observational sciences are divided into natural sciences and social sciences: natural sciences include chemistry, physics, and biology; the social sciences include economics, sociology, and anthropology.

Matter has certain general properties: mass, the quantity of matter; volume, the amount of space occupied by matter; weight, the force of the earth's gravity on matter; and inertia, the tendency of matter to resist any change in its state.

USES OF LISTS

In technical writing, lists are usually used to give details or examples.

1. Lists are used to give a string of characteristics, properties, or parts of a definition.

EXAMPLE   A solid has a definite volume and a definite shape. It resists deformation. Its molecules are in fixed positions. The molecules vibrate within these fixed positions.

SUBJECT OF LIST   Characteristics of a solid.

ITEMS IN LIST   Definite volume, definite shape, resists deformation, molecules in fixed position, molecules vibrate in fixed position.

2. Lists are used to give a long series of supporting examples or explanations. In this case, the author usually states an idea that all of the examples support.

EXAMPLE   Many of the units in which measurements are made originated from dimensions of parts of the human body. The width of the hand and the length of the foot are obvious sources of two such units. The height of a horse is measured in hands, the length of a room in feet.[1]

SUBJECT OF LIST   Units of measurement that originate from parts of the human body.

ITEMS IN LIST   Foot, hand

TAKING NOTES ON CLASSIFICATION AND LISTS

Entire passages or chapters may be organized as classification and lists. In such cases, it is important to be able to take simple notes on the topic and subtopics. The skill will aid you in remembering major divisions.

For instance, consider Fig. 3.1, in which two examples have been put side by side. The paragraph on the left is taken from a textbook; the notes on the right were made up by a student who read the paragraph. By writing out simple notes such as these, one can easily see how the author has organized the ideas; this in turn makes it easier to remember the information.

Textbook passage

The observational sciences are divided into natural sciences and social sciences. The natural sciences include chemistry, physics, biology, astronomy, and geology. The social sciences include economics, sociology, psychology, and anthropology.

Student's notes

Observational Sciences

A. Natural Sciences —
   chemistry, physics,
   biology, astronomy,
   geology.

B. Social Sciences —
   economics, sociology,
   psychology, anthropology.

Figure 3.1. Text and notes.

You can take notes on a classification-listing pattern in different ways. You can use short phrases, or you can use sentences in which some of the ideas are written out more fully. Later in this book you will study the differences between these two types of notes. For right now, use either sentences or short phrases. The answer key will indicate that either way is correct.

Follow these rules in taking notes:

1. Put the subject on a line by itself.
2. Put all the subcategories beneath the subject. List them, starting with the letter A.

Textbook paragraph

A solid has a definite volume and a definite shape. It resists deformation. Its molecules are in fixed positions. The molecules vibrate within these fixed positions.

Notes on the paragraph:
subject on first line, items below

Characteristics of a Solid

A. Definite volume, definite shape.
B. Resists deformation.
C. Molecules in fixed position.
D. Molecules vibrate in fixed positions.

Textbook paragraph

Many of the units in which measurement are made originated from dimensions of parts of the human body. The width of the hand and the length of the foot are obvious sources of two such units. The height of a horse is measured in hands, the length of a room in feet.

Notes on the paragraph:
subject on first line, items below

Origin of Units
Many of the units in which measurements are made, originated with the human body.
A. The width of the hand, which is used to measure the height of horses.
B. The lenght of the foot, which is used to measure length.

In the first example, only short phrases are used to take notes. In the second example, whole sentences are written out.

LOOKING AHEAD The exercises that follow will develop your ability to use classification-listing patterns to help understand and remember technical information. The exercises start short, and gradually lengthen out.

Refer back to these pages as you do the exercises.

By the time you finish the chapter, you should be able to do the following things:

1. Distinguish between the subject of a list and the items within the list.
2. Recognize typical words and punctuation that signal classifications and lists as they are used in technical writing.
3. Take simple notes on textbook material that uses a classification or listing form of organization.
4. Answer questions based on textbook information that is organized in classification-listing patterns.

SUMMARY

1. In a classification pattern, an author takes a general subject and breaks it down into subcategories.
2. Any classification has a subject and items. The subject is the topic about which something is written. The items are the subtopics or subcategories.
3. Certain words signal classification and listing relationships. These words include: *as follows, furthermore, moreover, also, and-and, either-or, neither-nor, in addition, first-second, next, many, the other, various, another.* Certain punctuation marks signal lists: the colon, which stands for the words "as follows," and the comma and semicolon, which are used to separate items in a list.
4. When you are required to read and remember information that is organized as a list, take notes. This will help you remember the information.
5. To take simple notes on information organized in this pattern, put the subject on the first line, and put all of the items beneath the subject. List them, starting with the letter A.

DIRECTIONS   Below are classification-listing sentences. (1) State the subject of each list. The subject is the topic about which each sentence is written. (2) State the items within each list. The items are the subdivisions the author has made of the main topic. (3) State any words or punctuation that signal a list. Note that signals are not always present, even though there is a list.

EXAMPLE   Matter may occur in three forms: solid, liquid, or gas.

SUBJECT OF LIST   Matter

ITEMS WITHIN LIST   Solid, liquid, gas

LISTING SIGNALS, IF ANY   : (Colon)

1. To express a measurement, two things are required: a number and a unit.

   a. Subject of the list: _____

   b. Items within the list: _____

   c. Listing signals, if any: _____

2. There are three fundamental units of measurement: length, mass, and time.

   a. Subject of the list: _____

   b. Items within the list: _____

   c. Listing signals, if any: _____

3. In the metric system, mass is expressed in kilograms, time in seconds, and distance in meters.

   a. Subject of the list: _____

   b. Items within the list: _____

   c. Listing signals, if any: _____

4. In the English system, mass is expressed in pounds, time in seconds, and distance in feet.

   a. Subject of the list: _____

   b. Items within the list: _____

   c. Listing signals, if any: _____

5. In the metric system, distance is measured in meters, centimeters, and kilometers.

a. Subject of the list: _____

b. Items within the list: _____

c. Listing signals, if any: _____

6. In the metric system, mass is measured in grams or kilograms.

a. Subject of the list: _____

b. Items within the list: _____

c. Listing signals, if any: _____

EXERCISE 3.2

DIRECTIONS   Here are eight sentences. Some of them are organized as listings; others are not. Circle the numbers of sentences that are organized as listings.

1. Matter may occur in solid state, but it may also occur in a liquid state or in a gaseous state.

2. Matter comes in three forms: solid, liquid, and gas.

3. A measurement cannot be expressed as "8", because a measurement requires more than a number.

4. To express a measurement, two things are required: a number and a unit.

5. There are three fundamental units of measurement: length, time, and mass.

6. In the metric system, mass is expressed in kilograms.

7. In the metric system, mass is expressed in kilograms, time in seconds, and distance in meters.

8. In the English system, mass is measured in pounds, time in seconds, and distance in feet. In the metric system, mass is measured in kilograms, time in seconds, and distance in meters.

EXERCISE 3.3

DIRECTIONS   Each of the following paragraphs is organized in a classification pattern. For each paragraph, state the subject of the classification. You may state it as a phrase or in a sentence. Then give the items in the classification and any signal words.

1   Energy is defined as the ability to do work. Energy may exist in many forms. It may be heat energy, or the energy of light or sound. Energy exists in mechanical, chemical, electrical, and nuclear forms.

a. Subject:_____

b. Items:_____

c. Listing signals of punctuation:_____

2   One form of energy is mechanical. But even this term "mechanical" is a broad one that may be further subdivided. Mechanical energy may be described in two categories: kinetic energy, the energy possessed by moving bodies, and potential energy, the energy of position or state.

a. Subject:_____

b. Items:_____

c. Listing signals of punctuation:_____

3   As the study of physics evolved, various specializations developed and separated themselves from the parent subject. Geology, the study of the origin and nature of the earth, is an example of a subject that was once part of physics. Astronomy, the study of celestial bodies, was also once considered part of physics.

a. Subject:_____

b. Items:_____

c. Listing signals or punctuation:_____

4   There are two widely used systems of fundamental units: (a) the metric system and (b) the English system. The metric system employs the meter as the unit of length, the kilogram as the unit of mass, and the second as the unit of time. The English system, sometimes called the engineer's system, employs the foot as the unit of length, the pound as the unit of mass, and the second as the unit of time.

a. Subject:_____

b. Items:_____

c. Listing signals or punctuation:_____

5   The metric system is subdivided into two systems: the centimeter-gram-second system (cgs) and the meter-kilogram-second system (mks).

a. Subject:_____

b. Items:_____

c. Listing signals or punctuation:_____

EXERCISE 3.4

DIRECTIONS   Here are two paragraphs organized as classifications. Please take notes on these two paragraphs. (1) Write the subject across the top. You may express it as a phrase or as a sentence. (2) List the items below the subject. Guidelines are provided.

1   No matter how complicated the machine you may observe, it is based on a combination of certain simple types of machines. There are six simple machines: (1) the wheel and axle, (2) the pulley, (3) the inclined plane, (4) the wedge, (5) the lever, and (6) the screw.

_____

A. _____

B. _____

C. _____

D. _____

E. _____

F. _____

2   There are two forces to consider in relation to machines: effort and resistance. Effort is the force applied by the person using the machine. Resistance is the weight being lifted or the obstacle being overcome.

_____

A. _____

B. _____

EXERCISE 3.5

DIRECTIONS   Here are two paragraphs organized as lists. In both cases, the author has defined a term or explained an idea and then given a list of supporting examples. Take notes on these two paragraphs. (1) Write the subject across the top. If it is a definition, write out the entire definition. (2) List the supporting items below the subject.

1   Friction is a word describing the opposing forces that occur when one surface passes against another surface. A car moving along encounters the frictional force of the wind; the tires encounter the resistance of the road.

_____

_____

2   It must not be assumed that friction is always bad just because it reduces the available energy. In many instances it is highly desirable.
Walking is difficult enough on icy pavements, but it would be wholly
impossible if there were no friction between the shoe and the pavement. In the case of a car, the wheels would spin without moving the
vehicle. If you managed to get the car moving, how would you stop it
without friction? . . . Nails would not hold in wood without friction and
would be useless.[2]

_____

_____

_____

_____

EXERCISE 3.6

DIRECTIONS   Here is a longer passage from a textbook. If you read it carefully, you will realize that it is made up of a definition of terms
and two examples. On a separate sheet of paper, take notes on
the passage. (1) Write the term and definition across the top.
(2) List the two supporting examples.

In everyday usage, the word *work* is used when referring to almost any
kind of useful activity which makes us tired. In mechanics, however, it
is understood in a more restricted sense: there it means *the effect that is
accomplished when a force is exerted upon some object and moves it a certain
distance.* If there is no motion, there is no work. A boy who sits down
quietly with a book to study does no mechanical work. A less studious
boy who goes outdoors and plays a game of tennis does work. The first
boy may have accomplished a much more useful result; he may have
conceived a new idea that will bring him fame and fortune as well as
help all mankind. But he has exerted no mechanical force, nor moved
an object; therefore, he has done no work. The other boy has probably
accomplished something useful too in terms of health, but that in itself
does not constitute work. The essential difference is that he has exerted
forces and moved objects.[3]

EXERCISE 3.7

DIRECTIONS   On a separate sheet of paper, take notes on this passage, which
is organized in a classification pattern.

FORMS OF ENERGY

. . . but there are many other kinds of energy that are capable of doing
useful work. The most common of these is *heat energy.* Steam, diesel,

and gasoline engines prove that heat is capable of doing work. The kind stored in coal and other fossil fuels is *chemical energy*. From this stored energy, we can accomplish may useful things. In a beam of sunlight, there is another form of energy; we call it *radiant* or *electromagnetic energy*. An electric current flowing in a wire possesses *electrical energy*, for it has the ability to run motors and do useful work. A nuclear reactor gets its energy from the loss in mass during the nuclear reactions; hence, we can consider *mass* a form of energy. . . .[4]

EXERCISE 3.8

DIRECTIONS   On a separate sheet of paper, take notes on this passage. The author makes a statement about the origin of units and then lists five illustrations of the statement.

ORIGIN OF UNITS

Man originally used the dimensions of parts of his body as units for length measurements. The width of a man's thumb, or from the knuckle to the tip of the forefinger, became our *inch*. The *foot* originated as the length of a man's foot. The width of the hand is a unit very familiar to horse lovers for the height of a horse is still measured in *hands*. A hand is about 4 inches. . . . A convenient unit for measuring cloth was found to be the distance from the tip of a person's nose to the tip of the middle finger of his arm outstretched sideways. This measurement for King Edgar of England has become our *yard*. . . . The *fathom*, used in measuring ocean depths, was originated by the Vikings as the distance from the tip of one middle finger to the other when the arms were outstretched in a straight line. From this it is clear that a fathom is equivalent to 2 yards.[5]

EXERCISE 3.9

DIRECTIONS   Here is a short listing passage in which the author uses both words and numbers. It is always difficult to handle this kind of language, because it requires the reader to switch back and forth from words to numbers. Take notes on this paragraph. Your understanding of listing patterns will help you organize this information. Remember that semicolons are used to separate items in a list.

MATHEMATICAL SHORTHAND

Scientists often deal with very large or very small numbers. To avoid the confusion of numerous zeros or a large number of decimal places, the scientists have devised a shorthand way of writing numbers. One hundred, we know, is 10×10, or 10^2; one thousand is $10 \times 10 \times 10$, or 10^3; one million is $10 \times 10 \times 10 \times 10 \times 10 \times 10$, or 10^6; one billion is $10 \times 10 \times 10 \times 10 \times 10 \times 10 \times 10 \times 10 \times \times 10$, or 10^9.[6]

A. _____

B. _____

C. _____

D. _____

EXERCISE 3.10

DIRECTIONS   Here is a longer textbook excerpt. You have read a portion of it earlier in this chapter. Read this passage and answer the questions based on classification and listing that follow. As you read, notice how the author defines "friction" and "efficiency," lists examples of both desirable and undesirable friction, and lists examples of the term "efficiency."

FRICTION

Any time friction is involved useful energy is lost. *Sliding friction* is the resistance encountered when one surface slides over another. The opposition is due to interlocking of irregularities in the two surfaces. The energy wasted in overcoming this opposition is always converted to heat. This loss can be reduced by carefully lubricating the surfaces or by the substitution of rollers or ball bearings.

It must not be assumed that friction is always bad just because it reduces the available energy. In many instances, it is highly desirable. Walking is difficult enough on icy pavement, but it would be wholly impossible if there were no friction between the shoe and the pavement. In the case of a car, the wheels would spin without moving the vehicle. If you managed to get the car moving, how would you stop it without friction? Belts are often used in conveying power from one part of a machine to another part or to another machine. In the absence of friction this could not be done. The driving wheel would not move the belt; neither would the belt run the pulleys or wheels to be driven. Nails would not hold in wood without friction and would be useless. Therefore, we often sacrifice the energy lost for the advantages derived from the friction.

Efficiency of Machines   The energy delivered by a machine in the form of useful work is always less than that supplied. In the case of a steam engine, this loss is about 90%. In the case of our automobile engines, the loss is less, but it is still 70 to 75%. In the car engine, about 25% of the heat energy is dissipated through the radiator to keep the engine from overheating. Another 25% is unavoidably lost by way of the exhaust. This loss is in the form of unburned fuel and heat produced by combustion. Still further losses occur within the engine in overcoming friction. Only 25 to 30% of the available energy is used to move the car.

The machines that utilize the greatest fraction of the energy supplied them are usually electrical. A well-designed electric motor, when running at its rated load, will deliver as useful work 80 to 85% of the energy supplied it. An alternating-current transformer, which has no moving parts, and consequently no frictional losses in the usual sense, is still more efficient. Such devices frequently utilize 98% or more of the energy with which they are supplied.

The term *efficiency* is used to indicate the fractional part of the energy received by a machine that is finally delivered from it in the form of useful work. It is defined as the ratio of the work output to the work input. The car engine transforms into useful work about 30% of the supplied energy, and so we say that it has an efficiency of 0.30 or 30%.[7]

QUESTIONS

1. All except one of the following items are listed as examples of useful friction. Mark the item that is not mentioned.
   a. nails in wood
   b. electricity in a wire
   c. machinery belts and machine parts
   d. shoes and pavement

2. How can one reduce the loss of energy that results from sliding friction?

   a. _____

   b. _____

3. Which of the following machines listed by the author is the least efficient?
   a. the electric motor
   b. an alternating-current transformer
   c. a steam engine
   d. a car engine

4. Rate the following machines in terms of their efficiency. Start with a 1 for the most efficient, a 2 for the second most efficient, and so on.
   _____ the electric motor
   _____ an alternating-current transformer
   _____ a steam engine
   _____ a car engine

5. Here are two statements. Indicate whether they are true (T) or false (F). Beside your answer, write out a quote from the passage that proves your answer.

  a. Since friction invariably reduces available energy, friction is *useless.*   T   F

  Quote from passage: _____

  b. The fewer moving parts a machine has, the more efficient it will be.   T   F

  Quote from passage: _____

REVIEW

6. Define the term *sliding friction.* _____

7. Define the term *efficiency.* _____

EXERCISE 3.11

DIRECTIONS   Read the selection and answer the questions that follow.

UNITS OF DERIVED QUANTITIES

All quantities in mechanics can be expressed in terms of the three fundamental quantities of length, mass, and time. Although these three are undefined, we nevertheless have an intuitive feeling for their meaning, and have units for measuring them. The mass of a body is a more fundamental property than its weight. The property called mass represents the amount of matter in an object while weight is the gravitational pull on that matter. Other quantities may be derived by combinations of the fundamental quantities. The units of all of these derived quantities depend upon the units of the three basic quantities. When the length is expressed in feet, the weight in pounds, and the time in seconds, we have the *foot-pound-second* or English system of units, which is used in the United States in industry and in daily living. In the metric system, there are two sets of units which only differ in size of units: the *centimeter-gram-second* (cgs) and the *meter-kilogram-second* (mks) systems. The mks system of units is widely adopted because it can be used in electricity as well as in all other phases of the physical sciences, whereas the English system has not been used in electricity because it isn't as convenient. The size of the mks units are more practical than those of the cgs system. From here on, in this book we shall use the metric system exclusively to acquaint the student with the units of the world.[8]

QUESTIONS

2. Define the term *weight.* _____

3. What are the two sets of units into which the metric system is divided?

4. Here are three statements. Indicate whether they are true (T) or false (F). Beside your answer, write out a quote from the passage that proves your answer.

   a. The mks and cgs systems are fundamentally different.   T   F

   Quote from passage: _____

   b. The author states that mass and weight are equally fundamental properties.   T   F

   Quote from passage: _____

   c. The units of derived quantities are based on the fundamental units of length, mass, and time.   T   F

   Quote from passage: _____

   _____

1. Define the term *mass.* _____

EXERCISE 3.12

DIRECTIONS   Here is a section taken directly from a physics book. As you read, notice how important classification-listing is. It is one of the main ways the author uses to present information.

BASIC UNITS USED IN PHYSICAL SCIENCES

Until the beginning of the nineteenth century, the situation in the field of weights and measures was not much better than the linguistic situation at the Tower of Babel. The units of length varied from country to country, from town to town, from one profession (such as tailor) to another (such as carpenter), and were mostly defined, rather loosely, by reference to various parts of the human body. Thus, an "inch" was defined as a thumb-width, a "hand" or "palm" (still used for measuring the height of race horses) as the breadth of a hand, a "foot" as the length of a British king's foot, a "cubit" as the distance from the elbow to the tip of the middle finger, a "fathom" (used in measuring ocean depths) as the distance between the tips of the middle fingers of the two hands when the arms are outstretched in a straight line, etc. In the year 1791 the French Academy of Sciences recommended the adoption of an international standard of length and suggested that the unit of length be based on the size of the Earth. *This unit, called a meter, was to be equal to one ten-millionth of the distance from the pole to the equator.* To prepare a standard meter it became necessary to measure, with all possible precision, at least a part of the earth's meridian, and two French scientists, M. Delambre and M. Méchain, were charged with the task. It took them seven years to measure, by an improved triangulation method, a stretch of meridian from Barcelona in Spain to Dunkirk in Normandy. On the basis of these measurements the academy prepared a "standard meter"—a platinum-iridium bar with two marks on it that was supposed to represent one ten-millionth part of a quarter of the Earth's meridian. The original meter is kept at the Bureau des Poids et Mesures in Sèvres (not far from Paris), and true copies are universally distributed. . . .

While it is a fact that in stores and factories in the U.S.A., length is customarily measured in yards (yd), feet (ft), and inches (in.), scientific measurements are always expressed in *kilometers* (km; 1,000 m or 0.62 mi, or miles), *meters* (m), *decimeters* (dm; one-tenth of a meter), *centimeters* (cm; one hundredth of a meter), *millimeters* (mm; one-thousandth of a meter), etc. . . .

Along with the standard unit of length, the metric system also introduced a new unit for the amount of matter, or mass. Disposing of "short and long tons," "pounds (lb)," "ounces (oz)," "drachms," "grains," etc., it uses a *gram* (gm), defined as *the mass of a cubic centimeter* (cc or cm³) *of water at the temperature (about 1° C) at which it has the greatest density.* A standard *kilogram* (kg; equal to 1,000 gm) equivalent to the mass of 1 liter (or to one cubic decimeter, 1 cu dm) of water under the above conditions was made of platinum and iridium alloy; the original is kept together with the original meter in Sèvres, and copies are distributed all over the world. While 1 gm is the standard unit used in physical measurements, we also use *milligrams* (mg; one-thousandth of a gram) and *micrograms* (μg; one-millionth of a gram) to express the mass of very small amounts of matter.

The clock symbolizes the third fundamental physical unit: a unit of time. A day is divided into 24 hours (hr), and each hour is subdivided into 60 minutes (min), with each minute further divided into 60 seconds (sec). This system of time measurement is based upon that used in ancient Babylon and Egypt, and even the French Revolution (not to mention the Russian one) was unable to convert it into a decimal system. Since we use a decimal system for length and weights, we should logically divide a day into "decidays" (2.4 hr each), "centidays" (8.4 min each), and "millidays" (59.4 sec each). This would necessitate, however, the introduction of "decadays" (10 days each), "hectodays" (3.3 months each) and "kilodays" (2.6 years, or yr, each) and would lead to chaos in speaking about the phases of the Moon or the seasons of the year. In the scientific measurement of time intervals much shorter than a second, however, the decimal system is used, and we speak about *milliseconds* (m-sec; one-thousandth of a second) and *microseconds* (μsec; one-millionth of a second).

Having defined the units for length, mass, and time, we can express through them the units for other physical quantities. Thus, the unit of velocity becomes *a centimeter per second* (cm/sec), the unit of material density, *a gram per cubic centimeter* (gm/cm³), etc. This system of units is known as the "CGS (centimeter-gram-second) system" and is always used in scientific literature. Being a unique system accepted by all scientists in the world, it represents a definite advantage over the Anglo-American systems of units where the velocity, for example, may be expressed at will in "feet per second," "miles per hours," or even in "furlongs per weekend." Thus in this book the metric system will be used exclusively. Readers who are not familiar with meters and kilograms should remember that one *meter* is about equal to one *yard* (1.093611), while one *kilogram* is about equal to two *pounds* (2.20462).[9]

QUESTIONS

1. Here is a set of notes on a part of this passage. Some of the items have been left blank. Please complete this set of notes.

   Basic Units for Length, for Mass, and for Time

   Basic unit for length: the meter
      A. Kilometer: 1,000 meters.
      B. Decimeter: one-tenth of a meter.

      C. Centimeter _____

      D. Millimeter _____

      _____

      A. _____

      B. _____

      C. _____

   Basic unit for time: the second
      A. Hour, minute, second

      B. Millisecond _____

      C. _____

SPRINGBOARD 3

Choose one chapter from your reading this week.
1. Pick out three passages where the author is listing information. Choose passages where it is difficult to understand and remember the information just from reading through it quickly.
2. Use a 3 × 5 card for each passage.
   a. Write the subject of the list across the top of the card.
   b. List the items beneath the subject, using A, B, C.
   c. Turn the card over and write one or two words on the back to remind you of the subject of the selection.

d. Then review the passage by saying the subject and items to yourself. Check the card to see if you are right.

Front   Back

NOTES

1. E. J. Cable et al., *The Physical Sciences,* 5th ed. Englewood Cliffs, N.J.: Prentice-Hall, Inc., 1969, pp. 36–40.
2. Willard J. Poppy and Leland L. Wilson, *Exploring the Physical Sciences,* 2nd ed. Englewood Cliffs, N.J.: Prentice-Hall, Inc., 1973, p. 187.
3. Poppy and Wilson, *Exploring the Physical Sciences,* p. 180.
4. Poppy and Wilson, *Exploring the Physical Sciences,* p. 186.
5. Poppy and Wilson, *Exploring the Physical Sciences,* p. 127.
6. E. J. Cable et al., *The Physical Sciences,* p. 16.
7. Poppy and Wilson, *Exploring the Physical Sciences,* pp. 187–88.
8. Poppy and Wilson, *Exploring the Physical Sciences,* p. 134.
9. George Gamow, *Matter, Earth, and Sky,* 2d ed. Englewood Cliffs, N.J.: Prentice-Hall, Inc. 1965, pp. 3–7.

QUICK PROGRESS TEST 1

DIRECTIONS   *Definition, example,* and *classification* are stepping stones to better comprehension. When you know how to combine these skills, you have mastered the first stage of a system for improving your ability to read and remember technical materials. Here is a quick test of *definition, example,* and *classification.* The two passages that follow are from a book on earth resources. As you read, (1) Identify all new terms by underlining the term and the definition. (2) Think through each example. Examples are designed to illustrate ideas. (3) Be prepared to take notes on the passages.

1   Resource is a word with many shades of meaning. Dictionary definitions range from "something in reserve" to "additional stores, ready if needed." But the definitions do not specify the "somethings" and the "stores." They could be resources of courage to face a personal crisis, of wood to fuel a stove through a winter, or of finances to meet a medical expense. The resources discussed in this book are all linked by a common factor. They are all *natural resources,* which means that they

are supplies we draw from a bountiful Earth, such as food, building and clothing materials, minerals, water and energy. . . .

Maintenance of the Earth's huge population is now totally dependent on continuing supplies of natural resources: fertilizers to increase crop yields, water to drink and to irrigate crops, metals to build machines, fuels to energize them, and a myriad other materials. Without continuing supplies civilized society must collapse and the population wither.

Natural resources fall into two distinct categories. Resources derived from living matter, such as food, clothing and wood, are *renewable resources* because they are replenished each growing season. Even if one season's crop is consumed, the next season brings a renewed larder. But *mineral resources* such as coal, oil, atomic energy, copper, iron and fertilizers are not renewed each season. They are nonrenewable. . . .[1]

QUESTIONS

a. What are the three important terms and definitions given in the passage?

_____

_____

_____

b. Cite examples of each term.

_____

_____

_____

c. Take simple notes on the last paragraph.

_____

_____

_____

THE EARTH

2   At the Earth's center is a metallic *core* consisting predominantly of iron and nickel, surrounded by a *mantle* of dense rock rich in iron and magnesium; the core and the mantle together account for more than 99.6 percent of the total mass of the Earth. Above the mantle is the Earth's *crust,* which is the only portion of the solid Earth we actually observe,

and which accounts for 0.375 percent of the Earth's mass. The crust is of two parts, one that projects above the oceans and one that lies below; the portion above, in addition to a narrow sea-covered fringe around each continent, is called the *continental crust;* the portion below the oceans is the *oceanic crust.*

At the Earth's surface are the oceans, lakes, and rivers that, together with the water trapped in holes and fractures in soil and near-surface rocks, are called the *hydrosphere* and account for 0.025 percent of the Earth's mass. Enclosing everything is the gaseous envelope of the *atmosphere,* which accounts for only 0.0001 percent of the mass. It is from the three outermost and smallest zones—the crust, hydrosphere, and atmosphere—that we draw our present resources, and to which we must look for those of the future. The mantle and the core are so inaccessible that they cannot ever be seriously considered as potential suppliers of resources.[2]

QUESTION:

Take simple notes on this passage. Include all the terms that are listed and defined.

NOTES

1. Brian J. Skinner, *Earth Resources,* 2nd ed. Englewood Cliffs, N.J.: Prentice-Hall, Inc., 1976, p. 1.
2. Skinner, *Earth Resources,* pp. 14–15.

4
CONTRAST

Some technical materials are hard to understand because the terms in them are difficult to "picture." For instance, the word "molecule" doesn't bring an instant picture to most people's minds. It isn't as easy to think about as "kitchen table," "hungry," "money," or other words and ideas that we know from our everyday lives.

There are some devices that writers use to make difficult ideas sharper and clearer in the reader's mind. The main device that you will find in technical writing is *contrast*. Authors put one idea up against another. The contrast makes both ideas clearer.

When you develop an eye for contrast, it will help you to analyze and remember technical information. There is another use for contrast—it will add to your growing ability to take notes on complicated materials.

This chapter will explain how to use contrast to understand and remember scientific information. The chapter is also designed to review the skills of definition, example, classification, and simple note-taking.

A contrast is a way of showing a *difference* or *distinction* between two or more factors.

For example, an author may contrast the nature of solids and fluids.

EXAMPLE   The molecules of a solid are in fixed positions in relation to each other. In contrast, the molecules of a liquid flow over one another.

If you had to break this brief paragraph into two parts and draw a circle around each part, you would probably do the following:

> The molecules of a solid are in fixed positions in relation to each other.
> In contrast, the molecules of a liquid flow over one another.

This paragraph really has two parts or factors. The first factor is "The molecules of a solid are in fixed positions in relation to each other." The second factor is "The molecules of a liquid flow over each other."

In contrast, one of the factors may be thought of as *x*, and the other as *y*. For example, the information in the paragraph you just read could be restated as follows:

x = molecules of a solid. These are in a fixed position.
y = molecules of a liquid. These flow over one another.

Authors use contrasts to highlight the *difference* between idea *x* and idea *y*.

EXAMPLE   The molecules of a solid are fixed in relation to one another. A solid has a definite shape. In contrast, the molecules of a liquid flow over each other. A liquid takes the shape of its container.

This information could be restated as follows:

x = Molecules of a solid have fixed positions. A solid has a definite shape.
y = Molecules of a liquid flow over each other. A liquid takes on the shape of its container.

The author has deliberately put these two ideas back to back so that the reader will begin to see the *difference* between a solid and a liquid. The contrast is used to make the distinction between the two states of matter clearer to the reader.

Many words signal contrasts, including the following: *however, but, yet, still, alternatively, in contrast, instead, the difference, on the contrary, on the other hand, conversely, although, despite, then-now.*

Here are two examples of contrasts, with the signal words underlined:

1. The molecules of a solid are in fixed positions, and they vibrate within these positions. The molecules of a liquid, <u>however</u>, are not in fixed positions. They flow over each other.

2. It was not possible for the ancient Greeks to measure precisely the amount of time a pebble took to drop from the hand to the earth. This is in sharp <u>contrast</u> to today, when measurements can be made with great accuracy. The development of sophisticated measuring tools is in part responsible for the rapid development of scientific knowledge since the seventeenth century.

Signal words are helpful when you are learning how to use contrast. However, as you practice, you will be able to identify contrasts whether or not the author has used signal words.

A contrast may be as brief as a sentence, or it may provide the basis for an entire selection. Usually contrasts are longer than one sentence, since at least two factors are needed to set up a contrast.

CONTRAST-LISTING

The most frequent pattern in technical writing is a combination of contrast and listing. In this pattern an author contrasts ideas and lists characteristics of each idea, as shown in the following selection:

CHARACTERISTICS OF MATTER

The molecules of a solid are fixed in relation to each other. They vibrate in a back-and-forth motion. They are so close that a solid can be compressed only slightly. Solids are usually crystalline substances, meaning their molecules are arranged in a definite pattern. This is why a solid tends to hold its shape and has a definite volume.

The molecules of a liquid are not fixed in relation to each other. They normally move in a flowing type of motion but yet are so close together that they are practically incompressible, thus having a definite volume. Because the molecules move in a smooth flowing motion and not in any fixed manner, a liquid takes the shape of its container.

The molecules of a gas are not fixed in relation to each other and move rapidly in all directions, colliding with each other. They are much farther apart than molecules in a liquid, and they are extremely far apart when compared to the distance between molecules in solids. The movement of the molecules is limited only by its container. Therefore, a gas takes the shape of its container. Because the molecules are far apart, a gas can easily be compressed and it has the same volume as its container.[1]

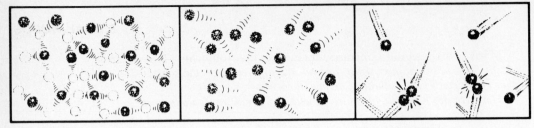

| Solid molecules vibrate in fixed positions | Liquid molecules flow over each other | Gas molecules move rapidly in all directions and collide |

Figure 1

Does this pattern look familiar to you? Entire passages in your technical books are organized in just this way. Technical authors like contrast-listing. It allows them to put down a great deal of information back to back, with the important differences highlighted.

Since contrast-listing passages contain a lot of information, take notes on these passages. This will help you understand and remember.

To take notes on contrast-listing, you can use the same method that you used for simple listing. However, since there is more than one major division or heading, use a Roman numeral I for the first heading, a Roman numeral II for the second heading, and so on. Here are simple notes based on the preceding passage:

CHARACTERISTICS OF MATTER

I. The molecules of a solid are fixed.

   A. They vibrate back and forth.

   B. They are close together, so a solid can't be compressed much.

   C. They are in a definite pattern, which therefore fixes the solid in a definite shape.

II. The molecules of a liquid are not fixed, but are close together.

   A. They can flow over one another, unlike the molecules of a solid.

   B. Since they are close together, a liquid is practically incompressible, and has a definite volume.

   C. They take the shape of the container.

III. The molecules of a gas are neither fixed, nor close together.

   A. They move rapidly in all directions, colliding with each other.

   B. They are far apart.

   C. Their movement is limited only by the container.

   D. They take on the shape of the container.

LOOKING AHEAD The exercises that follow will develop your ability to use contrasts to understand and remember technical information.

Refer back to the text of the chapter as you do the exercises.

By the time you finish the chapter, you should be able to do the following things:

1. Distinguish factors in a contrast.
2. Recognize typical words that signal contrasts.
3. Take simple notes on textbook material that uses a contrast-listing pattern.
4. Answer questions based on textbook information organized in a contrast-listing pattern.

SUMMARY

1. A contrast is a way of showing a *difference* between two or more factors.
2. One of the factors may be thought of as *x*, the other as *y*.
3. Certain words signal contrasts. These words include: *however, but, on the other hand, yet, still, in contrast, instead, the difference, on the contrary, conversely, then-now.*
4. Authors usually combine contrast and listing. Taking notes on such passages will help you understand and remember their content.
5. To take notes on contrast-listing patterns, use Roman numerals (I, II, III) for the major divisions, and capital letters (A, B, C) below for the items that are listed.

EXERCISE 4.1

DIRECTIONS Each of the following paragraphs is organized as a contrast. Write out the two factors in each contrast.

EXAMPLE In day-to-day usage, the word "work" refers to physical or mental effort designed to achieve a result. In mechanics, however, work is defined as the effect accomplished when a force is exerted upon an object to move it a certain distance.

Idea x: *Ordinary definition of work — physical or mental effort designed to achieve result.*

Idea y: *Mechanical definition of work — Effect of force exerted on object to move it a certain distance.*

1   Why does it rain? Is it because there is a goddess up in the sky who is crying for her lost daughter? Or is it because of water vapor that condenses and falls to earth?

Idea x: _____

Idea y: _____

2   Why do clouds move across the sky? Perhaps a storm god up there is pushing them. Or perhaps it is the winds that are caused by differences in air pressure.

Idea x: _____

Idea y: _____

EXERCISE 4.2

DIRECTIONS   Each of the following paragraphs is organized as a contrast. Consider one idea in the contrast *x*, and the other idea *y*. Read to distinguish the two factors in the contrast. Note signal words.

1   There are two very different ways of explaining such natural phenomena as storm clouds and rain. One way is by the use of myths. These are stories or tales that seek to explain natural phenomena. In contrast, rational explanations try to use reason to explain what happens in nature.

Idea x: _____

Idea y: _____

Word(s) signaling a contrast: _____

2   Primitive people used myths to analyze natural phenomena. Beginning about 600 years before the birth of Christ, however, Greek philosophers set about analyzing natural phenomena in a different way. They were the first physicists.

Idea x: _____

Idea y: _____

Word(s) signaling a contrast: _____

3   The Greek natural philosophers rejected myths as a way of explaining the world. Instead, they relied on reason and observation to formulate their theories.

Idea *x:*————————————————————————————

Idea *y:*————————————————————————————

Word(s) signaling a contrast: ——————————————————

EXERCISE 4.3

DIRECTIONS   Each of the following paragraphs is organized as a contrast. Read to distinguish the two factors in the contrast.

1   There is a difference between the molecules of a solid at low temperatures and at high temperatures. At high temperatures the molecules vibrate more rapidly. Their velocity and kinetic energy are greater.

Idea *x:*————————————————————————————

Idea *y:*————————————————————————————

Word(s) signaling a contrast: ——————————————————

2   There is a difference between the molecules of a cold gas and the molecules of a hot gas. In a cold gas the molecules move around slowly. At higher temperatures the molecules move faster. When the average speed of the molecules increases, the temperature rises.

Idea *x:*————————————————————————————

Idea *y:*————————————————————————————

Word(s) signaling a contrast: ——————————————————

EXERCISE 4.4

DIRECTIONS   Read the following paragraphs and answer the questions on contrast that follow.

1   Energy can be neither created nor destroyed. In a closed system the total amount of energy remains constant. However, energy can be converted from one form to another. For instance, when you flip on the toaster, electric energy is converted to heat energy. When coal burns, chemical energy is converted to heat energy.

a. The author contrasts two ideas about energy. What are these two ideas?

_____

_____

b. Give any signal words that indicate a contrast. _____

c. What two examples does the author give of the idea? _____

_____

2   There are different ways that heat is transferred. When a frying pan is placed on a gas burner, the molecules in the pan that are in direct contact with the flame start to vibrate faster. The process by which the heat passes from the hot part of the pan to the cold part is called conduction. Conduction is transfer of heat by molecular collision. In convection heating, in contrast, heat is transferred by means of currents in the liquid or gas. For example, right above a radiator, the warm air rises, cold air moves in to take its place, and circulation is set up.

a. Two methods of heat transfer are contrasted. What are the two methods?

_____

b. Give one example of each method of heat transfer. _____

_____

EXERCISE 4.5

DIRECTIONS   Read the following paragraph and answer the questions on contrast that follow.

ASTRONOMY AND ASTROLOGY

Ancient people looked to the sky for an explanation of the upsetting things that happened in their lives. They credited the stars with a direct force on their destiny. They believe that if you were born under a certain star, something would happen to you that would not occur if you were born at another time of the year. This was called astrology. Today we consider astrology to be a pseudoscience. ("Pseudo" means "false.") However, even then there were men and women who tried to analyze the motions of the planets and stars in a more rational way. They were the ancestors of today's astronomers. Astronomy is a branch of the physical sciences which treats the history and condition of the celestial bodies.

1. What two ideas is the author contrasting?_____

_____

2. Give any signal words that indicate a contrast. _____

3. Authors use contrast to show a difference between ideas. What is the

difference between the two ideas contrasted in this paragraph?_____

_____

DIRECTIONS Read the following paragraphs, which are taken from a textbook, and answer the accompanying questions on contrast.

OLD AND NEW SYSTEMS
OF THE WORLD

Thousands of years ago men looked at the stars with mystical admira-
tion. It was believed that stars govern the fate of men, and the pseudoscience *astrology* flourished far and wide through the ancient and
medieval worlds. It is shameful to admit that even today the number of
astrological magazines exceeds the number of scientific *astronomical* pub-
lications, and the total income of astrologers, who claim to be able to
predict your future if you tell them under which star you were born,
exceeds the combined salaries of all professional astronomers in the
world. . . .

But even at this early time in the history of human civilization there
were individuals who wanted to understand the motion of the Sun,
Moon, and planets in a more rational rather than a mystical way, and
who laid the foundation of modern astronomy.[2]

1. What two basic ideas are contrasted in this excerpt? _____

_____

2. Give any words that signal a contrast.
3. Authors use contrast to show a difference between ideas. What is the

difference between the two ideas contrasted in this excerpt?_____

_____

DIRECTIONS Here is a longer textbook excerpt, which lists and contrasts the
three forms of heat transfer. Read it, and answer the questions
that follow. As you read this passage, (1) Underline all new
terms and their definitions. (2) Pause to think about the exam-

ples the author gives for each idea. Do you understand the ideas that the examples illustrate? (3) Note the basic contrasts in the passage. Questions on definition, example, contrast, and simple note-taking follow the passage.

HEAT TRANSFER

To be useful, heat must be transferred from the device in which it is generated to the place where it is to be used. Our planet would be a cold, barren place if the heat from the Sun could not reach the Earth. There are only three ways by which heat is transferred from a warm to a cold region: conduction, convection, and radiation.

Conduction   A spoon placed in a cup of hot coffee soon becomes warm throughout. Heat has been transferred by the metal from the parts that touch the liquid to the parts that do not. The heat was transmitted from the hot part of the spoon through the metal to the cool handle, raising its temperature. The outside of the firebox of a furance becomes hot because of the fire inside. The heat is passed through the metal, from the hot inside to the colder outside. This method of heat transfer through the substance is called *conduction*. Silver and copper are the best of all heat conductors. Aluminum is much better than iron. For this reason, a burner heats the bottom on an aluminum pan more uniformly than that of an iron pan, and so there are no hot spots to burn the food.

Convection   The heating of a room by a radiator, or an entire house by a warm-air or hot-water furnace, involves a second method of heat transfer: *convection*. In heating the room, the air in contact with the radiator becomes warm, expands, and rises because it is less dense than the air around it. The cooler, heavier air moves in to take its place. The circulation set up in this way carries heat to every part of the room. In the case of a hot-air furnace, the air is heated by the furnace, expands and rises into the rooms through the pipes, carrying the heat with it. The cold, heavier air in the rooms drops through the cold-air ducts to the furnace, thus setting up a circulation. A forced warm-air heating system as shown in Fig. 1 has a blower to increase that circulation. In convection, the medium itself moves and carries the heat from the warm to the cool region.

Radiation   The third method of heat transfer is *radiation*. It is by this method that the heat of a bonfire reaches the people standing nearby, and that the Earth receives its heat from the Sun. Radiant heat is transmitted with the speed of light, 3×10^8 m/sec. The energy is carried by electromagnetic waves. These waves are emitted by a warm substance, pass through space, are absorbed by an object upon which they fall, and raise the temperature of that object. These waves are like light waves but are much longer; therefore, since the optic nerve is sensitive only to a narrow range of wavelengths, heat waves do not stimulate the nerves of the eye and are invisible.

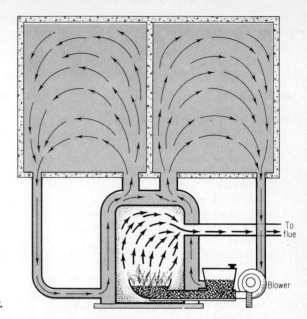

Figure 1. A warm-air heating plant.

Regardless of the method of transfer, heat always "flows" spontaneously from a warm object to a colder one.[3]

QUESTIONS

1. What three basic topics are contrasted in this passage?

   _____

2. What two examples does the author give of heat transfer by conduction?

   _____

   _____

3. How does the author define the term *conduction?* _____

4. What examples does the author give of heat transfer by convection?

   _____

5. Define the term *convection.* _____

   _____

6. What two examples does the author give of heat transfer by radiation?

   _____

   _____

7. Define the term *radiation.* _____

   _____

8. Here is a set of notes on this passage. These notes are not in order. Write them out in correct order in the guidelines provided.

Heat transfer

II. *Convection* — air in contact with heat becomes warm, expands, and rises. Cooler air takes it place. Circulation is set up in this way.
  A. Heat of bonfire reaching people nearby.
  B. Heat of sun reaching earth.

 I. *Conduction* — method of heat transfer through the substance by molecular collision.
  A. Radiator — air in contact with radiator rises. Cold air takes its place.
  B. Warm-air furnace — air heated by furnace expands and rises through pipes. Cold air drops through ducts to furnace setting up circulation.

III. *Radiation* — electromagnetic waves emitted by warm substances through space, absorbed by object on which they fall.
  A. A spoon in a hot cup of coffee — heat transferred from part of spoon that touches liquid to part that does not.
  B. Outside of the firebox on a furnace — heat passes through the metal.

Heat transfer

I. _____

_____

  A. _____

  B. _____

II. _____

_____

_____

  A. _____

  B. _____

III. _____

_____

_____

  A. _____

  B. _____

EXERCISE 4.8

DIRECTIONS   The following passage contrasts the achievements of two early civilizations. As you read the passage, note the basic contrasts. Questions on contrast and simple note-taking follow.

THE DAWN OF SCIENCE

The birthplace of man is believed to be somewhere in the eastern hemisphere, but in just what region or even on what continent it is still impossible to say. It is equally difficult to determine when or where the first, faint glimmerings of science appeared. The earliest notable scientific achievements are ascribed to the Egyptians and the Babylonians. It is certain, however, that the human race had made enormous strides of a scientific nature many centuries before the great pyramids began to rise on the banks of the Nile. . . .

Early Science.   By the middle of the fourth millennium B.C. at least two written languages had appeared, one in Babylonia and one in Egypt. It is also quite possible that two others had arisen in India and in China. As a result of their ability to record observations, these early peoples discovered that physical phenomena followed definite patterns from which they could predict future events. For example, from their records of solar eclipses, the Babylonians observed that the eclipses occurred at definite intervals of time, and thus they were able to predict future eclipses. Ardent and successful students of astronomy, they compiled lists of stars and noticed that some of these, the ones we call planets, did not remain fixed in the sky. They divided the year into 12 months, each month into 30 days, each day into 24 hours, and each hour into 60 minutes, and each minute into 60 seconds. . . . Mathematics was also highly developed by these people. Multiplication tables and tables of squares and cubes have been found in Babylonian ruins. To ensure that people received correct amounts of merchandise in their bartering, the Babylonians created standards for measuring length and weight, as well as time. . . .

The Egyptians did not develop their knowledge of astronomy to the extent of the Babylonians; however, by 4200 B.C. they had devised a calendar of 365 days. As indicated by carvings on their walls of surgeons performing various operations, they were more interested in medicine than astronomy. That the learning of the Egyptians was extensive and well organized is authenticated by two papyri, one dating from the middle of the nineteenth and the other from the middle of the seventeenth century B.C., each of which was copied from a still earlier text. These papyri and the great pyramids testify to the remarkable intellectual activity and the mathematical and engineering skills of these early Egyptians.[4]

QUESTIONS

1. What two basic topics are being contrasted in this passage?

_____

2. Contrast the achievements of the Babylonians with those of the Egyptians.

_____

_____

_____

3. Here is a set of notes on a part of this passage. These notes are not in the correct order. Write them out in correct order in the guidelines provided. Indicate the major divisions with Roman numerals I and II.

The Dawn of Science

Scientific achievements of Babylonians

Scientific achievements of Egyptians

Interest in medicine

Great engineering and mathematical skills—as evidenced by pyramids

Ability to predict eclipses

Divided calendar into months, days, hours, minutes, and seconds

Highly developed mathematics—including tables of squares and cubes

Standards for length, weight, and time

The Dawn of Science

A. _____

B. _____

C. _____

D. _____

A. _____

B. _____

EXERCISE 4.9

DIRECTIONS   In the following passage, the author contrasts three ways that mechanical energy is converted to heat energy: by friction, by concussion, and by compression. Read to distinguish the differences in the three ways mechanical energy is converted to heat energy. Questions on contrasts, definition, and note-taking follow.

ENERGY CONVERSION TO HEAT

When one surface rubs over another, the irregularities in the surfaces interlock, slide over each other, and interlock again. Since the molecules of one surface are continually striking against the molecules of the other surface, they are all set into rapid vibration. The more the surfaces are rubbed together, the faster the molecules vibrate, and the warmer the substance becomes. This can be illustrated by rubbing one's hands together and feeling the warming effect. Mechanical energy is therefore converted to heat energy.

A piece of metal resting on a solid support will become warmer if struck a few blows with a hammer, because the hammer imparts some of its energy to the atoms in the metal, increasing their linear kinetic energy and causing the temperature of the metal to rise. A person notices that his hands are much warmer after prolonged applause; sometimes they actually "burn." The impact of the hands increases the speed of the molecules in the skin, giving a sensation of warmth. Pounding a nail into hard wood heats the nail, which at times gets too hot to handle. The hammer sets the atoms of the nail into random vibrational motion, thus raising the temperature of the nail. The hammer head is also and similary heated in the process.

If a gas is compressed, its temperature rises, because some of its molecules are struck by the moving compressor piston and receive additional kinetic energy. This added energy is then distributed among the rest of the enclosed molecules, raising the temperature of the entire gas. If the gas is rapidly compressed, the molecules hit by the compressing piston are subject to tremendous increase in speed, and the gas becomes extremely hot. All of the work required to compress a gas is converted into random molecular energies.

In the cylinders of a diesel engine, air drawn in from the outside is quickly compressed by the piston to about one-sixteenth of its original volume. The pressure inside the cylinder increases to about 700 psi, and the temperature rises to almost 1100°F. A fine spray of oil is then injected into this hot air. Since the temperature is above the fire point of the oil, the oil burns and produces the power stroke. No other provision is made for the ignition of the fuel.

Heat energy produced by friction, concussion, and compression are all examples of mechanical energy being converted to heat.[5]

QUESTIONS

1. What are the three ways mechanical energy is converted to heat energy?

_____

2. How is heat energy produced by friction?_____

_____

3. What example of heat energy produced by friction does the author give?

_____

4. What examples of heat energy produced by concussion does the author give?

_____

5. What example of heat energy produced by compression does the author give?

_____

6. Here are a set of notes on this passage. These notes are not in the correct order. Write the notes out correctly. Indicate major divisions with Roman numerals (I, II, III). List examples and supporting points beneath the major divisions (A, B, C).

Three ways mechanical energy
is converted to heat energy

Three ways mechanical energy
is converted to heat energy

Heat produced by friction.

Hammer imparts kinetic energy to atoms in metal, raising temperature of the metal.

Heat energy produced by concussion.

Rubbing one's hands together.

Heat energy produced by compression.

Molecules of one surface interlock with molecules of other surface, slide over each other, and interlock again. Molecules vibrate faster and faster. Warmth is produced.

In a diesel engine, the piston strikes the mixture of air and oil vapor, heating it up and causing it to burn.

Pounding a nail into hard wood.

EXERCISE 4.10

DIRECTIONS   Read this passage on heat and answer the questions on contrast that follow.

HEAT

When a machinist drills a hole in a metal block, it becomes very hot. As the drill does mechanical work on the metal, the temperature of the metal increases. How can we explain this? We need to look at the difference between the metal at low temperatures and at high temperatures. At high temperatures the atoms in the metal vibrate more rapidly than at low temperatures. Their velocity is higher at high temperatures, and thus their kinetic energy (KE $= 1/2 \ mv^2$) is greater.

To raise the temperature of a material, we must speed up the atoms, that is, we must add energy to them. *Heat is the name given to this energy which is being added to or taken from a material.*

Drilling a hole in a metal block causes a temperature increase. As the drill turns, it collides with atoms of the metal, causing them to speed up. This mechanical work done on the metal has caused an increase in the energy (speed) of the atoms. For this reason, any friction between two surfaces results in a temperature rise of the materials.

Since heat is a form of energy, we could measure it in ft lb or joules, which are energy units. However, it was not always known that heat was a form of energy, and special units for heat were developed and are still in use.

These units are the BTU (British Thermal Unit) in the English system and the calorie in the metric system. The BTU is the amount of heat (energy) necessary to raise the temperature of 1 lb of water 1°F. The calorie is the amount of heat (energy) necessary to raise the temperature of 1 gram of water 1°C.[6]

QUESTIONS

1. According to this passage, what is the difference between metals at

low temperatures and at high temperatures? _____

_____

_____

2. Define the term "heat" as used in this passage. _____

_____

3. What example does the author use to illustrate the conversion of

mechanical energy to heat energy? _____

_____

4. Why does drilling a hole in a metal block cause a temperature increase? _____

EXERCISE 4.11

DIRECTIONS Here is a long passage on the beginnings of science taken directly from a textbook. You have read sections of this passage earlier in this chapter. As you read, look for basic *contrasts* the author makes. Then answer the questions on contrast that follow.

The Dawn of Science   Primitive man was primarily concerned about his survival. He was continually battling nature and preditory animals. In his struggle for life, he left the mysteries of nature to higher powers, the gods. To account for all phases of nature, he imagined a multitude of gods; he had a god of harvest, a god of thunder, a god of fertility, and so forth. This was very convenient, for whenever anything went wrong he blamed a god, which took the responsibilities out of his hands. He thought these same gods often punished him through floods, droughts, and famines. After each disaster, he felt the urge to go through some kind of a religious ceremony or to sacrifice something to appease the god who had punished him.

Man's first feeble attempt to control the mysteries of nature was through magic. He performed rituals and dances to try to control the amount of rain, or the amount of sunshine. These attempts by the "Witch Doctors" to control the environment, although in vain, gave primitive man the idea that by better understanding nature, he might somehow attain a measure of control over it, and thus make life more pleasant. This type of magic still appeals to modern man. To this day we rub a rabbit's foot or search for four-leaf clovers to bring us luck, and we drink a toast to a person's success. Some baseball players go through regular rituals when they come to bat, to enhance their probability of getting hits. This type of ceremony does not make them better batters, but it may remove the tension and give them more confidence in their own abilities.

By the middle of the fourth millenium B.C. man learned to read and write. At least two written languages appeared, one in Babylonia in the Tigris and Euphrates valleys and one in Egypt in the valley of the Nile. In all likelihood they were of equal antiquity. Both countries were in fertile valleys and were somewhat isolated and protected by nature. For example, the fertile valley of the Nile was protected by cataracts in the south, large deserts on both sides, and the Mediterranean in the north. Without fear of hunger or invasion, these two groups of people developed remarkable civilizations. It is also quite possible that two other written languages had appeared in China and India at about this time, but they contributed very little to our knowledge of the physical sciences.

By being able to record observations, these early people noticed that nature followed definite patterns from which they could predict future happenings. The Babylonians recorded the solar eclipes, and from the data, they observed that the eclipes occurred at definite intervals of time: from this, they predicted future eclipses. Knowing more about nature helped remove the fear of such physical phenomena. The Babylonians were ardent and successful students of astronomy. They divided the year into 360 days, 12 months of 30 days each. They also divided the week into 7 days, the day into 24 hours, the hour into 60 minutes, and the minute into 60 seconds. They believed that a person's life was controlled by the constellation of stars under which he was born; therefore they developed the theory of astrology. Bablonians called this a science, and for many of them it was the most important branch of science. Mathematics and engineering were also developed by these people during the approximately 3,000 years of their civilization. Multiplication tables and tables of squares and cubes have been found among the Babylonian ruins. They used a decimal system derived from their 10 fingers. They also realized the necessity of having standard units of length, weight, and time, and set up such standards.

By 4200 B.C., the Egyptians had developed their knowledge of astronomy, not to the extent of the Babylonians, because they did not believe in astrology, but enough to devise a calendar of 365 days. They were more interested in medicine, as some of their early carvings of Egyptian surgeons performing operations would indicate. By 3500 B.C., they were using the decimal number system, and each decimal unit was represented by a special symbol. The learning of the Egyptians was extensive and well organized, as authenticated by two papyri, one dating from about the middle of the nineteenth and the other from the middle of the seventeenth century B.C. Each of these, we are quite sure, was copied from a still earlier text. Together they give evidence of a remarkable intellectual activity in mathematics and medicine. Humanity will always remember these ancient Egyptians for their great pyramids. Such masterpieces show us the mathematical and engineering skills of the Egyptians. These great stone structures are still one of the seven wonders of the world.

During the fifteenth century B.C., the Euphrates and Nile valleys were invaded by tribesmen from the north, and under the ensuing military rule, the two civilizations gradually declined almost to oblivion.

Greek Civilization   It was fortunate for mankind that some of the ancient learning was passed on to the Greeks, and in the sixth century B.C. an intellectual awakening took place in these people. They employed the learning to such extent that the golden age of the Greek civilization is regarded by many as the highest level of achievement that the human species has yet attained.

The Greeks cultivated many of the sciences. Their most important contributions were in the fields of astronomy, mathematics, botany, physics, structure of matter, and medicine. They had a great love for abstract reasoning. To the Greeks, philosophy and science were the same thing. They relied on observations and logic rather than on experimentation, yet their achievements were truly remarkable. The earliest known scientist was Thales of Miletus (580 B.C.), who was a mathematician, an astronomer, an engineer, and a statesman. He felt that the Earth was flat, and was floating on water at the center of the universe. After studying in Egypt, he was much impressed by the rules set up for land surveying each spring after the floods. From this experience he derived certain postulates which were basic to the development of geometry later on. Pythagoras (530 B.C.) extended the work of Thales and gave the first deductive proof that the square of the hypotenuse of a right-angle triangle is equal to the sum of the squares of the other two sides. Pythagoras brought into prominence the abstract idea of a number. One of Pythagoras' disciples, Empedocles, introduced a new idea about matter. He proposed that matter was composed of four elements—earth, air, fire, and water. In 420 B.C., Democritus disagreed with this and introduced the one-element theory of matter. He believed that everything was made of indivisible, indestructible particles called *atoms* (Gr. uncut), and that all atoms were alike in substance but different in shape and size.

The greatest of all the Greek philosophers was Aristotle (384–322 B.C.). He was the son of the physician to King Philip of Macedonia. He had his schooling under Plato, the famous philosopher, and was the tutor of the king's son, who later became Alexander the Great. Because of Aristotle's high position in life, he could not do any experimenting himself, for this was considered manual labor, which was slave's work; therefore, he had to rely on reason and logic. He became known as the "father of logic." He reasoned that the Earth was spherical because a sphere is the most nearly perfect configuration. He believed the Earth to be at rest because rest is the most nearly perfect position. He also argued that a heavy object falls faster than a light one because things seek their natural places. He had his greatest success in biology, with much less success in the physical sciences. Nevertheless, Aristotle's views on all phases of science were accepted without question for nearly 2,000 years.

The only true scientist of the Greek period of whom we have a record was Archimedes (287–212 B.C.). He isolated a problem, gathered experimental data relating to that problem, drew his conclusions, and then checked his conclusions by experiments. He also combined mathematics with experimental inquiry. He was the first to consider the theoretical aspects of the levers that were used 2,000 years earlier by the Egyptians. He formulated the concept of density. The greatest of his discoveries was a physical principle which bears his name. The problem which led him to this discovery was that of determining the amount of silver and gold in the king's crown without taking the crown apart. One day while taking a bath and thinking about the problem, he noticed that his legs felt much lighter in the water, and, as the story goes, he jumped out of the bathtub and ran down the street shouting, "Eureka! Eureka!" which means, "I have got it! I have got it!" After some experimenting he observed that the buoyant force or lift on an object submerged in a liquid is equal to the weight of the liquid displaced by that object. This is known as Archimedes' principle. By weighing the crown in air and again submerged in water, and using his principle, he was able to compute the amount of each metal in the crown. With all of his ingenious inventions, Archimedes helped to keep the Romans from conquering Syracuse for a number of years, but eventually the city fell and Archimedes was killed by an invading soldier.

The Greeks were the first people to assume that nature was rational and understandable by man.

The Renaissance   By the sixteenth century, paper had been invented by the Chinese and appeared in Europe, the printing press had been invented in Germany, and the Spanish and Portugese had expanded commercial trade by discovering the Virgin Islands and America. All of these factors tended to change the outlook of mankind: reformations started in politics, religions, and science, as men began considering nature as something to understand instead of something to fear.

Galileo Galilei (1564–1642) was one of the great intellectuals of the Renaissance period. His father wanted him to study medicine, so he attended the University of Pisa. While there he became interested in physics and astronomy, and later became a professor at the university. He experimented with balls rolling down inclined planes of various slopes and lengths, and from his observations he established the laws of accelerated motion. He rejected Aristotle's theory of falling objects and proposed that heavy and light objects fall at the same rate. The story is told that, to prove his point, he dropped two stones of different weights from the top of the Leaning Tower of Pisa. When they struck the ground at the same time, his colleagues at the university could not believe what they had seen. They thought that he had pulled some kind of trick on them, and so he was released from the Pisa faculty. Whether this be true or legendary, Galileo left Pisa and went to the University of Padua as a mathematician. While there he heard of a new glass made by Lippershey, a Dutchman, that could magnify distant objects. This gave him the idea that he might magnify the heavens. He constructed a telescope, and what he discovered with this telescope (it has been estimated) would have won him at least nine Nobel Prizes, had they been granted at that time. From his observations he was convinced that Copernicus and Kepler were right—the Sun was the center of the planetary system. In 1632, he published "A Dialogue on the Two Principal Systems of the World," and it aroused a great deal of attention throughout Europe. The following year, Galileo was summoned to Rome and forced to renounce his findings. He was sentenced to an indefinite prison term and spent the remaining years of his life confined to his villa in Florence under constant surveillance.

Sir Isaac Newton (1642–1727), an English mathematician, physicist, and astronomer, was born the year Galileo died. Newton was the greatest scientific genius the world has ever known. He introduced the binomial theorem, formulated the three basic laws of motion, developed a differential calculus in order to use adequately his laws of motion, discovered the composition of light, and deduced the inverse-square law of gravitation. It is said that one day, while walking through an orchard, he saw an apple fall from a tree and he began to wonder why the apple fell. His curiosity led to the formulation of the law of gravitation. He also wondered how far out from the Earth the attraction extended, and thought that maybe the force that pulled the apple to the ground might be the force that held the Moon on its course around the Earth. From this assumption he calculated the motion of the Moon around the Earth and found it to agree with the observed facts. Assuming the Sun to have a similar gravitational force, he calculated the motions of the planets about the Sun and found that these motions satisfied Kepler's laws. In 1703 he was elected president of the Royal Society of London, which position he held until his death.[7]

QUESTIONS

1. How did primitive people account for natural phenomena?_____

_____

2. In both the Babylonian and Egyptian civilizations, people recorded their observations of the heavens and discovered that there were definite patterns. What was the result of this discovery?_____

_____

3. In what important way was the Greeks' view of nature different from that of others who had gone before them? _____

_____

4. Contrast Aristotle's and Galileo's theories of falling objects._____

_____

NOTES

1. Dale Ewen, et al., *Physics for Career Education.* Englewood Cliffs, N.J.: Prentice-Hall, Inc., 1974, p. 184
2. George Gamow, *Matter, Earth, and Sky,* 2d ed. Englewood Cliffs, N.J.: Prentice-Hall, Inc., 1965, pp. 462–63.
3. Willard J. Poppy and Leland L. Wilson, *Exploring the Physical Sciences,* 2d ed. Englewood Cliffs, N.J.: Prentice-Hall, Inc., 1973, pp. 202–4.
4. E. J. Cable et al., *The Physical Sciences,* 5th ed. Englewood Cliffs, N.J.: Prentice-Hall, Inc., 1969, p. 1.
5. E. J. Cabal et al., *The Physical Sciences,* p. 124.
6. Ewen et al., *Physics for Career Education,* p. 213.
7. Poppy and Wilson, *Exploring the Physical Sciences,* 1st ed. Englewood Cliffs, N.J.: Prentice-Hall, Inc., 1965, pp. 1–6.

5

CAUSE-EFFECT

People have always been curious about why things happen in the world. From earliest times, they looked for the *causes* of the events around them. It wasn't enough to know, "it's raining." The question was, "*Why* is it raining? What is the *cause* of the rain?"

If there is one relationship that is basic to science, it is the relationship of *cause* to *effect*. Cause-effect is the fundamental logical relationship in science, whether the subject is chemistry, physics, or one of the dozens of fields in which basic principles of chemistry and physics are put to work. These fields include electrical, mechanical, electromechanical, automotive, and construction technology, as well as many other areas.

An understanding of cause-effect relationships will be very helpful to you in the study of any scientific or technical subject. It will give a focus to your reading.

There is a special way—a kind of shorthand—that can be used to take notes on cause-effect. You can use this special shorthand in class lectures, to take notes on materials, and to organize many kinds of technical information in a logical way.

This chapter will explain how to identify cause-effect relationships and how to use cause-effect shorthand to organize and remember scientific information.

Here is an example of a sentence that expressses a cause-effect relationship:

> The energy of the water tumbling over the waterfall turns the waterwheel.

If you had to break this sentence into two parts, and draw a circle around each part, you would probably do the following:

> The energy of the water tumbling over the waterfall turns the waterwheel.

The sentence really has two parts. The first part is "The energy of the water tumbling over the waterfall." The second part is "The waterwheel turns."

The information in the sentence could be restated as follows:

CAUSE   Energy of water tumbling over the waterfall.
EFFECT   Waterwheel turns.

Here is an example of two sentences that together express a cause-effect relationship.

> The water tumbling over the waterfall possesses kinetic energy, the energy of motion. This energy may be used to turn the blades of the waterwheel, an example of mechanical energy.

The information in these two sentences could be restated as follows:

CAUSE   Water tumbles over the waterfall (this is kinetic energy).
EFFECT   The blades of the waterwheel turn (this is mechanical energy).

CAUSE-EFFECT NOTATION

There is a very useful way to take notes on cause-effect relationships. It is called cause-effect notation. Here is an example of cause-effect notation, side by side with the sentence on which it is based:

The kinetic energy of the waterfall is converted to the mechanical energy of the waterwheel

> *Kinetic energy of waterfall → mechanical energy of waterwheel.*

In cause-effect notation, the arrow ⟶ stands for the word "yields." The notation

> *Kinetic energy of waterfall ⟶ mechanical energy of waterwheel*

would be read, "The kinetic energy of the waterfall yields the mechanical energy of the waterwheel."

Here are two other examples of cause-effect sentences, side-by-side with cause-effect notation:

As the molecules of one surface rub against the molecules of another surface, they begin to vibrate more and more rapidly.

Molecules of surfaces rub against each other → vibration.

As the molecules vibrate more and more rapidly, warmth is produced.

Rapid vibration → warmth.

SIGNAL WORDS

Many words signal cause-effect relationships, including the following ones: *the consequence, consequently, so, as a result, therefore, thereby, yields, for this reason, thus, because, accordingly, hence, the cause, the effect, the result, that is why.*

Here are some examples of cause-effect relationships, with the signal words italicized:

The molecules of a solid are in fixed positions in relation to one another. *Therefore* a solid does not take on the shape of its container.

The molecules of a liquid flow over each other, somewhat like a pile of marbles. *As a consequence,* a liquid takes on the shape of its container.

Because the molecules of a liquid flow over each other, a liquid takes on the shape of its container.

The movement of molecules of a gas is limited only by the container. *Therefore* a gas takes on the shape of its container.
The molecules of a gas are far apart. *Consequently,* a gas can be easily compressed.

Signal words are helpful when you are first learning about cause-effect. However, as you practice identifying cause-effect relationships, you will be able to take notes on them whether the author has used signal words or not.

DIFFERENT KINDS OF CAUSE-EFFECT

Cause-effect relationships are written in many ways. The effect may be stated first, and then the cause, as in the following example:

When you are hammering a nail, the temperature of the nail rises. This is a result of the impact of the hammer, which imparts kinetic energy to the atoms in the metal.

Hammer gives kinetic energy to atoms in nail → temp. rises.

A cause can have more than one effect.

***EXAMPLE OF
ONE CAUSE,
TWO EFFECTS***

The electrical energy of a toaster is converted to both heat and light.

electric energy of toaster
→ *heat energy*
→ *light energy*

or

electric energy of toaster → *heat and light energy*

An effect can have more than one cause.

***EXAMPLE OF
TWO CAUSES,
ONE EFFECT***

Imagine someone twirling a tin can around on a string. The centripetal force on the stone is balanced by the centrifugal force on the hand twirling the string. Consequently, the can stays in orbit.

Centrifugal and centripetal forces balance → can stays in orbit.

CAUSAL CHAINS

A cause-effect relationship may be extended through many stages. This is called a *causal chain*. Here is an example of a causal chain.

Water stored behind a dam possesses potential energy, the energy of position. When the gates of the dam are released, the water spills over the waterfall. The water has now acquired what is called kinetic energy, the energy of motion. The energy of the waterfall will produce mechanical energy as the water turns the blades of the turbine. This mechanical energy will be converted to electrical energy in a generator.

This information could be expressed briefly as follows:

Potential energy   →   *kinetic energy* →
(water stored behind dam)   (waterfall)

Mechanical energy   →   *electrical energy*
(turbine)   (generator)

USES OF CAUSE-EFFECT NOTATION

Cause-effect notation is a way to "boil down" technical information. Here is an example of a paragraph; next to it, the information has been boiled down into a causal chain:

If you drill a hole in a metal block, the drill will collide with atoms of the metal. The kinetic energy imparted by the drill will cause the atoms in the metal to vibrate faster. Consequently, the temperature of the metal will rise.

Kinetic energy of drill → atoms vibrate faster → temp. rises.

Often it is very difficult to untangle or make sense of a technical passage. If you set about trying to distinguish causes and effects, and take notes on these relationships, you will have a much better understanding of them.

In the beginning, you may find that you sometimes put the effects *before* the causes in your notes. This is particularly true when the author states the effect before stating the cause:

One's hands grow warmer when one rubs the surfaces together.

Hands grow warmer → rubbing surfaces together.

However, the notation

Hands grow warmer → rubbing surfaces together.

makes no sense. Always check your cause-effect notation by substituting the word "yields" for the arrow, and checking to see if what you have written is logical. The notation should read *Rubbing surfaces together → warmth.*

This is an important step. In the logic of science, a cause cannot be preceded by an effect. A given event cannot cause another event that happened earlier. For example, in the cylinders of a diesel engine, air is drawn in and compressed. As it is compressed, the temperature of the air rises. When oil is sprayed into the hot air, it ignites and produces the power stroke. The power stroke cannot cause the compression of the gas. When we say that something is not "logical," we often mean that any particular event cannot cause another event that occurred earlier in time.

There are many ways of expressing cause-effect relationships—in single sentences or in long chains. No matter how the cause-effect relationship is arranged, understanding and taking notes on it will be very useful to you. Cause-effect notation is a logical way to approach material in a technical text. Using this system, you will be able to untangle difficult passages and boil the information down to essential phrases. In doing this, you will be able to understand and remember the information.

> **LOOKING AHEAD**   The exercises that follow will develop your ability to use cause-effect notation to understand and remember technical information.
> By the time you finish this chapter, you should be able to
>
> 1. Distinguish causes from effects.
> 2. Recognize typical words that signal cause-effect relationships.
> 3. Use cause-effect notation on sentences, paragraphs, and longer textbook passages.
> 4. Answer questions based on an understanding of cause-effect relationships.

SUMMARY

1. Cause-effect is a fundamental relationship in technical writing.

2. Use cause-effect notation to express this relationship. Write the cause in the briefest way possible. Use an arrow $\longrightarrow$ to connect cause to effect. This arrow stands for the word "yields," "leads to," or "results in."

3. Many words signal cause-effect relationships, including *the consequence, consequently, as a result, the cause, the effect, therefore, yields, for this reason, thus, because, accordingly.*

4. Cause-effect relationships may be expressed in many ways. There may be multiple causes or multiple effects. There may be a long chain of causes and effects.

5. Check your notation to make sure you haven't put an effect before a cause.

6. Use cause-effect notation to boil down information in a technical text. This will help you both understand and remember the information.

EXERCISE 5.1

DIRECTIONS   Each of the following statements about rock decay can be divided into two parts. One part can be labeled "cause" and one part "effect." Write out the cause and the effect for each sentence. Then express the information in cause-effect notation.

EXAMPLE   Temperature changes may cause rock to crumble.

Cause: *Temperature changes.*

Effect: *Rock may crumble.*

Cause-effect notation: *Temperature change → rock may crumble.*

1. The sun's rays heat up rock during the day, and the rock expands.

   Cause:_____

   Effect:_____

   Cause-effect notation: _____ → _____

2. When the air cools off at night, the surface of the rock contracts.

   Cause: _____

   Effect:_____

   Cause-effect notation:_____ → _____

3. Heat during the day plus cooling at night results in alternating expansion and contraction.

   Cause: _____

   Effect: _____

   Cause-effect notation: _____ → _____

4. Alternating periods of expansion and contraction lead to fragmentation.

   Cause:_____

   Effect: _____

   Cause-effect notation: _____ → _____

5. The crumbling of rock can also be caused by the freezing of moisture present in the cracks of rocks.

   Cause: _____

   Effect: _____

   Cause-effect notation: _____

6. Rocks fragment because ice forms in cracks within the rock, and then exerts great pressure on the surrounding rock.

Cause: _____

Effect: _____

Cause-effect notation: _____

7. Rock crumbles because of temperature change and because of freezing.

Cause: _____

Effect: _____

Cause-effect notation: _____

EXERCISE 5.2

DIRECTIONS Use cause-effect notation on each of the following items. Indicate signal words.

EXAMPLE A temperature rise results from friction.

Cause-effect notation: *friction → temperature rise*

Signal word(s): *results*

1. If you drill a hole in a metal block, the metal becomes hot.

Cause-effect notation: _____

Signal word(s): _____

2. At high temperatures the atoms vibrate more rapidly than at low temperatures, and thus their kinetic energy is greater.

Cause-effect notation: _____

Signal word(s): _____

3. As the drill turns, it collides with the metal, causing the atoms to speed up.

Cause-effect notation: _____

Signal word(s): _____

4. Greek natural philosophers did not usually test out their theories by direct observation. As a result, they acquired little empirical information.

Cause-effect notation: _____

5. The experimentalists' method, in which theories were tested out by direct observation, began to flourish during the Renaissance. As a result, empirical evidence began to accumulate rapidly.

Cause-effect notation:_____

Signal word(s):_____

EXERCISE 5.3

DIRECTIONS   The atom is composed of a nucleus, which has protons and neutrons, and of electrons. The electrons are negatively charged particles that travel around the nucleus (see Fig. 5.1). All the following sentences and short paragraphs describe the atom. Answer the questions on cause-effect that follow each item.

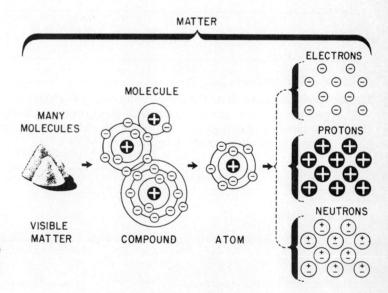

Figure 5.1. Breakdown of visible matter to electric particles.

EXAMPLE   The behavior of electric circuits is a direct result of the behavior of electrons.

Cause: *behavior of electrons*

Effect: *behavior of electric circuits*

Signal word: *result*

Cause-effect notation: *behavior of electrons → behavior of electric circuits.*

1. The nucleus of an atom is composed of neutrons and protons. The neutrons are neutral. The protons have a positive charge. Therefore the nucleus has a positive charge:

   Cause: _____

   Effect: _____

   Signal word(s): _____

   Cause-effect notation: _____

QUESTION

Why does the nucleus have a positive charge?_____

_____

2. The nucleus of an atom has a positive charge. This is because it is composed of neutrons (neutral) and protons (positive).

   Cause: _____

   Effect: _____

   Signal word(s): _____

   Cause-effect notation: _____

3. The normal atom has the same number of electrons (negative charges) as protons (positive charges). The positive charges of the protons balance the negative charges of the electrons. Therefore in the normal atom there is no charge.

   Cause: _____

   Effect: _____

   Signal word(s): _____

   Cause-effect notation: _____

QUESTION

Why is there no charge in the normal atom?_____

_____

4. If a neutral body loses some of its electrons (negative charges), it will have a positive charge.

   Cause: _____

   Effect: _____

   Cause-effect notation: _____

5. If a neutral body gains electrons, it will have a negative charge.

Cause: _____

Effect: _____

Cause-effect notation: _____

6. The electrons that are in the farthest shell from the nucleus are called valence electrons. These valence electrons are very important: the electrical and chemical properties of materials depend on the number of valence electrons.

QUESTIONS

a. What are valence electrons? _____

b. Why are valence electrons important? _____

EXERCISE 5.4

DIRECTIONS   Read the following paragraph, which is excerpted from a textbook on electrical theory. Then answer the questions that follow. Note that each sentence in the passage has been numbered.

VALENCE ELECTRONS

(1) The electrons in the last shell are called *valence* electrons, and the electrical (and chemical) properties of a material are dependent on the number of such electrons. (2) A filled last shell (eight valence electrons) produces an inert material. (3) The electrons are tightly bound to their nucleus. (4) Atoms with less than four valence electrons tend to give up one or more electrons, and the fewer the valence electrons, the greater this tendency. (5) Conversely, atoms with more than four electrons in their last shell have a tendency to acquire one or more additional electrons. (6) In elements with atomic valences of four, adjacent atoms form into a crystal structure sharing their electrons in *covalent bonds*. (7) Such bonding fills the valence shell, and the material is electrically inert. (8) This creates the *semiconductor* properties that are fundamental to solid-state (transistor) electronics.[1]

QUESTIONS

1. Express the first sentence of this paragraph as a cause-effect relationship.

_____   _____

2. Express the second and third sentences as a cause-effect relationship.

_____   _____

3. Express the fourth sentence as a cause-effect relationship.

_____ → _____

4. Express the fifth sentence as a cause-effect relationship.

_____ → _____

5. Express the sixth and seventh sentences as a cause-effect relationship.

_____ → _____

EXERCISE 5.5

DIRECTIONS The following items are based on the preceding passage on valence electrons. The left-hand column lists causes. The right-hand column lists effects. Please match causes and effects. Then list matched pairs below the columns, using cause-effect notation.

Causes	*Effects*
Number of electrons in last shell (valence electrons)	Tendency to share electrons with adjacent atoms
A filled last shell (eight valence electrons)	Inert material
Atoms with less than four valence electrons	
Atoms with more than four valence electrons	Tendency to give up valence electrons
	Tendency to acquire additional valence electrons
Atoms with valences of four	Electrical and chemical properties of a material

1. _____ → _____

2. _____ → _____

3. _____ → _____

4. _____ → _____

5. _____ → _____

EXERCISE 5.6

DIRECTIONS Express the information in the following paragraphs in causal chains.

EXAMPLE When oil burns, it heats up the water in a hot-water furnace. The water boils, producing steam. The steam rises through the pipes until it reaches a radiator in a room. The steam heats the metal radiator.

Oil burns → water in furnace heats up → steam → hot radiator.

1   The sun's heat during the day combined with rapid cooling at night re-
     sults in alternate expansion and contraction of the constituent materials
     in rock. This in turn may lead to fragmentation.

_____   _____   _____

2   We are all familiar with examples of energy conversion. For instance,
     the sun's energy causes lake water to evaporate. This vapor rises. Be-
     cause of its high position, it has potential energy. The water falls as
     rain and travels in a river to a waterfall. The kinetic energy of the wa-
     terfall turns the waterwheel, itself an example of mechanical energy.
     The mechanical energy drives the generator, an example of electrical
     energy. When you flip on the light switch, you convert this electrical
     energy to light and heat.

_____   _____

_____   _____

_____   _____

3   The following items are based on the preceding paragraph. The left-
     hand column lists causes. The right-hand column lists effects. Match
     causes and effects. Then list the matched pairs below to make a causal
     chain.

Sun's rays   Electrical energy of generator

Potential energy of water vapor in   Kinetic energy of streams and spillways
clouds
                                        Evaporation of surface water into clouds
Mechanical energy of waterwheel

_____ → _____

_____ → _____

_____ → _____

EXERCISE 5.7

DIRECTIONS   Read the following passage and answer the questions on cause-
               effect that follow.

               If we carry a heavy parcel against the force of gravity up several flights
               of stairs, we soon become aware that we are expending a considerable
               amount of energy. Strangely enough, this conversion of the chemical

energy stored in the tissue of our body to mechanical energy, which, in turn, moves a mass against the force of gravity, is called *work.*

> *Work is the accomplishment of motion against the action of a force which tends to oppose the motion.*

Because the energy needed to perform this work was present before we climbed the stairs,

> *Energy is the capacity to do work.*

One further basic concept which we must note before we investigate the electrical property of matter is the principle of conservation of energy, which states that

> *In any closed system, the total energy remains constant.*

Energy can be transformed from one form into another, but the total energy after the transformation must exactly equal the total energy going into the transformation. Consequently, energy and work are numerically the same, and we may use the same unit of measurement for both.[2]

QUESTIONS

1. Define *work.* _____

2. Define *energy.* _____

3. Express the information in the last paragraph of the passage as a causal chain. Notice the signal word "consequently." _____

_____

_____

EXERCISE 5.8

DIRECTIONS   Read the following textbook passage and answer the questions on cause-effect that follow. Each sentence in the paragraph has been numbered.

ELECTROSTATIC FIELDS

(1) Suppose we have a piece of glass rod. (2) It is composed of atoms. (3) Each atom has the same number of electrons and protons and therefore no charge. (4) If we take a piece of silk and rub it on the glass rod, we find that the rod can now pick up pieces of paper. (5) It has ability to do work. (6) In other words, it has energy. (7) Where did this energy come from? (8) We ate breakfast—chemical energy. (9) Our bodies converted this into mechanical energy in our muscles. (10) In rubbing, we converted some of this mechanical energy into friction, or

heat energy, but the rest remained as energy in the glass rod. (11) Exactly what has taken place? (12) By rubbing, the silk has removed electrons from the glass rod. (13) The silk now has an excess of electrons, or a negative charge. (14) The glass has a deficiency of electrons, or a positive charge. (15) These charged bodies have energy. (16) The energy is not in the charged body itself, but in a field of force surrounding the body. (17) This assertion can readily be proved as follows: charge your hard-rubber or plastic fountain pen by rubbing it on your sleeve. (18) The pen is now surrounded by an energy field. (19) This field can do work. (20) Tear up some paper into small pieces. (21) The pen can pick up these pieces, but notice that you do not have to touch the paper. (22) If the pen is held close to the paper, the pieces will jump up to the pen. (23) The energy is therefore in a field surrounding the body. (24) This energy is stored in what is called a *dielectric* or *electrostatic* field.[3]

QUESTIONS

1. Express the first three sentences as a cause-effect relationship. _____

2. Express sentences 8, 9, and 10 as a causal chain. _____

_____

3. Express sentences 12, 13, and 14 as a cause-effect relationship. _____

EXERCISE 5.9

DIRECTIONS Read this passage and answer the questions on cause-effect that follow.

Some 2500 years ago, Thales of Miletus was one of the first to discover a means of disturbing the normal electrical balance of matter. He noted that when he rubbed a piece of amber, it acquired an ability to attract light pieces of straw and dust. However, it was not until the eighteenth century that serious experiments were conducted in an effort to learn the nature of this force which attracted small particles of straw and dust.

We can duplicate Thales' experiment by rubbing a glass rod with a silk cloth, or an ebonite rod with a piece of cat's fur. Since these rods can then attract bits of paper against the force of gravity, work is being accomplished and energy is being expended. Rubbing the rods must have provided them with some form of energy which they did not reveal in their normal state. We say that we "placed" an electric *charge* on the rod, using the term charge to imply potential energy in much the same sense that we speak of a charge of dynamite placed in a drill hole for a blasting operation.

We can investigate the effect of the force produced by rubbing glass or ebonite rods by means of lightweight balls suspended by silk threads, as shown in Fig. 1. We discover that we can transfer some of the charge from the rods to the balls by touching them with a charged rod. If we touch a charged glass rod to both balls, we discover that they tend to *repel* one another, as in Fig. 1(a). However, if we touch a charged glass rod to the left ball and a charged ebonite rod to the right ball, we find that they tend to *attract* one another, as in Fig. 1(b).

From these observations, we can state that the force between the charged balls is a *field* force, since the balls are not in contact. But the force is *not* gravitational force, since gravitational force is always a force of attraction, never repulsion. Secondly, the charge on the ebonite rod must be different from that on the glass rod, since in one example we produce a force of repulsion, and in the other a force of attraction. Since both balls in Fig. 1(a) were charged from the same glass rod, the two balls must possess *like charges.* With no knowledge of the exact nature of these charges, the eighteenth-century scientists could only label the charges in Fig. 1(b) as *unlike charges,* and state that

Like charges repel, unlike charges attract.[4]

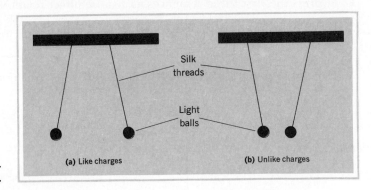

**Figure 1. Coulomb's demon-
stration of electric force.**

(a) Like charges   (b) Unlike charges

QUESTIONS

1. What is the effect of rubbing a glass rod with a silk cloth?
a. The rod can attract pieces of paper against the force of gravity.
b. We have provided the rod with energy.
c. We have placed an electric charge on the rod.
d. All three of the above.
2. The repulsive force between charged bodies
a. may be gravitational, since all bodies have gravitational force between them.
b. is a field force, since charged bodies do not have to be in direct contact.
c. received no experimental investigation in the eighteenth century.

3. What effect do like charges have on each other?_____

4. What effect do unlike charges have on each other? _____

DIRECTIONS   Here is a long selection on electron theory taken directly from a textbook. Questions on cause-effect follow the selection. As you read: (1) Identify all important terms; these include *nucleus, proton, electron, valence electron, covalent bonds,* and *energy.* (2) Use examples to make sure you understand the ideas that they illustrate.

ELECTRON THEORY

At one time, students of electricity used to be told: "We don't know what electricity is, but—. We don't know what current is, but—. We don't know how electricity goes through a solid wire, but—."

The electron theory, though only a theory, explains these things clearly and simply. In addition, it explains the true meaning of voltage, resistance, insulation, magnetism, induced voltage, and vacuum tubes. Therefore, an understanding of the fundamentals of the electron theory is basic to the understanding of electrical and electronic theory.

Scientists now agree that our universe is fundamentally dependent on two factors, one of which is matter, the other, energy. Let us consider matter first, then energy.

Matter is anything that occupies space and has weight. It can exist in any of three forms: solid, liquid, or gaseous.

The composition of matter is divided into three ingredients: protons, neutrons, and electrons. Let us see what each of these in turn is. The word "proton" gives us a clue that the proton is a positive charge. (Now don't ask at present what a positive charge means. It will be explained later.) This ingredient has very little weight. The neutron, as the name indicates, is neutral; that is, it has no charge. But what is it there for? It supplies practically all the weight of matter. The electron charge is opposite to the proton; that is, it has a negative charge. In turn, it also has very little weight. These are our basic ingredients. If we could examine the structure of a piece of copper, we would find that it consists of a specific number of protons, neutrons, and electrons arranged in some particular manner. In a piece of iron, a certain number of protons, neutrons, and electrons are arranged in a different way. The proton of iron is identical to that of copper, and similarly for the other elements. They are all made up of the same ingredients. Since the arrangement of these ingredients is so important, let us consider the structure of matter.

The structure of the atom   When we take protons, neutrons, and electrons and make up a small part of iron or copper, we call it an atom. We can say that the atom is the smallest recognizable part of any element.

Nucleus   We find that the atom has, first of all a nucleus. The nucleus is composed of the protons and neutrons. All the protons and all the neutrons which that material has are grouped into one small mass which we call the *nucleus*. ... What would the charge of the nucleus be? It consists of protons which are positive, and neutrons which have no charge; therefore the nucleus must be positive. In addition, we find that the nucleus spins on its own axis.

Those of you who have studied chemistry may recall atomic weights and atomic numbers. The word "weight" tells us that atomic weight has something to do with the number of neutrons in the atom. The atomic number corresponds to the number of protons in the atom, and also the number of electrons.

Electrons   The electrons are the remaining ingredients of our atom. You may have seen or heard that these electrons are arranged in shells around the nucleus. Let us see what that statement means. One electron may be a certain distance away from its nucleus. That electron is rotating around the nucleus, making a ring around it. This ring may be elliptical. At the same time, the plane of the electron shifts a few degrees, so that we get another ring, and then another and another, so that we finally have the electron tracing the path of a complete sphere or shell. We may have some more electrons a greater distance away also shifting their planes or orbits of rotation. They are arranged in a similar fashion, forming a second shell (see Fig. 1). The maximum number of shells for any known element is seven. (The shells are labeled alphabetically K through Q starting with the innermost shell.) Each shell has a definite maximum limit as to the number of electron orbits it can have. This limit is given by

$$\text{Maximum orbital paths} = 2n^2$$

where $n =$ the shell number.

Obviously, the K, or first shell, has a maximum electron quota of two,

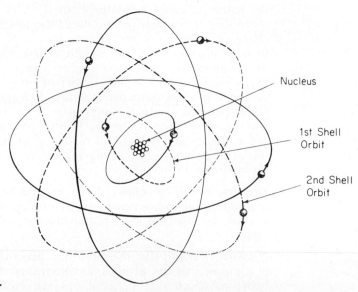

Figure 1. Electron orbital shells.

(2×1^2); the second shell, eight (2×2^2); the third shell, eighteen; and so on.

However, there are two other limitations. The *outermost* shell is filled when it reaches eight electrons; and the next to the last shell cannot contain more than eighteen regardless of its quota. Some examples follow:

1. Argon (Ar), atomic number 18, has an electron grouping of 2-8-8. The last shell is filled. (Yet, as the third shell, its maximum quota is 18.)
2. Potassium (K), atomic number 19, has four shells, with an electron grouping of 2-8-8-1.
3. Iron (Fe), atomic number 26, has an electron grouping of 2-8-14-2. Notice that since the third shell is no longer the last shell, it can build up toward its quota of 18.
4. Cesium (Cs), atomic number 55, has an electron grouping of 2-8-18-18-8-1. The last electron cannot go into shell 4, because it would then be the next to the last shell and its maximum is 18; nor can this electron go into shell 5, because that would exceed the last shell limitation of 8.

The electrons in the last shell are called *valence* electrons, and the electrical (and chemical) properties of a material are dependent on the number of such electrons. A filled last shell (eight valence electrons) produces an inert material. The electrons are tightly bound to their nucleus. Atoms with less than four valence electrons tend to give up one or more electrons, and the fewer the valence electrons the greater this tendency. Conversely, atoms with more than four electrons in their last shell have a tendency to acquire one or more additional electrons. In elements with atomic valences of four, adjacent atoms form into a crystal structure sharing their electrons in *covalent bonds*. Such bonding fills the valence shell, and the material is electrically inert. This creates the *semiconductor* properties that are fundamental to solid-state (transistor) electronics.

What else are these electrons doing? They spin on their own axes and at the same time they revolve around the nucleus. Also, in any one shell, of the number of electrons revolving around the nucleus, some move in a clockwise direction, whereas others revolve in a counterclockwise direction. The number revolving clockwise may or may not be equal to the number revolving counterclockwise. These motions compare very well to our own solar system. The sun is the center of the universe and revolves on its own axis. The planets revolve around the sun and rotate on their own axes. So the picture is very clearly seen when we compare the atom with the solar system (see Fig. 1).

There is one more point about the structure of the atom: In a normal atom the number of electrons is equal to the number of protons. What is the total charge in the atom? It's balanced. There are just as many positive charges as negative, so that a normal atom has no charge.

Atomic dimensions   At this point a word about atomic dimensions is in order. Atomic dimensions are necessary to explain such a phenomenon as conductance. (These figures do not have to be memorized, but the relative dimensions are important.)

Consider the electron's weight: If we take 5×10^{19} electrons, put them all together, and weigh them, they equal one pound. As to diameter, if we take 1×10^{13} electrons and line them up, one alongside the other, we have one inch. The proton is heavier than the electron. This fact is obvious when we recall that the proton contains the neutron, which is the heaviest part of the atom. To obtain a pound's weight, we require only 1×10^{16} protons. On the other hand, the proton is smaller than the electron in diameter: 2×10^{16} protons equal one inch. This time we need 2,000 times as many to equal one inch. The radius of the orbit from the electron to the nucleus is equal to 10,000 times the diameter of the electron. So if you were asked to state what the major portion of the atom consists of, the only answer would be "empty space."

If a powerful microscope could be obtained to magnify an electron to the size of a basketball, its proton would look like a pea and the space between them would equal three miles! When later we consider a piece of "solid" copper wire and say that electrons flow through it, we can see that there is plenty of room for electron motion.

Forces within the atom   You may wonder what prevents the electron, which is minus, from crashing into the proton, or nucleus, which is positive. Why does it stay in a circular path? Why doesn't it fly out? Let's consider the forces in the atom. First, there is a definite force of attraction between the positive nucleus and negative electron. Secondly, did you ever tie a tin can to a string and whirl it around your head? There is a tendency for the can to fly off. You must pull on the string to keep the can in its circular path. Our electron rotating around the nucleus develops a similar force. This centrifugal force tends to make the electron fly away. So if the electron stays in its orbit, it's obvious that the two forces must be balanced (see Fig. 2).

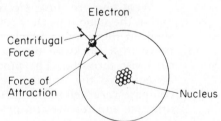

Figure 2. Balance of forces within the atom.

Let's consider an electron in the second shell. It is farther away from the nucleus. The force of attraction is weaker, but the electron is rotating at a slower speed. The centrifugal force is also weaker. The two forces are still balanced. The forces in the third and fourth shell must be still weaker; that is, the forces on the outer shells decrease.

Energy   In talking about forces we come to the next fundamental factor of the universe—energy. Energy has been defined as the ability to do work. We cannot see or feel energy itself, but we can notice its effects. At one time it was thought that energy could be created or destroyed, but careful analysis has proven that energy is actually being liberated or converted from one form to another. For example, the sun's rays fall on a lake, causing the water to evaporate. The water rises as vapor to the clouds. The water, because of its high position in the clouds, has *potential* energy. Water falls as rain on the mountain top and forms a stream; then it comes to a waterfall, where the energy changes to *kinetic* energy as the water falls. This type of energy may be used to turn a water wheel, which in turn might produce *mechanical* energy that drives a generator. The generator would produce *electrical* energy, which now can be used to light a bulb, which in turn gives off *light* energy. Some of the *electrical* energy is also converted to *heat,* as you well know if you have ever tried to remove a large bulb from its socket just after switching off the electrical supply. The bulb's energy is similar to the original rays of the sun, being composed of light and heat.

QUESTIONS

1. Define:

nucleus _____

proton _____

electron _____

valence electron _____

energy _____

2. Why does the nucleus of the atom have a positive charge? _____

_____

3. Atomic weight is related to
   a. number of electrons
   b. number of protons
   c. number of neutrons

4. What is the charge in a normal atom? Why? _____

_____

5. Why is there room for electron motion in a piece of "solid" copper?

_____

6. Why doesn't the electron, which is negative, crash into the proton,

which is positive? _____

1. J. J. DeFrance, *Electrical Fundamentals.* Englewood Cliffs, N.J.: Prentice-Hall, Inc., 1969, p. 6.
2. Herbert W. Jackson, *Introduction to Electric Circuits,* 4th ed. Englewood Cliffs, N.J.: Prentice-Hall, Inc., 1976, p. 5.
3. DeFrance, *Electrical Fundamentals,* p. 8.
4. Jackson, *Introduction to Electric Circuits,* 4th ed., pp. 5–6.
5. DeFrance, *Electrical Fundamentals,* pp. 3–11.

6

WRITING OUT MAIN IDEAS

You have learned that an author may develop ideas in the following ways:

1. By *defining* and further explaining a term.
2. By the use of *examples*.
3. By *classification and listing*.
4. By a *contrast* of different ideas.
5. By use of the relationship of *causes to effects*.

In this chapter you will practice using these five relationships to help you determine and write out main ideas of passages.

The "main idea" of a passage is the key point that the author is making. Your ability to write out this point and recognize how other information backs it up will greatly aid you in understanding and remembering technical material.

Most technical writing is dense; a great deal of information is compressed into a small space. It is necessary to read this kind of writing very carefully.

Often we think that if someone reads slowly, it is bad. This simply is not true in relation to technical materials. For instance, many studies have shown that engineers read technical information very, very slowly. Each word counts. Technical material is saturated with ideas; it is not written to be sped through. Every definition has to be thought about;

the examples have to be imagined. One has to understand basic contrasts and the relations of particular causes to particular effects.

If you read technical material carefully in this way, taking advantage of your knowledge of definitions, examples, listing, contrast, and cause-effect, you will be able to determine the main ideas of passages and write them out. You will also be able to show how other information in passages backs up the main ideas.

This is slow work and requires a lot of care. The reward is that you will understand and remember the basic points in your textbook. In later chapters you will build on this skill of writing out main points to do informal note-taking and outlining.

DEFINITIONS PASSAGES

We have said that a main idea is the key point that the author is trying to make in any particular passage. It answers the question, "What points is the author making?" or "What is the author saying about this subject?"

A main idea may be a definition. Consider the following passage:

> We have discussed how mechanical energy is converted to heat energy by friction, concussion, and compression. There is an important point here: all energies may be converted from one form to another, but by themselves they go to a less usable form. This is called *degradation of energy*. Other forms of energy naturally transform themselves into heat energy, and since heat energy is associated with random motion, it is less usable than the other, more organized forms.[1]

To determine the main idea, ask yourself, "What point is the author making in this passage?"

In this case, your knowledge of definitions of terms is helpful. The author is defining a term, *degradation of energy*. The "main idea" or point would simply be an explanation of the term *degradation of energy*.

Degradation of energy — by themselves, energies go to less usable forms. Other forms of energy naturally transform themselves into heat energy.

What about the rest of this paragraph? It provides examples of the main idea. If you were taking notes on the passage, the main idea would be written across one line and some of the examples put below.

Definitions passage

We have discussed how mechanical energy is converted to heat energy by friction, concussion, and compression. There is an important point here: all energies may be converted from one form to another, but

Main idea written out; examples listed below

I. Degradation of Energy — by themselves energies go to less usable form — heat.

by themselves they go to a less usable form. This is called *degradation of energy*. Other forms of energy naturally transform themselves into heat energy, and since heat energy is associated with random motion, it is less usable than the other, more organized forms.

A- Mechanical energy → heat energy by friction, concussion, compression.

Consider this passage, which is also a "definition-of-terms" paragraph:

> Elasticity is the ability of a solid to regain its shape after a deforming force has been applied. For example, if you pull on a rubber ball, it will stretch out of shape until you release it, whereon it will return to its original shape.

To determine the main idea, ask yourself, "What point is the author making in this passage?" As in the last example, the main idea is a definition of a term: "Elasticity is the ability of a solid to regain its shape after a deforming force has been applied." The rest of the paragraph contains examples of the main idea.

Definitions passage

Elasticity is the ability of a solid to regain its shape after a deforming force has been applied. For example, if you pull on a rubber ball, it will stretch out of shape until you release it, whereupon it will return to its original shape.

Main idea/examples listed below

I. Elasticity – ability of solid to regain shape after deforming force.
A. Rubber ball – stretches, then returns to original shape.

LISTING PASSAGES

Most passages list something, as we have seen. In this section, we will look at passages that state important points and then list examples of the point. Consider the following passage:

> Electrical machines utilize a greater fraction of the energy supplied them than steam turbines, gasoline engines, and diesel motors. A well-designed electric motor will deliver as useful work up to 85% of the energy supplied. An alternating-current transformer utilizes 98% or more of the energy with which it is supplied.

To determine the main idea, ask yourself, "What point is the author making?" or "What point do the examples illustrate?"

Listing passage

Electrical machines utilize a greater fraction of energy supplied them than steam turbines, gasoline engines, and diesel mo-

Main idea/examples listed below

I. Electric machines more efficient than steam turbines, gas engines, diesel motors.

tors. A well-designed electric motor will deliver as useful work up to 85% of the energy supplied. An alternating-current transformer utilizes 98% or more of the energy with which it is supplied.

a. Elec. motor — 85% of energy delivered as work.
B. Alternating current transformer — 98% of energy utilized.

CONTRAST PASSAGES

The main idea may be the difference between two factors in a contrast. In this case the contrast is written out across the top; the factors in the contrast are written out below.

Contrast passage

There are two types of forces, each very different from the other. A *contact force*, which is easy to imagine, is one in which there is a direct physical contact. The push we give to a stalled car is an example of a contact force. However, there are also forces that interact at a distance without contact. These are called *field forces*. Gravity is an example of a field force.

Main idea/factors listed below

I. Contact Forces vs. Field Forces
a. Contact force — direct physical contact.
B. Field forces — forces that interact at a distance, e.g., gravity.

CAUSE-EFFECT EXPLANATIONS

The author may use cause-effect explanations to prove a particular point.

Passage with cause-effect explanation

Unlike contact forces, field forces cause objects to interact without touching. For example, masses interact without touching as a result of a gravitational force. As a result of electrical force, charged bodies interact without touching.

Main idea/cause-effect listed below

I. Field forces cause objects to interact without touching
a. Gravity → masses interact
B. Elec. force → charged bodies interact.

Authors of technical books combine definitions, examples, lists, contrasts, and cause-effect. We have tried to simplify many of the examples to give you an idea of how to use these patterns to take notes. By the end of this chapter, however, we will "mix" many of these five elements together in the same passages and ask you questions about all of them.

LOOKING AHEAD The exercises that follow will develop your ability to write out main ideas and supporting information.

By the time you finish this chapter, you should be able to do the following things:

1. Write out the main ideas of passages.

2. Write out the supporting points, explanations, or examples beneath the main points.

3. Answer questions based on your understanding of main ideas.

SUMMARY

1. The main idea of a passage is the key point that the author is making. It answers the question: (a) "What point is the author making?" or (b) "What point do the examples illustrate?" or (c) "What is the point of the contrast?" or (d) "What point does this causal chain prove?"

2. You can use your understanding of definition, example, listing, contrast, and cause-effect to determine the main idea of a passage.

3. The main idea may be a definition, the difference between two ideas, the point that a list illustrates, or the point that a chain of cause-effect illustrates.

4. Write the main idea out by itself. List below it the examples or supporting details. Examples are not the same as the ideas; they are illustrations of the ideas.

5. When writing out the main idea, try to boil down your language as much as possible. You won't need more than two or three sentences to express most of the key ideas in these exercises.

EXERCISE 6.1

DIRECTIONS Read each of the following short definitions paragraphs. (1) Ask yourself, "What point is the author making?" or "What point do the examples illustrate?" (2) Write this point out. It is the main idea of the passage. (3) List the support examples (A, B, C) beneath the main ideas, using as few words as possible.

EXAMPLE A variable is a characteristic or set of characteristics that can change or vary. If a coin is flipped many times, for example, the flip can produce either a head or a tail. The two variables are the number of heads and the number of tails.

I. *Variable — characteristic that can change or vary.*

   A. *Flip of coin → heads or tails.*
     These are both variables.

1. A process is a series of actions or operations that contribute to the reaching of a definite end, or maintain a repetitive or continuous function. Growth is an example of a natural process. The manufacture of steel is an example of an artificial process.

    I. _____

      A. _____

      B. _____

2. A variable is a characteristic or set of characteristics that can change or vary, and to which a number can be assigned. In a steam heating system, the flow of steam into a room could be considered a variable. The temperature of the room being heated would be another variable.

    _____

    _____

3. The flow of steam into a room can be controlled directly; that is, it can be increased or decreased by the controller. A variable that can be acted on directly in this way is called a *manipulated variable*.

    _____

    _____

EXERCISE 6.2

DIRECTIONS   Read the following paragraphs. (1) Ask yourself, "What point is the author making?" or "What point do the examples illustrate?" (2) Write this point out. It is the main idea of the passage. (3) List supporting examples (A, B, C) beneath the main idea, using as few words as possible.

1   When you remove the top from a bottle of soda pop, some of the gas comes out and escapes into the air. Vapor steaming out of a teakettle condenses on a cold plate placed nearby. The water vapor, a gas, moves from the teakettle in all directions. If a gas spreads all by itself, one has to conclude that its molecules must be in motion.

    _____

    _____

    _____

2   Heat energy produced by friction, concussion, and compression are all examples of mechanical energy being converted to heat. We are all

familiar with other transformations. Chemical energy is converted into heat energy when substances burn. Electrical energy is transformed into heat energy in electric toasters, stoves, and flatirons. Radiant energy is converted to heat energy when sunlight strikes a dark surface. All energies may be converted from one form to another, but by themselves they only go to a less usable form. This is called *degradation of energy*. Since heat energy is associated with random motion, it is less usable than the other, more organized forms, and other forms of energy naturally transform themselves into heat energy.

a. Friction, concussion, and compression (mechanical energy) → heat energy.

EXERCISE 6.3

DIRECTIONS   Here are two paragraphs introducing the "molecular hypothesis." After you read each paragraph, write out the main idea.

MOLECULAR HYPOTHESIS

1   Surveying the physical properties of different substances encountered in nature, we find a great deal of variety. Some of the substances are normally solid, melting and turning into gas only at extremely high temperatures. Others are normally gaseous, becoming liquid and freezing only when the temperature drops close to absolute zero. Some liquids are of high fluidity, while others are very viscous. Some substances, generally known as metals, possess a high degree of electric and thermal conductivity, while others, the so-called dielectrics, are very good insulators. Some substances are transparent to visible light while others are completely opaque; some possess a high refractive index and some a low one.

Main idea: _____

2   We ascribe all these differences between substances to differences in their internal structure and attempt to explain them . . . as being due to different properties and interactions of the structural elements of matter. We assume that such seemingly homogeneous substances as air, water, or a piece of metal are actually composed of a multitude of extremely small particles known as *molecules*. All molecules of a given pure substance are identical, and the differences in physical properties between various substances are due to the differences between their mole-

cules. . . . There are the molecules of oxygen and of mustard gas, the molecules of water, alcohol, and glycerine, the molecules of iron, asbestos, and camphor, the molecules of gelatine, insulin, and fats. . . .[3]

Main idea: _____

_____

EXERCISE 6.4

DIRECTIONS   Here is a passage in which a point is stated and then explained in terms of causes and effects. Read the passage and answer the questions that follow.

BIMETALLIC STRIPS

Temperature changes cause metals to expand or contract. This property is called thermal expansion. Thermal expansion is the basis for the *bimetallic strip*, which is made up of two different metals welded together. One strip may be brass, which has a relatively high coefficient of expansion, and the other may be invar, an alloy of iron and nickel with a relatively low coefficient of expansion. When this bimetallic strip is heated, it will bend. In which direction will it bend? Since the brass expands more than the invar, the strip will bend toward the invar (see Fig. 1).

Bimetallic strips are often used in a coiled form (see Fig. 2).

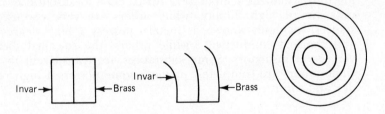

QUESTIONS

1. What happens to metal when it is exposed to a temperature change?

_____

2. What happens when two metal strips with different coefficients of expansion are welded together and then heated? _____

_____

EXERCISE 6.5

DIRECTIONS   Each of the following passages is organized as a contrast of two ideas. Take notes on these passages.

1   Electric motors and electric generators are counterparts of one another. An electric motor is a machine that converts electrical energy to rotary mechanical motion. Conversely, the electric generator converts rotary mechanical energy to electrical energy.

I. Electric motors and electric generators are counterparts.

a. _____ — _____

B. _____ — _____

2   There are two distinct hypotheses for the origin of the earth: the nebular hypothesis and the comet-produced hypothesis. The nebular hypothesis maintains that our planet began in an aggregation of interstellar gas and dust. This theory is gaining more and more acceptance. The other hypothesis is that the earth began as a piece of sun that was ripped out by a comet.

3   We are really the products of two inheritances. Our biological inheritance includes that which is genetically transmitted to us through our parents. This includes our vastly expanded brain, our opposable thumb, our hair type, the color of our eyes. However, we are also the product of our cultural inheritance. This includes our arts and sciences, our humanities, our laws, the sum of the social knowledge that is passed on and added to in generation after generation.

4   There are two types of variables, manipulated variables and controlled variables. A variable that can be acted on directly is called a manipulated variable. The flow of steam into a room is an example of a manipulated variable, as it can be directly controlled. In contrast, a variable that can't be acted on directly is called a controlled variable. The temperature of a room is an example of a controlled variable, because it must be achieved through manipulating another variable. In this case, it must be achieved through manipulating the flow of steam.

EXERCISE 6.6

DIRECTIONS   The following passage is organized as a listing, in which an idea is stated and then divided into subcategories. Write out the main idea of the passage. Beneath it, list the subcategories and any supporting details.

EXAMPLE   Machines have certain common elements. The rotor is the rotating member of an electric machine. The stator is the stationary member of the electric machine.

> I. Common elements in machines
>   A. Rotor — moves
>   B. Stator — stationary

ELECTROMECHANICAL TRANSDUCERS

A transducer is a device which converts energy from one form to another. In particular, an electromechanical transducer converts a mechanical quantity into an electrical signal, or vice versa. Some of the mechanical quantities which can be converted into electrical signals include rotary position, temperature, pressure, and sound.

There are three common transducers used to convert rotary shaft position to electrical signals: the potentiometer, the synchro, and the resolver. The latter is similar to the synchro. One of the most commonly used temperature transducers is the thermocouple. Another is the bimetallic strip. The bourdon tube is an example of a pressure transducer. Piezoelectric ceramics or crystals are also used as pressure transducers. These crystals convert pressure or mechanical motion into electrical signals and vice versa. The microphone is an audio transducer, converting electrical signals into sound waves.

I. _____

A. Rotary shaft position → electrical signal: potentiometer, synchro, resolver.

B. _____

   _____

C. _____

   _____

   _____

D. _____

   _____

EXERCISE 6.7

DIRECTIONS In each of these passages the author makes two points. As you read, ask yourself, "What points is the author making?" and "What points do the examples illustrate?"

1   In an open-loop system, no return or feedback path exists for sending information on the controlled variable back to the input. For example, the valve on the side of a radiator is part of an open-loop system. The valve cannot sense the room temperature; it has no information on this controlled variable, and no way of sending information on the controlled variable back to the furnace. An on/off switch on a light is another example of an open-loop control. In this case, the controlled variable is the lighting of the room. The switch is not equipped to sense whether the light bulb actually lights up. There is no feedback device for sending information back on the actual condition of the controlled variable. In an open-loop system, the actuating signal is independent of the controlled variable.

QUESTIONS

a. What important points does the author make about open-loop systems?

_____

_____

b. Give two examples the author has used to back up the points.

_____

_____

2   Open-loop control systems may be manually or automatically actuated. For example, timers may automatically open or close the steam valves on radiators. However, the inclusion of a timer on a steam valve does not change the basic design of the system. *The actuator still cannot sense the condition of the controlled variable* (the room temperature). The timer—not the temperature of the room—controls the opening and closing of the valve. The system is still an open-loop one, despite the addition of an automatic device for actuation.

QUESTIONS

a. What important point(s) does the author make in this passage? _____

_____

b. Give one example the author uses to back up this point. _____

_____

3   A closed-loop system is one in which the actuating signal is dependent upon the condition of the controlled variable. The autopilot of an airplane provides an example of closed-loop control. The autopilot is a device which is able to sense and respond to changes in general flying conditions, such as gusts of wind or drops of temperature. The general flying conditions are the controlled variable; directions or commands issued by the controller of the autopilot depend directly on these conditions. A gust of wind at 60 mph results in an automatic compensation of a certain amount; a gust of wind at 40 mph results in a different compensation. In this system, there is a feedback path for sending information on the controlled variable back to the input.

QUESTIONS

a. What important point(s) about closed-loop systems does the author make?

_____

_____

b. Cite one example the author uses to illustrate the point(s). _____

_____

EXERCISE 6.8

DIRECTIONS   Read the following passage and answer the questions on main idea and cause-effect that follow.

HOME HEATING SYSTEMS

One of the luxuries we find in most modern homes today is a device called a *thermostat*. The thermostat is used to control the temperature inside the house automatically. The occupant of the house need only set the thermostat to the desired temperature and then forget about it. During the winter months, the thermostat does all the work in controlling the furnace. But how is this possible?

The operation of the thermostat is often made possible through the use of a type of temperature transducer that we investigated earlier called a *bimetallic strip*. In Fig. 1, study the control system used to regulate the furnace. As the temperature cools, the movable contact mounted on the larger coiled bimetallic strip moves toward the fixed contact until both contacts meet. When they meet, the closing of the circuit sends an electrical signal to the furnace controller to turn on the furnace. The heat from the furnace heats up the larger bimetallic strip until it begins to expand. As it expands, the movable contact breaks its connection with the fixed contact when the force is sufficient to overcome the force exerted by the permanent magnet. This opening of the circuit is an electrical signal to the furnace controller to shut off the furnace.[4]

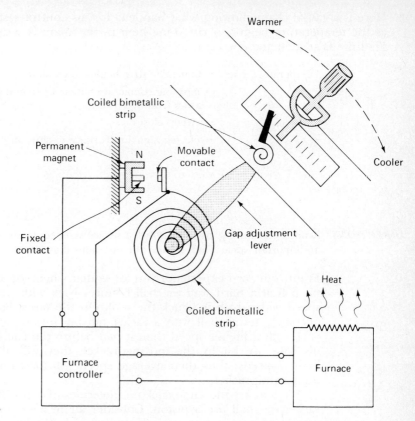

Figure 1. Home heating system.

QUESTIONS

1. The important point the author is making is that
    a. the thermostat is one of the luxuries of modern life.
    b. the operation of the thermostat is often made possible by the properties of the bimetallic strip.
    c. the heat from the furnace heats up the larger bimetallic strip.
    d. none of the above.

2. Here is a causal chain showing what happens to this control system as the temperature cools. One item in the chain is wrong. Find the false item and correct it.

    Temperature cools → movable contact on bimetallic strip moves toward fixed contact and they meet
    → circuit closes
    → electric signal goes to furnace
    → furnace is shut off

3. Here is a causal chain showing what happens in this control system as the temperature begins to rise. One item in the chain is wrong. Find the false item and correct it.

> Temperature rises → bimetallic strip begins to expand
> → movable contact on bimetallic strip moves away from fixed contact
> → circuit closes
> → electric signal to furnace to shut off

EXERCISE 6.9

DIRECTIONS   Read the following passage, which uses cause-effect to explain an important idea. Then answer the questions that follow.

From your own experience you know that when you throw a good tennis ball at a hard wall the ball bounces back with practically the same speed with which it struck the wall. On the other hand, if you hit an oncoming tennis ball with a racket moving toward it, the ball bounces back with a higher speed than it had before the collision. If many tennis balls are hit by the moving racket, they will all bounce back at higher speeds; thus their average speed will increase by collision with the moving racket.

We may try the same trick on molecules of a gas. Instead of a tennis racket we shall use a piston. Consider air in a tube closed at one end and fitted with a piston at the other end. While the piston is being pushed in, the molecules striking it will bounce back at higher speeds. In speeding up the molecules, the piston is acting like the moving tennis racket. Hence, when we compress a gas, we expect its temperature to rise. . . .

To sum up, we have seen that the temperature of a gas is related to the average speed of its molecules. When the average speed of the molecules increases, the temperature rises.[5]

QUESTIONS

1. What is the main idea of this passage?_____

_____

2. How many examples of the main idea does the author give?_____

3. List the supporting examples the author gives to back up the main idea.

_____

_____

EXERCISE 6.10

DIRECTIONS   Here is a long selection taken directly from a textbook on automatic control systems. You have read parts of this selection
earlier in this chapter. Read to distinguish main points from
explanations of these points. Underline key definitions and
important points as you read. Then answer the questions that
follow.

CONTROL SYSTEMS

• How is an unmanned satellite controlled?
• How are machine parts manufactured to tolerances closer than
those a human being can measure?
• How can we control an airplane flying faster than the speed of
sound?

The beginning of answers to these questions lies in an understanding of control theory. The control or regulation of mechanical
processes is the subject of this chapter.

CONTENTS
Processes and Variables
Two Types of Control Systems
Open-loop Systems
Closed-loop Systems
Negative Feedback

Processes and Variables   A *process* is a series of actions or operations
that contribute to the reaching of a definite end, or maintain a repetitive or continuous function. Growth is an example of a *natural process*.
The manufacture of steel is an example of an *artificial process*.

The existence of a process implies the existence of *controls* on the
process. The endocrine glands are part of the *control system* for growth.
Thermometers and other regulatory mechanisms are part of the *control
system* in the manufacture of steel.

The control of a process implies the existence of at least one variable.
A *variable* is a characteristic or set of characteristics which can change
or vary and to which a number can be assigned. If the characteristic
does not vary, it is referred to as a *constant*. The flip of a coin, for example,
produces either a head or a tail. The result is not constant. In this case,
the two variables are the number of heads and number of tails.

A process implies the existence of many variables. Consider a steam-
heating system. One variable is the desired temperature of the room
being heated. Another variable is the flow of steam into the room. How
are these two variables controlled?

The flow of steam into a room can be controlled directly; that is, it
can be increased or decreased by the controller. A variable that can be

acted on directly is called a *manipulated variable*. The temperature of the room, however, cannot be acted on directly by the controller. The temperature of the room is achieved through manipulating another variable. A variable which is acted upon indirectly is called a *controlled variable*. The controlled variable (in this case, the room temperature) is achieved through the manipulated variable (the flow of steam).

Two Types of Control Systems   We will consider two control systems for processes: open-loop control systems and closed-loop control systems. An open-loop control system is one in which the actuating signal is independent of the resulting condition of the controlled variable. A closed-loop control system is one in which the actuating signal is dependent upon the condition of the controlled variable.

Open-Loop Systems. Open-loop systems are common in our society. The valve on the side of a radiator is an example of part of an open-loop control system. The valve is not capable of sensing room temperature; accordingly, it cannot adjust the flow of steam into the room as the room heats up. The valve (actuating signal) is *independent* of the room temperature (controlled variable).

In the open-loop system, no return or *feedback* path exists for sending information about the controlled variable back to the input. For example, the valve has no sensing device that could detect room temperature (the controlled variable) and transmit such information back to the controller. This is how the system got the name "open." The path of control or loop is open because no return or feedback path exists for sending information about the controlled variable back to the input.

The ON/OFF switch on a light is another example of open-loop control. In this case, the illumination of the room is the controlled variable. The actuating signal (ON/OFF switch) is independent of the condition of the controlled variable (illumination of room). The switch is not equipped to sense whether the light bulb actually lights up, or how brightly it illuminates the area. There is no feedback device for sending back information on the actual condition of the controlled variable to the controller.

An open-loop control system may be further classified as either *continuous* or *discontinuous*. The ON/OFF control on a television set illustrates these two systems. This switch usually includes a volume control. After turning on the set, the control can be continuously rotated to vary the volume of sound produced. The ON/OFF control, which is discontinuous, is often referred to as a *bang-bang* control. The volume control is *continuous*.

Open-loop control systems may be manually or automatically actuated. For example, timers may automatically open or close the steam valves on radiators. However, the inclusion of a timer on a steam valve does not change the basic design of the system. *The actuator still cannot sense the condition of the controlled variable.* The timer controls only the opening and closing of the valve, not the temperature of the room. The system is still an open-loop one, despite the addition of an automatic device for actuation.

There is a brain-teaser based on the idea that open-loop control systems have limits, even though they may be automatically actuated. If you set your alarm clock for 8:00 A.M., and go to sleep at 7:00 P.M., how many hours of sleep will you get? The answer is, only one hour. The alarm clock has no way of "sensing" whether it is morning or evening. An open-loop system is independent of the controlled variable. The clock sets off an alarm based on the position of its hands. Unfortunately, the clock hands pass the 8:00 position twice in 24 hours.

Close-Loop Systems   A closed-loop system is one in which the actuating signal is dependent upon the condition of the controlled variable. The autopilot of an airplane provides an example of closed-loop control. The autopilot is a device which is able to sense and respond to changes in general flying conditions such as gusts of wind or drops of temperature. The general flying conditions are the controlled variable; directions or commands issued by the controller of the autopilot depend directly on these conditions. A gust of wind at 60 mph results in an automatic compensation of a certain amount; a gust of wind at 40 mph results in a different compensation. *The signals to the controller depend upon the condition of the controlled variable.*

The chief advantage of the closed-loop system is its adaptability. The fixed program or schedule of control occurring in the open-loop system is inadequate for circumstances in which there are *randomly varying conditions.* For instance, the drive motors in elevators are subject to shift in load condition. The drive motors in power tools must adjust to varying circumstances. An autopilot must function in relation to random gusts of wind. No open-loop system can handle random circumstances; by definition its actuating signals are *independent* of the controlled variable.

Feedback is a general term. It refers to information on the controlled variable which is sent back to the controller. When feedback results in decreased error, it is referred to as *negative feedback.*

In a closed-loop system, the controller functions to reduce the error between the desired and actual conditions of the controlled variable. The *desired* condition of the controlled variable is referred to as the *reference.* For instance, if one wants to maintain the temperature of a room at 68°, this temperature is the reference. The *actual* condition of the controlled variable is referred to as the *sensed* condition. If the temperature of the room is 70°, the sensing device will pick up this information, the information will be fed back to the controller, and the controller will automatically adjust the flow of heat sent to the room.

The *error signal* represents the difference between the *desired* and *actual* values of the controlled variable. When the actual and desired values of the controlled variable are made to correspond, the error signal is reduced to zero and the controller is no longer actuated.

Note that in a negative feedback system, the *controller is actuated by the existence of error.* Such a system will strive to eliminate *all* error, regardless of the source. The advantages of such a control system are extensive. For instance, there are many possible causes for malfunction in an elevator. A system with negative feedback control will attempt to compensate for whatever errors are detected. Errors caused by aging of system components will be handled. Errors caused by random external influences will also be handled. The autopilot of an airplane provides another example. If the airplane is blown off course by a sudden wind gust, the negative feedback incorporated within the control system will handle the deviation. Control surfaces will be activated by the error signal produced. They in turn will maneuver the plane until the error has been eliminated. At this point the surfaces will be back to their original position. In summary, it is possible to make the following statements about a closed-loop control system:

1. There is a means of sensing the actual condition of the controlled variable, or one related to it.
2. Feedback exists; the sensed condition of the controlled variable may be reported back for comparison with the reference condition.
3. The controller can act to reduce the error between the desired and actual condition of the controlled variable.[6]

QUESTIONS

1. What is the principal advantage of a closed-loop system? Include one example to illustrate your point. _____

_____

_____

2. What actuates the controller in a negative feedback system? Why is this so important? _____

_____

_____

3. Define the following terms:

Manipulated variable: _____

Controlled variable: _____

Closed-loop control system: _____

Negative feedback: _____

Reference condition: _____

Sensed condition: _____

Error signal: _____

SPRINGBOARD 6

Choose one chapter from your reading this week.

    1. Pick out a passage of one or two pages where it is difficult to understand the information just from reading through it quickly.

    2. Take notes on this passage.

        a. Write each main idea out by itself.

        b. List the supporting details or examples below the main point.

NOTES

1. E. J. Cable et al., *The Physical Sciences*, 5th ed., Englewood Cliffs, N.J.: Prentice-Hall, Inc., 1969, p. 124.
2. Cable et al., *The Physical Sciences*, p. 124.
3. George Gamow, *Matter, Earth, and Sky*, 2d ed., Englewood Cliffs, N.J.: Prentice-Hall, Inc., 1965, pp. 205-6.
4. Dewey A. Yeager and Robert L. Gourley, *Introduction to Electron and Electro-Mechanical Devices*. Englewood Cliffs, N.J.: Prentice-Hall, Inc., 1976.
5. *College Introductory Physical Science*. Education Development Center, Inc., Newton, Mass., 1969, p. 290.
6. Arthur Roitstein and Anne Eisenberg, *Control Systems*, New York City Community College, 1975.

QUICK PROGRESS TEST 2

Part One

DIRECTIONS   Read the following passage and answer the questions that follow.

    To push a door open, we must apply sufficient mechanical force to overcome the mechanical force tending to keep the door closed. This opposing force might be the tension of the spring in the door-closer, or it might be just the friction of the door hinges. The force we apply with our hand in this example is a *contact force*, since it does not act on the door until our hand touches the door. Gravitational force, on the other hand, is not a contact force. Gravitational force can act at a considerable distance, as for example the gravitational force between the mass of the Moon and the mass of the Earth which governs the orbit of the Moon around the Earth. A force, such as gravitational force which can act at a considerable distance without contact is called a *field force*.[1]

QUESTIONS

1. What two terms are contrasted in this selection?_____

2. Define each of the terms that is contrasted._____

3. Give an example of each term that is contrasted. _____

4. Here are notes on this passage. The notes are incomplete. Please finish them.

  I. Contact force
    A. Force that comes about by physical contact.

    B. Example: _____

 II. _____

    A. _____
    B. Example: gravity. Force of gravity between Earth and Moon governs Moon's orbit.

Part Two

DIRECTIONS   Here are three sentences describing the behavior of valence electrons. Valence electrons are those in the last shell of the atom. Express the information in each of these sentences in cause-effect notation.

1. The number of valence electrons determines the electrical properties of a material. _____

2. If an atom has less than four valence electrons, it will tend to give up its electrons. _____

3. If an atom has more than four electrons in its last shell, it tends to acquire electrons. _____

Part Three

MAGNETIC FIELDS AND LINES OF FORCE

If a bar magnet is dipped into iron filings, many of the filings are attracted to the ends of the magnet, but none are attracted to the center of the magnet. As mentioned previously, the ends of the magnet where the attractive force is the greatest are called the *poles* of the magnet. By using a compass, the line of direction of the magnetic force at various points near the magnet may be observed. The compass needle itself is a magnet. The north end of the compass needle always points toward the south pole, S, as shown in Fig. 1(a), and thus the sense of direction (with respect to the polarity of the bar magnet) is also indicated. At the center, the compass needle points in a direction that is parallel to the bar magnet.

    When the compass is placed successively at several points in the vicinity of the bar magnet the compass needle alines itself with the field at each position. The direction of the field is indicated by the arrows and represents the direction in which the north pole of the compass needle will point when the compass is placed in this field. Such a line along which a compass needle alines itself is called a *magnetic line of force.* (This magnetic line of force does not actually exist but is an imaginary line used to illustrate and describe the pattern of the magnetic field.) As mentioned previously, the magnetic lines of force are assumed to emanate from the north pole of a magnet, pass through the surrounding space, and enter the south pole. The lines of force then pass from the south pole to the north pole inside the magnet to form a closed loop. Each line of force forms an independent closed loop and does not merge with or cross other lines of force. The lines of force between the poles of a horseshoe magnet are shown in Fig. 1(b).

Although magnetic lines of force are imaginary, a simplified version of many magnetic phenomena can be explained by assuming the magnetic lines to have certain real properties. The lines of force can be compared to rubber bands which stretch outward when a force is exerted upon them and contract when the force is removed. The characteristics of magnetic lines of force can be described as follows:

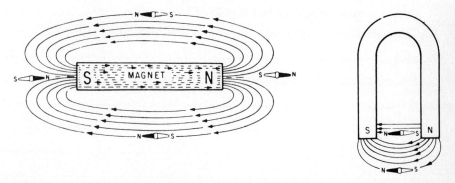

Figure 1. (a) Bar magnet and (b) horseshoe magnet.

1. Magnetic lines of force are continuous and will always form closed loops.

2. Magnetic lines of force will never cross one another.

3. Parallel magnetic lines of force traveling in the same direction repel one another. Parallel magnetic lines of force traveling in opposite directions tend to unite with each other and form into single lines traveling in a direction determined by the magnetic poles creating the lines of force.

4. Magnetic lines of force tend to shorten themselves. Therefore, the magnetic lines of force existing between two unlike poles cause the poles to be pulled together.

5. Magnetic lines of force pass through all materials, both magnetic and nonmagnetic.

The space surrounding a magnet, in which the magnetic force acts, is called a *magnetic field.*

QUESTIONS

1. What instrument is used to observe the direction of magnetic forces
   around a bar magnet? _____

2. Write out the main point of the first paragraph. You should not
   need more than one sentence. _____
   _____

3. Define the terms
   Pole of a magnet: _____
   Magnetic lines of force: _____
   _____

4. Place compass needle beside bar magnet $\longrightarrow$ _____
   Place compass needle by south pole of bar magnet $\longrightarrow$ _____

5. Take simple notes on characteristics of magnetic lines of force.
   _____
   _____
   _____
   _____
   _____
   _____
   _____

NOTES

1. Herbert W. Jackson, *Introduction to Electric Circuits,* 4th ed. Englewood
Cliffs, N.J.: Prentice-Hall, Inc., 1976, p. 5.

USING A TECHNICAL BOOK

7
USING ILLUSTRATIONS

Authors of technical books explain their ideas in two ways: they use words, and they use illustrations.

In a technical book the illustrations are side-by-side with the text. The author expects the reader to go back and forth from the words to the picture until the point is clear.

This is different from the way that illustrations are usually used in magazines and newspapers; you are not expected to sit and study each photograph in the newspaper. In contrast, illustrations in technical books are there so that the reader can match up ideas with illustrations of the idea. Many times it is easier to understand an idea, or the description of a process, through looking at a picture. If you skip an illustration because you don't understand it, you will be losing a valuable source of information, one that the author is counting on to help you understand important points.

Technical books usually have five types of illustrations: line drawings, graphs, tables, block diagrams, and photographs. All these types of illustrations are extremely important for the reader.

This chapter suggests ways to study illustrations and use them to understand and remember information in a technical book.

Line drawings are the most common form of illustration in technical books. They are often called figures or diagrams. The word "diagram" is a general one used to refer to illustrations that are not graphs, charts, or tables.

Line drawings are used to introduce broad distinctions or categories. For instance, Fig. 7.1 is an illustration used to introduce types of roofs.[1]

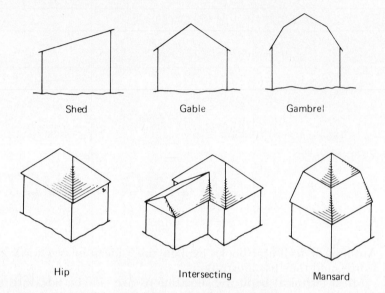

Shed   Gable   Gambrel

Hip   Intersecting   Mansard

Figure 7.1. Types of roofs.

Line drawings are used to introduce terminology. Figure 7.2 is a drawing used to introduce most of the terms used to describe rafters.[2]

Line drawings are used to illustrate important principles and pro-

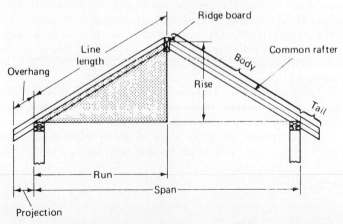

**Figure 7.2.
Common rafter terminology.**

cesses. For instance, when the battery is explained as a device to convert chemical energy to electrical energy, the explanation is accompanied by line drawings giving the parts of the battery and indicating the process of conversion. When the operation of a solenoid is explained, it is accompanied by an illustration such as Fig. 7.3, which is intended to aid your understanding of a process.[3]

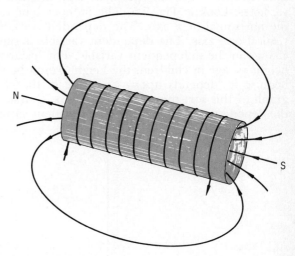

Figure 7.3. Magnetic field produced by an electron current flowing through a solenoid.

Line drawings may rely on special symbols, such as electrical symbols. When symbols are used and many of the details are removed so that the reader can concentrate on an important point, the drawing is called a *schematic*. For example, Fig. 7.4 is a schematic drawing of the cutaway end view of an armature.[4]

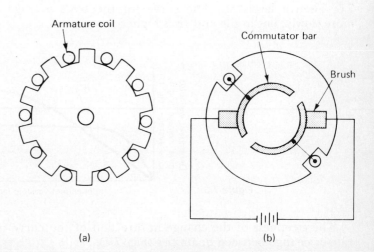

Figure 7.4.
D-C armature construction.   (a)   (b)

There are line graphs, circle graphs, and bar graphs. These are often called charts.

Line Graphs   The line graph is used to show a relationship between variables. Look at Fig. 7.5. The independent variable is plotted along the horizontal or x axis. The dependent variable is plotted along the vertical or y axis. The dependent variable is one that depends upon a change in the independent variable. For instance, if you were plotting height vs. age in children, the height would be the dependent variable, because it "depends upon" a change in the child's age. Usually in a graph of this sort the title is stated y vs. x; that is, the title is stated as the dependent variable vs. the independent variable.

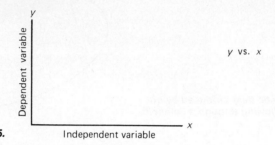

Figure 7.5.

A graph may have more than one curve plotted on it. In cases like this, it is possible to compare two or three dependent variables in terms of the same independent variable. Figure 7.6 is an example of this kind of graph.

Note how steeply the curve for the girl's average height rises in Fig. 7.6. Then it levels off. The curve for the boy's average height rises more slowly, but in the end rises higher.

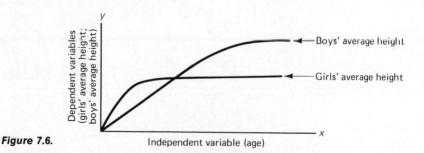

Figure 7.6.

The steepness of the change in direction of the curve indicates the rate of change between quantities (Fig. 7.7).

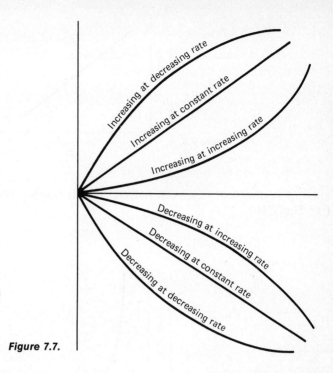

Figure 7.7.

Two relationships are particularly important in line graphs: direct proportion and inverse proportion.

Direct proportion. A direct proportion is shown by a straight line that moves up to the right (see Fig. 7.8). For example, if doubling *x* amount causes *y* amount to double, then *x* and *y* may be in direct proportion.

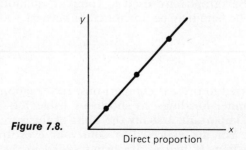

Figure 7.8.

Direct proportion

Inverse proportion. When the straight line moves down to the right, then the variables plotted are *inversely* proportional to each other (Fig. 7.9).

A concave, upward curve may indicate an inverse proportion. If *x*

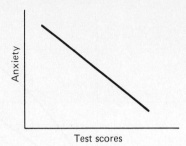

Figure 7.9.   Test scores

amount is doubled, then y is halved. If x is halved, then y is doubled (see Fig. 7.10).

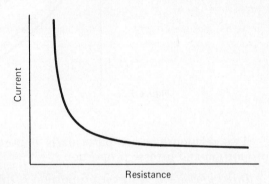

Figure 7.10.   Resistance

Circle Graphs Circle graphs, often called pie graphs or pie charts, are used to show the relation of parts to the whole, and to each other.

Bar Graphs Bar graphs are used to compare quantities by means of lines or bars. The bars may be horizontal or vertical.

TABLES

    Tables are used to present comparisons. Information is given in vertical columns under headings, as shown in Table 7.1. The heading of each column is important. Usually the units of measurement are given in the heading. You are expected to skim your eyes up and down the vertical column first. If figures are being added in the table, they will be added based on the vertical column. To make comparisons between columns, you would read horizontally across the different columns.

Table 7.1 Voltage vs. Current.
Resistance Constant at 10 Ohms.

Voltage *(volts)*	*Current* *(amperes)*
0	0.0
5	0.5
10	1.0

BLOCK DIAGRAMS

Block diagrams are charts that show steps in a process, or parts of a whole. When these charts are used to illustrate a process, the order in which the steps occur is important. The arrows indicate the direction in which the chart "flows." Figure 7.11 is a block diagram of power-systems technology.

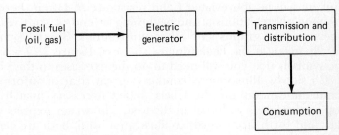

Figure 7.11. Power systems technology.

PHOTOGRAPHS

Photographs are used in many of the same ways as line drawings. Photographs of equipment are common. Often they are labeled in detail, so that when a term is used in the text, the reader can refer back to the illustration to help with the definition. Photographs are often used to illustrate steps in a process.

PARTS OF ILLUSTRATIONS

Whether it is a graph or chart, line drawing or photograph, study the illustration carefully. Each piece is important. Here is a list of the main parts of illustrations:

Caption The caption refers to the words printed beneath the illustration. There may be only a brief identification or as much as two sentences or more explaining the point of the illustration.

Labels The different parts of the drawing will be clearly labeled. Match up the labels with the information in the text. Go back and forth until you are clear on what the labels represent. If the caption is the "main idea" of the illustration, then the labels are the "important details."

Arrows These are important in technical drawings. Note the directions in which arrows point in each illustration. This is often the main way a process is explained. If you are looking at drawings of how automobile valves work, for instance, the arrows will do a lot of the "explaining."

Abbreviations and Symbols Abbreviations and special symbols are common in drawings. Units of measurements are almost always expressed in abbreviated form; this is true whether the units are at the top of a column in a table or along the x and y axes of a line graph. For instance, ohms will appear as Ω, pounds per square inch as psi. Current will be abbreviated I and resistance R. Often there is a table of common abbreviations at the beginning or end of your textbook. Use it when reading graphs and other illustrations. Special symbols are also usually given at the beginning of the text. Figure 7.12 is a table of electric symbols that you will need to do the exercises in this chapter.

Go slowly. Illustrations contain a great deal of information. Think about the caption and the labels. When necessary, match the information in the labels with that in the text. The writer expects you to shuttle back and forth from words to illustration until both are clear.

DRAWING YOUR OWN ILLUSTRATION

One of the best ways to test your understanding of a point is to draw an illustration of your own and then check it with the one in the book. You will not be able to do this for complicated line drawings or photographs, but you can do it in many cases.

LOOKING AHEAD By the time you finish this chapter, you should be able to:

1. Identify direct and inverse proportions in line graphs.
2. Identify dependent and independent variables in line graphs.
3. Write out descriptions of objects using a combination of information in the text and information in the illustration.
4. Use graphs to make comparisons between variables.
5. Use tables to make comparisons between variables.
6. Test your understanding of certain ideas by making simple drawings that illustrate the ideas.

SUMMARY

1. Illustrations in technical books are not decorations. They are at the core of explanations. Use the captions, the labels, and the directional arrows. Match the information in the illustration with the words in the text. Together the words and illustrations provide an explanation. The author expects you to go back and forth until both words and illustrations are understood.

2. Test your understanding of difficult ideas by drawing an illustration of your own and then checking yours with the one in the book.

3. Graphs and tables are used to picture relationships between variables and to show comparisons. Read to understand the relationship between the variables.

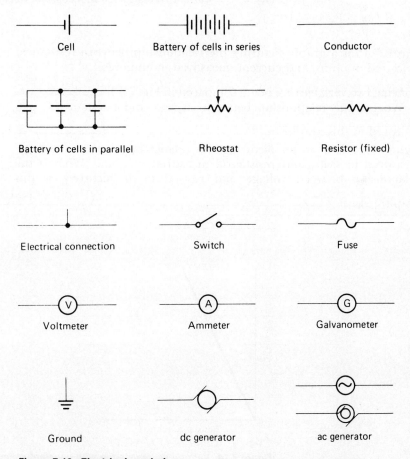

Figure 7.12. Electrical symbols.

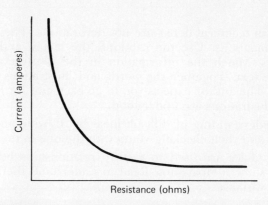

Figure 7.13. Current vs. resistance with constant voltage.

1. Figure 7.13 is a graph picturing the relationship between resistance, measured in ohms, and current, measured in amperes.

   a. What two variables are being compared in Fig. 7.13? _____
   b. What is the relationship between current and resistance as pic-

   tured in this graph? _____
2. Figure 7.14 is a graph picturing the relationship between voltage, measured in volts, and resistance, measured in ohms. What is the relationship between voltage and resistance, as pictured in this

   graph?_____

   _____

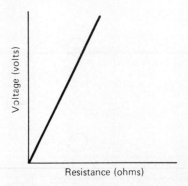

Figure 7.14. Voltage vs. resistance with constant voltage.

1. What is the relationship of amperes to volts in the graph in Fig. 7.15?

_____

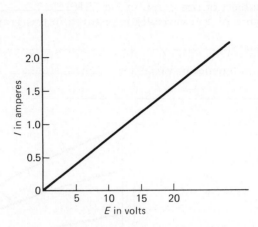

R = 10 Ω

E	I
0	0.0
5	0.5
10	1.0
15	1.5
20	2.0

Legend
 I = Current (measured in amperes)
 E = Voltage (measured in volts)
 R = Resistance (measured in ohms)
 Ω = ohm
 R = 10 Ω means that the resistance is 10 ohms and is kept
    constant at that figure.

Figure 7.15. Amperes vs. volts with constant resistance.

2. According to the graph, what happens if you double the voltage?_____

3. Data on two variables are given in the table. What two variables are

   described? _____

4. According to the table, what is the current when the voltage is 5 v? _____

   What is the current when the voltage is 10 v? _____

   What happens when you double the voltage? _____

QUESTIONS

1. What is the subject of the graph in Fig. 7.16? _____
2. The relationship of two variables is pictured in this graph. What are

the two variables?_____

Which is the independent variable?_____

Why?_____

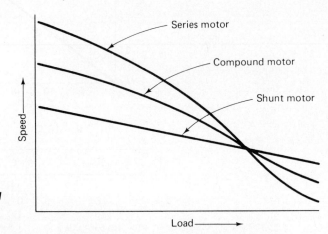

**Figure 7.16. Speed vs. load
for dc motors.**

3. What happens to the speed of a series motor when the load increases?

_____

4. What happens to the speed of a compound motor when the load increases?

_____

5. What happens to the speed of a shunt motor when the load increases?

_____

6. Which of the three motors drops off the most drastically as the load increases?

_____

7. Which of the three motors has the most gradual decrease in speed

as the load increases? _____

QUESTIONS

1. What is the subject of the graph in Fig. 7.17? _____

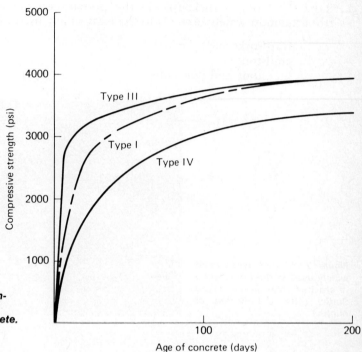

Figure 7.17. Representative comparison of the development of strength in three types of concrete.

2. What two variables are being compared in this graph?_____

Which is the independent variable?_____

Why? _____

3. What compressive strength does Type III concrete reach by 200

days?_____

4. Which two types of concrete have the greatest compressive strength

by 200 days? _____

5. If you need a concrete that hardens to 2,500 psi or more within 10

days, which of the three types of concrete should you use? _____

6. Could you expect either Type I, Type III, or Type IV concrete to

get significantly harder after 180 days? Why?_____

QUESTIONS

1. What subject is compared in the circle graph in Figure 7.18?

_____

2. Rank the types of rock used in the preparation of crushed stone from the most widely used (1) to the least widely used (3).

_____ trap rocks and granite
_____ sandstone
_____ limestone and dolostone

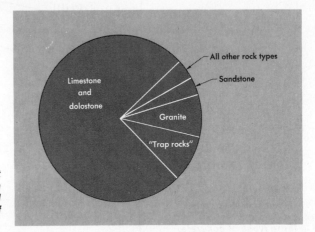

Figure 7.18. Rock types most widely used in the preparation of crushed stone in the United States. (After U.S. Bureau of Mines.)

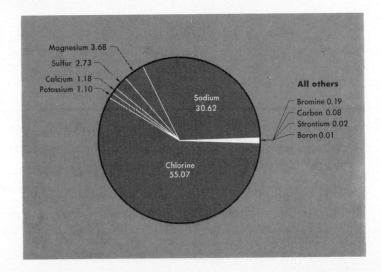

Figure 7.19. Major elements in the continental crust expressed as percentages. (After K. K. Turekian, 1969.)

QUESTIONS

3. What subject is compared in the circle graph in Fig. 7.19?

_____

4. Rank the major elements in the continental crust from the most common (1) to the rarest (9).

_____ silicon
_____ oxygen
_____ aluminum
_____ magnesium
_____ sodium
_____ potassium
_____ titanium
_____ calcium
_____ iron

EXERCISE 7.6

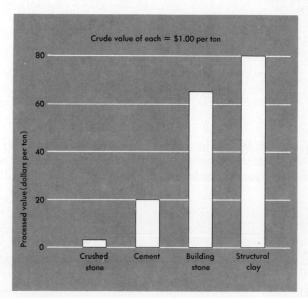

Figure 7.20. Processing of building materials adds greatly to their value. (After W. L. Fisher, 1965.)

QUESTIONS

1. What effect does processing building materials have on their value?

_____

2. What is the crude value of cement?_____

3. What is the processed value of cement? _____

4. Estimate the processed value of building stone. _____

5. Which of the building materials shows the greatest increase in value

when it is processed? _____

Block diagrams are used by authors to show the order in which processes occur. Often they trace the path of materials through a system. They show how one event "flows" into the next. The process will usually include a chain of cause-effect.

Block diagrams have a second use. If you read a description of a process that is difficult to understand, try drawing your own diagram and fitting in the information. This will help you to understand the steps in the process the author is describing.

DIRECTIONS   All the following passages describe steps in a process. Complete the block diagrams describing the processes.

EXAMPLE

SI ENGINES

Gas and air are the fuel for most automobiles. A spark plug ignites the gas-air mixture at the correct moment in the cycle. This is called spark ignition (SI). The process is diagramed in Fig. 7.21.

Note that in this example, the ingredients (air, gas, spark) are shown as arrows coming into the blocks. The blocks themselves (mixed, ignited) are used to tell what happened to the ingredients.

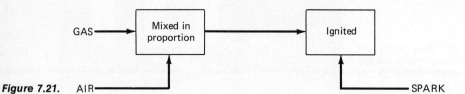

Figure 7.21.   AIR ———————————————— SPARK

1   CI ENGINES

Heavy duty vehicles may use a different ignition system. In this system, as the air is drawn into the cylinders, it undergoes a considerable compression. This compression causes the air to become very hot. Near the end of the compression stroke, a fine spray of fuel is injected into the hot, compressed air. It ignites spontaneously owing to the tremendous heat. This is compression ignition (CI). The process is diagramed in Fig. 7.22.

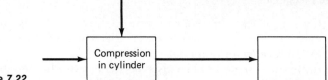

Figure 7.22

2   LIQUID COOLING SYSTEM

. . . Most automobile engines use a liquid, usually water, plus an anti-freeze, to maintain the engine at a constant operating temperature. This is done by transferring heat from the metal surrounding the combustion chamber to the liquid. The cooling liquid flows to a radiator where it runs through thin-walled tubes that are exposed to a flow of atomspheric air, which removes the heat. This system is called a liquid cooling system (Fig. 7.23).

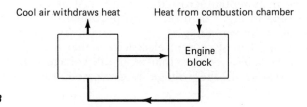

Figure 7.23

3   AIR COOLING SYSTEM

Some automobile engines maintain a constant operating temperature by transferring heat from the metal around the combustion chamber directly to the air without an intermediate liquid cooling medium. This is done by ducting air across fins that surround the combustion chamber. Cooling the engine by this method is called air cooling (Fig. 7.24).[10]

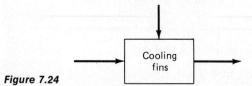

Figure 7.24

EXERCISE 7.8

DIRECTIONS   The illustration in this selection is designed to help you understand the basic principle of the passage. Read the selection and answer the questions that follow.

DIFFERENCE IN POTENTIAL

That force that causes free electrons to move in a conductor as an electric current may be referred to as follows: (1) Electromotive force (emf). (2) Voltage. (3) Difference in potential.

When a difference in potential exists between two charged bodies that are connected by a conductor, electrons will flow along the conductor. This flow is from the negatively charged body to the positively charged body until the two charges are equalized and the potential difference no longer exists.

An analogy of this action is shown in the two water tanks connected by a pipe and valve in Fig. 1. At first the valve is closed and all the water is in tank A. Thus, the water pressure across the valve is at maximum. When the valve is opened, the water flows through the pipe from A to B until the water level becomes the same in both tanks. The water then stops flowing in the pipe, because there is no longer a difference in water pressure between the two tanks.

Current flow through an electric circuit is directly proportional to the difference in potential across the circuit, just as the flow of water through the pipe in Fig. 1 is directly proportional to the difference in the water level in the two tanks.

A fundamental law of current electricity is that the *current is directly proportional to the applied voltage;* that is, if the voltage is increased, the current is increased. If the voltage is decreased, the current is decreased.[11]

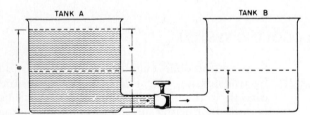

Figure 1. Water analogy of electric difference in potential.

QUESTIONS

1. What force causes electrons to move in a conductor as electric current? _____

2. What happens to the current if you increase the voltage? _____

3. Why did the water in Tank A stop flowing into Tank B? _____

_____

4. Would current flow through an electric circuit if there were no differences in potential across the circuit? Explain your answer. _____

_____

EXERCISE 7.9

DIRECTIONS   The illustration in this selection labels the parts of a device and helps explain a process. Read the selection and answer the questions that follow.

VOLTAGE PRODUCED BY HEAT

When a length of metal, such as copper, is heated at one end, electrons tend to move away from the hot end toward the cooler end. This is true of most metals. However, in some metals, such as iron, the opposite takes place and the electrons tend to move *toward* the hot end. These characteristics are illustrated in Fig. 1. The negative charges (electrons) are moving through the copper away from the heat and through the iron toward the heat. They cross from the iron to the copper at the hot junction, and from the copper through the current meter to the iron at the cold junction. This device is generally referred to as a thermocouple.[12]

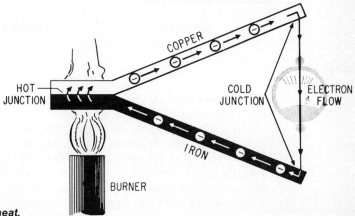

Figure 1. Voltage produced by heat.

QUESTIONS

1. What happens to the electrons in most metals when the metals are heated?

_____

2. What happens to the electrons in iron when iron is heated? _____

3. Test yourself. Close the book, and then draw a sketch of a thermocouple. Label the hot junction, the cold junction, the copper, the iron, and the direction in which the electrons flow.

DIRECTIONS   The illustrations in this passage label the parts of the cell and indicate their function. Read the passage and answer the questions that follow.

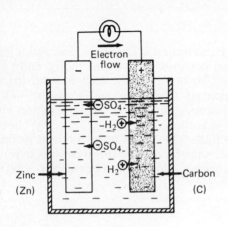

Figure 1.   Voltaic cell.

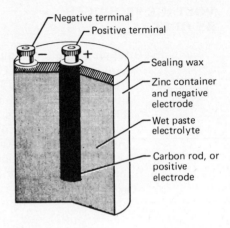

Figure 2.   Dry cell.

THE CELL

The battery is made up of two or more cells put together in a container and connected to serve as a source of electrical power.

In the wet galvanic or voltaic cell (Fig. 1) a strip of carbon and a strip of zinc are dropped into a solution of water and sulfuric acid. These two strips are electrodes. They are conductors; current leaves or returns to the liquid by means of the electrodes. The liquid is called the electrolyte; in the wet cell, it may be salt, acid, or alkaline solution.

In the dry cell (Fig. 2) the electrodes are the carbon rod in the center, and the zinc container that holds the cell. The electrolyte is not a liquid. Instead, it is a moist paste.

When a conductor is connected externally to the electrodes, electrons will flow from the negative zinc electrode through the external conductor to the positive carbon electrode, returning in the solution to the zinc.[13]

QUESTIONS

1. Test yourself. Close the book and then draw a picture of a wet voltaic cell. Label the positive carbon strip, the negative zinc strip, the water, and the sulfuric acid. Show the direction of electron flow. Then check your drawing with the one in the text.

2. Draw a cross-sectional view of a dry cell. Label the negative terminal, the positive terminal, the zinc container (negative electrode), the carbon rod (positive electrode), and the paste electrolyte. Then check your drawing with the one in the text.

EXERCISE 7.11

DIRECTIONS   Read the following passage and answer the questions that follow.

ELECTROSTATIC FIELDS

The electrostatic field is the space around charged bodies in which the influence of the charged bodies is felt. The fields are usually represented by lines of force. In reality, there are no such lines; the lines are used as a device to represent the direction and strength of the field. Figure 1 has two illustrations of the use of electrostatic lines to represent the field around charged bodies. Lines of force exerted by a positive charge are shown leaving the charge; lines of force exerted by a negative charge are shown entering the charge.[14]

EXERCISES

1. Describe an electrostatic field. _____

2. Test your understanding of electrostatic fields. Close the book and then draw figures representing electrostatic lines of force for (a) the repulsion of two like-charged bodies (b) the attraction of two unlike-charged bodies.

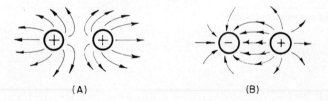

(A)   (B)

Figure 1. Electrostatic lines of force.

EXERCISE 7.12

DIRECTIONS   The illustration in this passage is designed to make the basic principle of the passage clearer.

CENTRIFUGAL AND CENTRIPETAL FORCES

In the case of a car turning a corner, the road must exert a frictional force on the car toward the center of the curved path, while the car, due to its tendency to travel in a straight line, exerts an outward force on the road. These two forces are equal and opposite. The inward force on the car is the centripetal force, whereas the outward force on the road is the centrifugal force. Note that the centripetal force is the only force acting upon the moving object. If a stone is whirled at the end of a string, the string pulls inward on the moving stone to keep it on a circular path, and the stone, due to its tendency to fly off tangentially, exerts an outward force on the string, which is felt by the hand whirling the stone. These two forces do not act upon the same object: the centripetal force is on the stone while the centrifugal force is on the hand (see Fig. 1). From these two examples we see that the *centripetal force is always on the moving object*, while the *centrifugal force is on the object producing the circular motion*.

According to Newton's third law, these forces are exactly equal in magnitude but opposite in direction.[15]

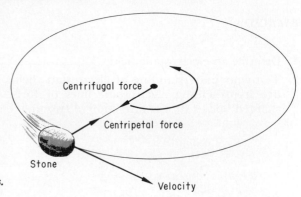

Figure 1. Centrifugal and centripetal forces.

QUESTIONS

1. Define "centripetal force." _____
2. Define "centrifugal force." _____
3. Test yourself. Draw a figure of a stone being twirled on a string. Label centrifugal and centripetal force. Include arrows.

EXERCISE 7.13

DIRECTIONS   Refer to the drawings as you read the following passage. Note the directions of the arrows.

ENGINE CYCLES

A basic automotive engine has a piston that moves up and down, or reciprocates, in a cylinder. The piston is attached to a crankshaft with a connecting rod. This arrangement allows the piston to reciprocate in the cylinder as the crankshaft rotates. The pressure developed in the combustion chamber will push the piston downward and, thereby, force the crankshaft to rotate.

The combustion chamber above the piston must be recharged with a fresh combustible mixture after each combustion, so valves are provided. The intake valve allows a fresh charge to enter for the combustion cycle. An exhaust valve releases the spent gases after the piston has moved to the bottom of the stroke. Valves are opened and closed at the correct time by a camshaft driven from the crankshaft. . . .

Engine cycles are identified by the number of piston strokes required to complete the cycle. A piston stroke is a one-way piston movement between top and bottom of the cylinder. Most automobile engines use a four-stroke cycle (see Figs. 1 and 2).

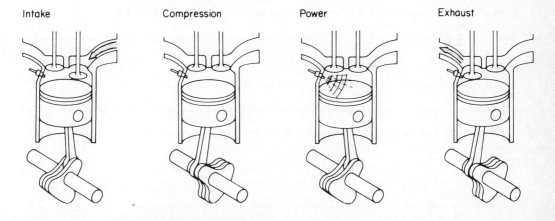

Intake   Compression   Power   Exhaust

Figure 1. Typical four-stroke cylinder engine.

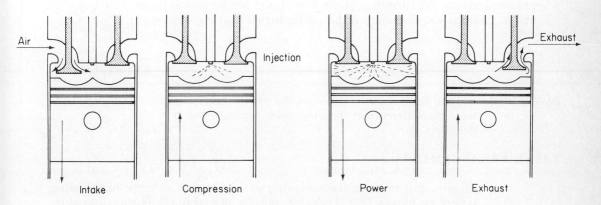

Air   Injection   Exhaust

Intake   Compression   Power   Exhaust

Figure 2. Typical open-chamber four-stroke cycle diesel.

145

The four-stroke cycle starts with the piston at top of the stroke. An intake valve opens as the piston moves down on the first, or *intake stroke,* allowing the combustible charge to enter the cylinder. The intake valve closes near bottom center and the piston then moves up on the second stroke, or *compression stroke,* to squeeze the charge into a small space. Near the top of the compression stroke, the spark plug ignites the charge so the fuel will burn. The heat released raises the charge pressure and the pressure pushes the piston down on the third, or *power stroke.* Near the bottom of the stroke, the exhaust valve opens to release the spent exhaust gases as the piston moves up on the force or *exhaust stroke* to complete the 720° four-stroke cycle. The piston is then in a position to start the next cycle with another intake stroke. The four-stroke cycle is repeated every other crankshaft revolution.[16]

QUESTIONS

1. Why does the crankshaft in the basic automotive engine rotate? Express your answer as a chain of cause-effect. _____

_____

2. What is the function of valves in a combustion chamber? _____

_____

3. Describe each of the four strokes in a four-stroke cycle. _____

_____

_____

_____

4. Test yourself. Without looking at the illustration, make a sketch showing each of the four strokes: intake, compression, power, and exhaust. Indicate the direction of air flow in the intake and exhaust strokes. Indicate the direction of the piston for all four strokes.

EXERCISE 7.14

DIRECTIONS   Use the illustrations as you read the text to help you understand the difference in the three valve arrangements that are described.

VALVE ARRANGEMENT

Engines may be classified according to the location and type of the valve system employed (Fig. 1). Valves may be placed in the block adjacent to the cylinder. This allows the inlet and outlet passages, called ports, to be short and surrounded by coolant. The head is a simple top for the cylinder. It includes a passage for coolant, an opening for a spark plug, and a cast impression that forms the top of the combustion chamber. With both valves located on one side of the cylinder, a cross-sectional

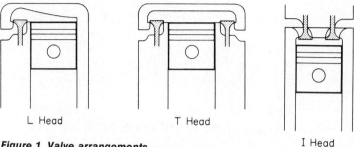

L Head   T Head

I Head

Figure 1. Valve arrangements.

view would be an L-shape. This type of valve arrangement is, therefore, called an *L-head* or *flat-head* engine.

A modification of this type of engine has one valve on each side of the cylinder. It is called a *T-head* engine because of its appearance in a cross-sectional view.

Most current automotive engines have both valves in the cylinder head. This reduces the cost of the engine block and allows better engine breathing by providing a large inlet port on one side of the head and a large exhaust port on the other side. The head is a large complex casting that provides openings for valve ports, coolant, valve actuating devices, and lubricant. The added cost and complexity of this type of cylinder head is offset by the reduced cost of the block and by the added performance produced by better engine breathing. This type of engine may either be called an *overhead-valve* engine or an *I-head* engine.[17]

QUESTIONS

1. List and describe each of the three types of valve arrangements discussed in the passage. Draw a sketch of each arrangement next to the description.

2. What are the two advantages of the I-head engine?_____

_____

Choose one chapter from your reading this week.

1. Pick out one long passage that goes with an illustration. The illustration may be a line drawing, graph, chart or diagram.

2. Read the passage carefully, using the illustration to help you understand what the author is saying.

3. Test your understanding. Close the book and make a simple sketch of the drawing. Label the parts of the illustration. Then check your drawing with the one in the book.

NOTES

1. Stanley Badzinski, Jr., *Carpentry in Residential Construction.* Englewood Cliffs, N.J.: Prentice-Hall, Inc., 1972, p. 120.
2. Badzinski, *Carpentry in Residential Construction,* p. 122.
3. Willard J. Poppy and Leland L. Wilson, *Exploring the Physical Sciences,* 2d ed. Englewood Cliffs, N.J.: Prentice Hall, Inc., 1973, pp. 202–4.
4. Dewey L. Yeager and Robert L. Gourley, *Introduction to Electron and Electro-Mechanical Devices.* Englewood Cliffs, N.J.: Prentice-Hall, Inc., 1976, p. 70.
5. Yeager and Gourley, *Introduction to Electron and Electro-Mechanical Devices,* p. 74.
6. W. J. Patton, *Construction Materials.* Englewood Cliffs, N.J.: Prentice-Hall, Inc., 1976, p. 77.
7. Brian J. Skinner, *Earth Resources,* 2d ed. Englewood Cliffs, N.J.: Prentice-Hall, Inc., 1976, p. 121.
8. Skinner, *Earth Resources,* p. 18.
9. Skinner, *Earth Resources,* p. 119.
10. Herbert E. Ellinger, *Automechanics,* 1st ed. Englewood Cliffs, N.J.: Prentice-Hall, Inc., 1972, p. 10.

11. Bureau of Naval Personnel, *Basic Electricity*. Washington, D.C.: U.S. Government Printing Office, 1969, p. 27.

12. Bureau of Naval Personnel, *Basic Electricity*, p. 30.

13. Bureau of Naval Personnel, *Basic Electricity*, p. 35.

14. Bureau of Naval Personnel, *Basic Electricity*, p. 17.

15. Poppy and Wilson, *Exploring the Physical Sciences*, p. 156.

16. Ellinger, *Automechanics*, pp. 8–9.

17. Ellinger, *Automechanics*, p. 12.

18. Dale Ewen et al., *Physics for Career Education*. Englewood Cliffs, N.J.: Prentice-Hall, Inc., 1974, pp. 302–4.

8

USING YOUR TEXTBOOK: STEP 1

OVERVIEW AND STUDY NOTES

The skills you have developed in Chapters 1–7 add up to a vital end-product: the ability to take all the information you need out of your textooks, organize it, study it, and learn it.

The best way to do this is to *take notes* as you read. You can use your ability to identify definitions, examples, contrast, cause-effect, and classification patterns, and your ability to write out main ideas and supporting details to take notes.

Taking notes requires you to pull all of the main points and supporting details together in an organized way. Making this effort and writing them out sharply and clearly will help you remember the material.

These next three chapters will show you how to use your textbook to the maximum in this way. This chapter concentrates on the first step: overview and section-by-section study notes.

LOOKING THE CHAPTER OVER

Remember what we said about looking a textbook over before you begin to read? The same idea applies for each chapter in a book. Before you read a chapter, or take notes on it, you should look it over and get an idea of its contents.

We have said that scientific and technical information is usually written in a dense manner that requires careful, thorough reading. It is not light information that you can glide through quickly. However, you can scan this information *before* you read to give yourself an overview of what the chapter will be about.

This is similar to what you do before you read a newspaper article. If you're like most people, you look at the headlines, pictures, and picture captions before you read the article. This process makes it much easier to understand the story. You can test this out by trying to read a story in the newspaper without looking at the headlines first. You'll find that it's much more difficult.

The information in your technical textbooks is more complicated than the information in a newspaper. However, you can use an overview to help you focus on the important points you are about to encounter. The ten minutes you spend looking the chapter over in this way will help you understand it more readily and thoroughly.

The title, subtitles, illustrations, captions, boldfaced and italicized print, introduction, conclusion, and chapter questions can all be used as part of a chapter overview.

Title and Subtitles   The title and subtitles give a clear overview of how the author has divided up the subject. By looking these over first, you can form a simple list in advance showing how the chapter is organized.

For instance, a chapter on "DC Sources" might include the following subtitles: "The Lead Storage Cell," "The Dry Cell," "Cells in a Series," and "Cells in Parallel." This information might be put as follows:

DC SOURCES

    I. Lead Storage Cells
   II. Dry Cells
 III. Cells in Series
 IV. Cells in Parallel

What else do the titles and subtitles tell you? Based on what you have already learned, you can assume that the author will *define* and *explain* all terms. You can assume that there will be *contrast* of important points. You can assume that much of the explanation will be in terms of *causes and effects.* You can use this knowledge for your overview. Looking just at the title and subtitles in the example of "DC Sources," you could predict that the author will:

   1. Define and explain both types of cells.
   2. Contrast the two kinds of cells.
   3. Define and explain series connections and parallel connections.
   4. Contrast the two kinds of connections.

Illustrations and Captions These will give you a further introduction to the main points in the chapter. In the example of "DC Sources," the sources will be pictured. The pictures will provide information on the difference between the cells, and the ways that they can be connected.

It is possible to write out a list of questions that a chapter will answer based solely on a look at the title, subtitles, and illustrations. Each of the section headings can be turned into a question; the information in the section will answer this question. For instance, the heading "Lead Storage Cell" could be turned into the question, "What is a lead storage cell?" or "How does a lead storage cell work?"

Figure 8.1 is a chart showing the different kinds of information available from a title and subtitles.

Title/Subtitles

DC sources/lead storage cell, dry cell, cells in series, cells in parallel

↓

Organization of Chapter

DC sources
  I. Lead storage cell
  II. Dry cell
  III. Cells in series
  IV. Cells in parallel

↓

Questions

What is a lead storage cell? How does it work?
What is a dry cell? How does it work?
What is a series connection?
What is a parallel connection?
What is the difference between a lead storage cell and a dry cell?
What is the difference between a series connection and a parallel connection?

↓

Contents

Definition and explanation of lead storage cell
Definition and explanation of dry cell
Contrast between lead storage cell and dry cell
Definition and explanation of series connection
Definition and explanation of parallel connection
Contrast between series and parallel connection

Figure 8.1. Information available from titles and subtitles.

Introduction and Conclusion   Technical books do not always have either of these two sections. If there is an introduction, however, it is worth reading as part of your overview. Introductions generally give a broad view of the problem before the author focuses on each part. Often the introduction gives the pattern of organization for the chapter. It may also serve to introduce the key terms that will be used throughout the chapter.

There are sometimes conclusions to chapters, in which the author sums up major points. If there is a conclusion, it should be read as part of the overview.

Here is an example from an introduction in which the author gives a clear account of what the chapter will be about:

ELECTROMECHANICAL TRANSDUCERS

Introduction   A device that converts energy from one form to another is often called a transducer. A electromechanical transducer can be defined as any device that converts a mechanical quantity into an electrical signal or vice versa; however, there may be intermediate stages of this conversion, as we will see later. Various quantities may be measured and converted to electrical signals. Some of these quantities are:

1. Rotary position
2. Linear position
3. Temperature
4. Pressure
5. Sound
6. Velocity
7. Acceleration
8. Brightness

This chapter will examine the first five quantities listed and investigate some of the transducers most commonly used to convert these quantities to electrical signals and vice versa.[1]

Opening Statements of Sections   Authors often open a section with a key statement. For instance, here is the opening statement from a chapter section: "Different construction methods are used by manufacturers." When your eye catches a statement like this, you know that the entire section will grow out of this statement: first the author will discuss construction method A, then method B, then method C, and so on.

Special Kinds of Print   Italic and boldfaced print are a "must" in an overview. They give major divisions, definitions, laws, and other points that the author thinks are particularly important. Sometimes definitions are printed in different colors, or in capital letters. Rules or laws may have special borders or boxes printed around them.

Questions Look to see what you have to do when you have finished reading the chapter. Usually there are review questions on the text, as well as problems involving mathematics. Sometimes there is a multiple-choice test as well.

TAKING TWO-LEVEL NOTES SECTION BY SECTION

After your overview, read the chapter section by section. As you finish each section, take notes on the most important points.

These notes are "informal"; that is, they are a study aid for you, not an assignment that will be graded on appearance.

Here is a very simple system for informal note-taking:

1. Identify each main idea or point. There may be one or two main ideas in each paragraph, or there may be three paragraphs in a row with no information that is important to remember. Write out each main point that you want to remember.

2. Indicate major points by putting Roman numerals (I, II, III) before each one.

3. Write out below each main idea any supporting details or examples you want to remember.

4. Indent each supporting point or subcategory to show that it is subordinate to the main idea.

5. Indicate the order of the supporting details by putting capital letters (A, B, C) before each indented item.

Here is a section from a chapter on automotive design, which we'll use to give an example of how to take section-by-section study notes.

Different construction methods are used among the manufacturers and their vehicle models (see Fig. 1). Separate body and frame construction has been used for the longest time. In this type of construction, the engine, drive line, and running gear are firmly fastened to the frame; then the body is mounted to the frame with insulators to minimize noise and vibration transfer.

A second type of construction is the unitized body, in which the frame is part of the body structure. Body panels add strength to the frame pieces that form part of the structure. The running gear and drive line are attached with large soft insulators to minimize noise and vibration. If the insulators are too soft they tend to give the vehicle a spongy ride, and if they are too hard they do not insulate properly. Careful insulator design and location will produce a vehicle that is satisfactory to drive and ride in.

A third type of construction combines features from both of the preceding types. It uses a stub frame from the fire wall forward and a unitized body from the fire wall back. The unitized portion is very rigid, while the stub frame provides an opportunity for good in-

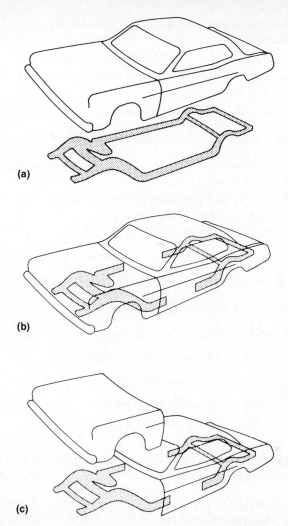

Figure 1. Body and frame construction. (a) Separate body and frame, (b) unitized construction, (c) unitized body and stub front frame.

(a)

(b)

(c)

sulation. This construction method is generally applied to larger body styles.

Manufacturers select their construction method by deciding which type is most economical for them to build, while still providing the noise, vibration, and ride characteristics they want to have in their vehicle. The largest number of standard-size vehicles are separate body and frame construction. The majority of small vehicles use unitized construction.[2]

If we follow the system for informal note-taking using this section, here is what happens:

1. Find each main idea or point. Write each one out.
2. Indicate major points by putting a Roman numeral before each one.

I. Different body and frame construction methods used by manufacturers.

3. Find the supporting details or examples that you want to remember and write them out *below* the main idea.
4. Indent each supporting point or subcategory to show that it is subordinate.
5. Indicate the order by A, B, C, before each indented item.

I. Different body and frame construction methods used by manufacturers.
A. Separate body and frame — used for most standard-sized vehicles.
B. Unitized body — used for most small vehicles.
C. Combination of stub frame and unitized body — for larger body styles.

Here is the way the text, and the informal notes on the text, would look if they were placed side by side:

Different construction methods are used among the manufacturers and their vehicle models. Separate body and frame construction has been used for the longest time. In this type of construction, the engine, drive line, and running gear are firmly fastened to the frame: then the body is mounted to the frame with insulators to minimize noise and vibration transfer.

A second type of construction is the unitized body, in which the frame is part of the body structure. Body panels add strength to the frame pieces that form part of the structure. The

I. Different body and frame construction methods used by manufacturers.
A. Separate body and frame — used in most standard-sized vehicles.

B. Unitized body — used in most small cars.

running gear and drive line are attached with large soft insulators to minimize noise and vibration. If the insulators are too soft they tend to give the vehicle a spongy ride, and if they are too hard they do not insulate properly. Careful insulator design and location will produce a vehicle that is satisfactory to drive and ride in.

A third type of construction combines features from both the preceding types. It uses a stub frame from the fire wall forward and a unitized body from the fire wall back. The unitized portion is very rigid, while the stub frame provides an opportunity for good insulation. This construction method is generally applied to larger body styles.

Manufacturers select their construction method by deciding which type is most economical for them to build, while still providing the noise, vibration, and ride characteristics they want to have in their vehicle. The largest number of standard-size vehicles use separate body and frame construction. The majority of small vehicles use unitized construction.[3]

C. Combination of stub frame and unitized body — for larger cars.

The information has been "boiled down" to a minimum.

These notes clearly show how the information is organized. This note-taking system is a two-level one. It shows the relationship of ideas that are *major* to those that are *minor*. It is possible to take much more complicated types of notes. These will be considered later.

LOOKING AHEAD   By the time you finish this chapter, you should be able to do an overview of a chapter and take section-by-section notes by:

1. Turning the titles of chapter sections into questions that information in the section will answer.

2. Using section headings, italic and boldface type, and picture captions to make simple lists of how the information in the section will be divided.

3. Using an introduction to predict the content of a chapter that will follow.

4. Taking two-level notes on paragraphs.

5. Taking two-level notes on typical textbook sections.

SUMMARY

1. To do an overview, combine quick reading with slow reading. Scan quickly until you find what you want; then read slowly and carefully.
2. Use titles, subtitles, illustrations, captions, boldface and italic type, introduction, conclusion, and chapter questions as part of the overview.
3. When you've finished the overview, read each section slowly.
4. Before you begin the section, turn the heading into a question. Read to answer the question.
5. When you finish reading each section, take two-level notes on the information you want to remember.
6. Indicate major ideas with Roman numerals. Indent supporting details, examples, or subcategories beneath major points. Use capital letters (A, B, C) to indicate they are subordinate to the major ideas.

EXERCISE 8.1

Directions   Here is a section from a chapter on "Characteristics of Construction Materials." Do an overview of this section. Do not read the text word-for-word. Note (1) the title, (2) any subheads, (3) all italic or boldface type. After you have scanned the section, answer the questions on overviewing that follow.

CHARACTERISTICS OF CONSTRUCTION MATERIALS

Three Fundamental Groups of Construction Materials With few exceptions, construction materials are solid materials or harden into solid materials. Solid materials are grouped into three fundamental types: ceramics, metals, and organics.

The *ceramic* materials are rock or clay minerals, or are compounded from such minerals. Examples are sand, limestone, glass, brick, cement, gypsum, plaster, mortar, and mineral wool insulation. These are materials dug from the earth's crust with or without further processing and purification. Since they are extracted from the earth, they are relatively inexpensive as compared to metals or the organic materials. The ceramics have been used as building materials from time immemorial, and their virtues will ensure their use in the future: they are enduring, hard, and rigid. Their outstanding disadvantages are brittleness and their heavy weight.

Metals are extracted from natural ores, which of course are also ceramic materials. Such metallic ores are usually oxides or sulfides of metals. The metals are not as hard as the ceramic materials and, because they must be extracted from the ore by complex smelting processes, they are more expensive. Ceramic materials are brittle, and so are restricted to the carrying of compressive forces in buildings and structures. Metals are ductile and are used where tensile forces must be carried.

Ceramic materials do not corrode in the atmospheric conditions to which buildings are exposed; metals do. The corrosion process returns the metal to its original state as a mineral. When iron and steel rust, they oxidize to iron oxide, Fe_2O_3, which is the iron ore hematite. Aluminum oxidizes to Al_2O_3, which is the ore bauxite.

The *organic* materials with the notable exception of wood and bitumens, are largely a development of the twentieth century. These are the numerous and increasing synthetic materials based chemically upon carbon. The organics include wood, paper, asphalts, plastics, and rubbers.[4]

QUESTIONS

1. Turn the section heading into a question that the entire section will

answer. _____

2. Based on your *overview only,* fill in the simple outline below. Give the section heading across the top. Below it list the three major subdivisions of the subject, which are indicated in the text by italics.

I. _____

   A. _____

   B. _____

   C. _____

EXERCISE 8.2

DIRECTIONS

Here is the next section from the chapter on "Characteristics of Construction Materials." Scan this section. Do not read the text word-for-word. Note (1) the title, (2) any subheads, (3) all italic or boldface type. After you have overviewed the section, answer the questions that follow.

INTRODUCTION TO THE MATERIALS

Of all the available building materials, *rock* and *stone* are traditionally associated with permanence. These are the enduring materials of the earth's crust, the oldest being perhaps 4 billion years old. But there is a remarkable difference in service requirements between a relatively static and protected position in the earth's crust and a building wall, and no rock will effectively last forever when incorporated into a building. All rocks are porous to some degree and can absorb water, with all the possibilities of water for damage and deterioration.

Concrete is a man-made conglomerate rock material of stone aggregate, sand, and a cement adhesive. It has a more complex structure and chemistry than rock and hence is exposed to a greater variety of modes of deterioration. It is weaker than rock in tension and compression and is not expected to support tensile forces. Like any other composite material, it is only as strong as its bonding material, the cement. Finally, it must be emphasized that the quality of concrete is dependent on the skill with which it is compounded and handled on the job site.

The architect's problem with concrete as a building facing material is that of satisfactory appearance. Its color is drab gray. But as a construction material it offers substantial advantages:

1. Concrete may be formed into virtually any shape.
2. It is both hard and rigid.
3. It is inexpensive.

Brick is a burned ceramic product somewhat similar in chemistry to concrete and cement. It is made in modular sizes in a range of colors. It is more attractive in color, texture, and general appearance than concrete, and quite elaborate designs are possible in brick.

The outstanding characteristic of *glass* is its transmission of light and other radiation.

Metals offer the advantages of high strength in compression, tension, or shear, ductility, rigidity, hardness, and dimensional stability. Their susceptibility to corrosion has been mentioned, although certain alloys such as the stainless steels are not corroded by the service conditions found in buildings.

The American architect Frank Lloyd Wright expressed the appeal of *wood* in the following words: "Wood is universally beautiful to man. It is the most humanly intimate of all materials. Man loves his association with it, likes to feel it under his hand." Wood is highly corrosion-resistant and remarkably durable, weathering away at a rate of about 1/4 inch per century. Although plastics and metals have increasingly displaced wood in building products and manufactured products, it is not conceivable that wood will become obsolete because of its unique advantages over other materials:

1. Trees are a self-perpetuating natural resource.
2. Wood is, or can be made, relatively abundant in most geographical areas.
3. Wood can be shaped with ease and with the use of simple tools.
4. Wood, like all organic materials, is light in weight.
5. It is perhaps the most beautiful of construction materials, with a variety of natural designs and textures.
6. It is the strongest and until recently the cheapest of the cellular construction materials.

Wood, clay, and stone have been standard construction materials for at least 100,000 years. Brick and concrete have a history of thousands of years. By comparison, the *plastics* and *rubbers* are recent additions to the range of construction materials. They have been serious contenders in construction for only about 20 years. They are a special case, and call for some special remarks.[5]

QUESTIONS

1. Based on your overview, fill out this simple listing of the contents of the section.

I. *Building Materials*

  A. rock and stone

  B._____

  C._____

  D._____

  E._____

  F._____

  G._____

2. Will the author use contrast? How?_____

_____

EXERCISE 8.3

DIRECTIONS   Do an overview of the following chapter section.

EARLY CONCEPTS OF MAGNETISM

Magnetism dates further back than the electrification of amber, but the origin of the term *magnet* is questionable. According to the Roman scholar Pliny, a Greek shepherd, Magnus, observed that the nails in his shoes and the iron on the tip of his staff adhered to certain black stones, and those "magic" rocks were named after him. But the Roman poet Lucretius referred to those stones as magnets because they came from a large deposit of this black rock in Magnesia, a province of Asia Minor. Those rocks, which had the ability to attract iron, were also called *lodestone* (*lode* meaning "attract" or "lead"). The Greeks called this black mineral *magnetite*, which consists mainly of iron ore. The ability of a lodestone to communicate with iron and to transfer its power to iron was considered as a supernatural power, more like a spiritual behavior than a physical phenomenon. The Greeks could not see how a lodestone could attract iron without any visible connection between them unless it was spiritual, and they wondered why it showed its affection only for iron. Thales even thought that a lodestone possessed a soul. Plato once praised his friend by saying: "There is a divinity moving you like that in a stone which Euripides calls a magnet." Many fantastic stories were written about the powers of the lodestone. According to one story, Archimedes used a very strong lodestone to pull the nails out of a number of the enemy's ships, sinking them. These black rocks were also believed to possess the secrets of good health. They were ground into powder and then taken internally as medicine to improve one's physical condition. The Greeks thought that the magnets emitted invisible emanations that pushed the air away from the magnets, and then iron moved into this void. Because of its magic powers, magnetism was one of the first natural phenomena to be investigated.

The earliest users of magnets were the Chinese. According to a Chinese dictionary completed in A.D. 121, they observed that a lodestone when floated on a bit of wood in water assumed a north-south position. They also found that needles rubbed with magnetite pointed north-south when allowed to swing freely. Such magnetic compasses were employed by the Chinese for journeying over land as early as A.D. 900. By the twelfth century, compasses were used for maritime navigation in Europe as well as in China. In the thirteenth century, Pierre de Marincourt (Petre Peregrine), a French nobleman who was a friend of Roger Bacon, became interested in the magic powers of the lodestone, and wrote a remarkable document on the subject. He was the first to locate and identify the so-called poles of a magnet—the regions near the ends of a magnet where the magnetic property seemed to be concentrated. He also noticed that when a magnet was broken in two, new unlike poles appeared at the broken ends. These magnetic poles seemed to come in pairs, and the poles of a magnet are equal and opposite. Unlike electric charges, there seemed to be no single poles. It was later learned that unlike poles attract each other, and like poles repel. Marincourt was the first to shape a lodestone in the form of a sphere and have it retain its magnetic properties. He also introduced the idea that there is a "field of influence" around a magnet where it affects magnetic substances as indicated by sprinkling iron filings around a lodestone. This we now call a *magnetic field*.

The first real scientific study of magnetism was started by Dr. William Gilbert near the end of the sixteenth century. His work was published in 1600 in his *De Magneta Magneticique Corporibus*. He refuted most of the magnetic superstitions with experimental facts. For centuries man had wondered why lodestones or compasses always pointed toward the north. Some thought that the north end of a compass was attracted by the Pole-Star, Polaris, while others thought that it pointed toward a submerged magnetic island someplace near Greenland. Gilbert settled the problem when he, like Marincourt, shaped a lodestone in the form of a sphere, but he identified the magnetic properties of it with that of the Earth. He noticed that a compass placed anywhere around his so-called *terrella* ("little earth") always pointed toward a fixed point on the sphere. He argued that the only difference between the Earth and his terrella was size. The end of the compass which pointed toward the north he called the north-seeking or north (N) pole and the end pointing south he called the south-seeking or south (S) pole. Before this time the poles of a magnet had not been named.

His view that the Earth acts like a big magnet is now universally accepted, but we feel that the magnetism is produced by some activity within the mantle or outer core of the Earth instead of the Earth being a big permanent bar magnet. We find that the Earth's magnetic poles are several degrees from the geographic poles; therefore, compasses at various places on the Earth do not point directly north. Columbus, on his voyage across the Atlantic Ocean, observed that the compass pointed west of north as determined by Polaris when he left Europe, and east of north when he arrived in the New World. This deviation of the compass from true north is called the *angle of declination*. The Chinese knew about this phenomenon, but made no scientific study of it.[6]

QUESTIONS

1. Turn the subtitle into a question that the entire section will answer.

2. Which are some of the earlier civilizations that investigated the nature of magnets? _____

3. Who wrote the first scientific study of magnetism? _____

EXERCISE 8.4

DIRECTIONS   Here is the introduction to a chapter on dc and ac machines. Read the introduction carefully. It is intended to be a foundation for the chapter that follows.

DC AND AC MACHINES

Introduction   An *electric motor* is a machine or transducer that converts electrical energy to rotary mechanical motion. The converse of the electric motor is the *electric generator,* which converts rotary mechanical energy to electrical energy. The generator differs only slightly from the motor in construction, and in most cases a motor may be used as a generator and vice versa. We will use the term *electric machine* or *machine* to refer to an electric motor or generator.

Machines may be excited by an ac or dc voltage; however, all machines have some common elements. The rotating member of an electric machine is called the *rotor.* In dc machines the rotor may contain several coils of wire known as the *armature winding.* Voltage is applied to these windings via *brushes,* which are connected to the armature winding by the *commutator.* The rotor connections in ac machines are made via brushes which maintain contact with *slip rings* if connection to the rotor is required.

   The stationary member of an electric machine is called the *stator*. The stator often contains the field windings of an electric machine, which set up a stationary or rotating magnetic field. In small dc machines the field may be produced by a permanent magnet. In dc machines the field is stationary, and in ac machines the field rotates.

   The interaction of the magnetic fields of the rotor and stator produces a force that causes the motor to rotate. This interaction produces an induced or generated voltage in the case of a generator.[7]

QUESTIONS

1. What basic terms are provided in this introduction?_____

_____

2. Define each of the following terms:

 a. Electric motor _____

 b. Electric generator _____

 c. Rotor _____

 d. Armature winding _____

3. Why does the author define these terms in the introduction?_____

_____

4. Why should the introduction be read slowly?_____

EXERCISE 8.5

DIRECTIONS Take notes on the following paragraphs.

1 We often interchange the terms "concrete" and "cement." However, concrete and cement are not identical. Concrete is an artificial stone made up of cement, water, and some type of stone aggregate. Cement is the substance that, in combination with water, makes up an adhesive that binds together the stone aggregate.

I. _____

 A. _____

 B. _____

2 Concrete has been extremely popular in the building industry. However, concrete has certain limitations as a construction material. It is somewhat permeable; that is, it allows the penetration of a certain amount of fluid. It is subject to expansion and contraction. Also, it must be reinforced if its tensile strength is to be increased.

I. _____

  A. _____

  B. _____

  C. _____

3   All five types of portland cement contain the same ingredients: iron, lime, alumina, and silica. The iron is obtained from iron ore. Lime comes from limestone, marl, oyster shells, and other calcareous materials. Alumina and silica are obtained from clay, shale, sand, and other argillaceous materials.

I. _____

  A. _____

  B. _____

  C. _____

EXERCISE 8.6

DIRECTIONS   Take notes on the following paragraphs. A form is provided.

1   Rocks have been used as a building material for millennia. Scientists classify rocks in three major categories: igneous, sedimentary, and metamorphic. The first group is igneous or primary rock. Igneous rock is formed when magma, the plastic material that lies beneath the earth's crust, wells up to the earth's surface and then cools. The second group is sedimentary rock. This rock results from the breakdown of primary rock by water, wind, or ice. The small particles are then deposited in layers called sediments. Eventually these layers harden, forming sedimentary rock. The third type of rock is metamorphic. This is a new stone formed when igneous or sedimentary rock is transformed as a result of heat or chemical energy.

I. _____

  A. _____

  B. _____

  C. _____

2   Wood is a building material whose use extends from antiquity. It is classified in two major categories: deciduous woods and conifers. The deciduous or hardwoods are categorized on the basis of their broad leaf and the fact that their seeds are usually in a seed case. The conifers or softwoods are distinguished by a needlelike leaf and the fact that their seeds are in the form of cones.

I. _____

  A. _____

  B. _____

3   Two properties of solids are particularly important. *Tensile strength* refers to a solid's resistance to being pulled apart. Steel is valued as a construction material for its high tensile strength. Concrete, in contrast, has a limited tensile strength; it is often reinforced with steel. *Ductility,* a second property of solids, refers to the ability to be drawn out without shattering. Copper, favored as a material for electrical wiring, is ductile, as is platinum.

I. _____

  A. _____

  B. _____

---

4   There is a difference between physical change and chemical change. For instance, if there are sharp shifts in temperature, rock will contract with cold and expand with heat. Eventually the rock may crumble. When it does, the smaller pieces of the rock will be of the same mineral composition as the original rock. The nature of the substance is not altered. When iron is heated, it expands, but it is still iron. A physical change is one in which the nature of the substance has not been altered. If, however, minerals in the rock interact with dissolved salts present in water to form a new mineral, a chemical change has occurred. If rust forms, a chemical change has occurred. A chemical change is one in which the nature of the substance is altered.

I. Difference between physical change and chemical change.

  A. _____

      _____

  B. _____

      _____

EXERCISE 8.7

DIRECTIONS   Here is a section from a textbook. You overviewed this section in Exercise 8.2. Read it carefully and take study notes on the important points on a separate sheet of paper.

INTRODUCTION TO
THE MATERIALS

Of all the available building materials, *rock* and *stone* are traditionally associated with permanence. These are the enduring materials of the earth's crust, the oldest being perhaps 4 billion years old. But there is a remarkable difference in service requirements between a relatively static and protected position in the earth's crust and a building wall, and no rock will effectively last forever when incorporated into a building. All rocks are porous to some degree and can absorb water, with all the possibilities of water for damage and deterioration.

Concrete is a man-made conglomerate rock material of stone aggregate, sand, and a cement adhesive. It has a more complex structure and chemistry than rock and hence is exposed to a greater variety of modes of deterioration. It is weaker than rock in tension and compression and is not expected to support tensile forces. Like any other composite material, it is only as strong as its bonding material, the cement. Finally, it must be emphasized that the quality of concrete is dependent on the skill with which it is compounded and handled on the job site.

The architect's problem with concrete as a building facing material is that of satisfactory appearance. Its color is drab gray. But as a construction material it offers substantial advantages:

1. Concrete may be formed into virtually any shape.
2. It is both hard and rigid.
3. It is inexpensive.

Brick is a burned ceramic product somewhat similar in chemistry to concrete and cement. It is made in modular sizes in a range of colors. It is more attractive in color, texture, and general appearance than concrete, and quite elaborate designs are possible in brick.

The outstanding characteristic of *glass* is its transmission of light and other radiation.

Metals offer the advantages of high strength in compression, tension, or shear, ductility, rigidity, hardness, and dimensional stability. Their susceptibility to corrosion has been mentioned, although certain alloys such as the stainless steels are not corroded by the service conditions found in buildings.

The American architect Frank Lloyd Wright expressed the appeal of *wood* in the following words: "Wood is universally beautiful to man. It is the most humanly intimate of all materials. Man loves his association with it, likes to feel it under his hand." Wood is highly corrosion-resistant and remarkably durable, weathering away at a rate of about 1/4 inch per century. Although plastics and metals have increasingly displaced wood in building products and manufactured products, it is not conceivable that wood will become obsolete because of its unique advantages over other materials:

1. Trees are a self-perpetuating natural resource.

2. Wood is, or can be made, relatively abundant in most geographical areas.

3. Wood can be shaped with ease and with the use of simple tools.

4. Wood, like all organic materials, is light in weight.

5. It is perhaps the most beautiful of construction materials, with a variety of natural designs and textures.

6. It is the strongest and until recently the cheapest of the cellular construction materials.

Wood, clay, and stone have been standard construction materials for at least 100,000 years. Brick and concrete have a history of thousands of years. By comparison, the *plastics* and *rubbers* are recent additions to the range of construction materials. They have been serious contenders in construction for only about 20 years. They are a special case, and call for some special remarks.[8]

EXERCISE 8.8

DIRECTIONS   Take two-level notes on the following chapter section on a separate sheet of paper.

TYPES OF WEATHERING

Mechanical Weathering   Mechanical weathering, which is also called *disintegration,* is the process by which rock is broken down into smaller and smaller fragments as the result of the energy developed by physical forces. For example, when water freezes in a fractured rock, enough energy may develop to pry off pieces of rock. Or a boulder moved by gravity down a rocky slope may be shattered into smaller fragments. Note that in mechanical weathering the size of the material changes from large to small, but the composition remains unchanged.

Expansion and Contraction Resulting from Heat   Changes in temperature, if they are rapid enough and great enough, may bring about the mechanical weathering of rock. For instance, in areas where bare rock is exposed at the surface, unprotected by a cloak of soil, forest or brush fires can generate enough heat to break up the rock. The rapid and violent heating of the exterior zone of the rock causes it to expand, and if the expansion is great enough, flakes and larger fragments of rock are split off. Lightning often starts such forest fires and in rare instances may even shatter exposed rock by means of a direct strike.

Variations in temperature from day to night and from winter to summer cause expansion and contraction of rock material. Occasionally these changes are known to cause mechanical failure of rock. . . .

Frost Action   Frost is much more effective that heat in producing mechanical weathering. When water freezes, its volume increases about 9 percent. So when water that trickles down into the cracks, crevices, and pores of a rock expands as it passes from the liquid to the solid state, it sets up pressures that are directed outward from the inside of the rock.

And these pressures are great enough to dislodge fragments from the rock's surface. In fact, by the time the temperature has fallen to about −7.6°F, the resulting pressure may be as great as 30,000 pounds per square inch, equivalent to the pressure produced by a 15-ton granite block. This temperature is not unusually low and is experienced several times a year even in temperate latitudes.[9]

EXERCISE 8.9

DIRECTIONS   Here are the first two sections of a chapter on direct-current electricity. (1) Do an overview of these two sections and answer the questions on overviewing. (2) Then read each section carefully and take study notes on a separate sheet of paper.

OVERVIEW   Using only the title, subtitles, and illustrations, fill out the chart in Fig. 8.2.

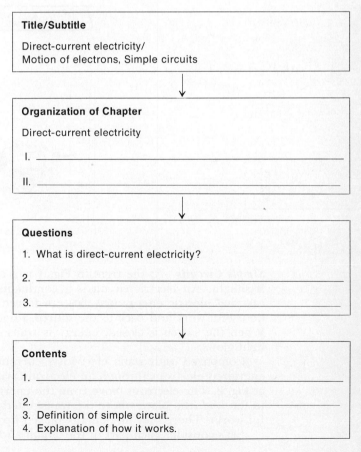

Title/Subtitle

Direct-current electricity/
Motion of electrons, Simple circuits

↓

Organization of Chapter

Direct-current electricity

I. _____

II. _____

↓

Questions

1. What is direct-current electricity?

2. _____

3. _____

↓

Contents

1. _____

2. _____

3. Definition of simple circuit.

4. Explanation of how it works.

Figure 8.2. Overview of two sections of chapter.

Motion of Electrons   Electrons moving in a wire make up a current in the wire. When the electron current flows in only one direction, it is called *direct current* (dc). Current which changes direction is called *alternating current* (ac). Alternating current will be considered in later chapters.

An electric current is a convenient means of transmitting energy. Technicians face many situations every day which require energy to do a particular task. To drill a hole in a metal block, energy must be supplied and transformed into mechanical energy to turn the drill bit. The problem the technician faces is how to supply energy to the machine being used in a form which the machine can turn into useful work. Electricity is often the most satisfactory means of transmitting energy. We will first study the use of electricity in transferring energy by looking at an example.

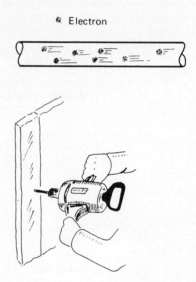

Electron

Simple Circuits   At the right in Fig. 1 is a circuit like that of a simple flashlight. An electric circuit is a conducting loop in which electrons carrying electric energy may be transferred from a suitable source to do useful work and back to the source. Energy is stored in the battery. When the switch is closed, energy is transmitted to the light and the light glows.

Compared with static electricity, current electricity is the flow of energized electrons through an electron carrier called a *conductor*. Look at Fig. 2. The electrons move from the energy *source* (the battery, here) to the *load* (the place where the transmitted energy is turned into useful work). There they lose energy picked up in the source.

Let's consider each part of the circuit and determine its function.[10]

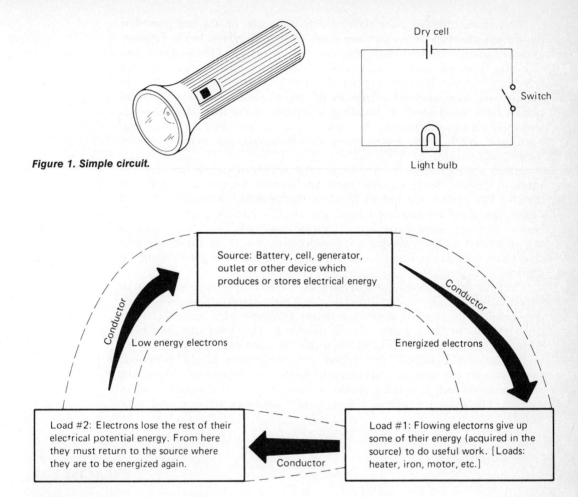

Figure 1. Simple circuit.

Dry cell

Switch

Light bulb

Source: Battery, cell, generator, outlet or other device which produces or stores electrical energy

Conductor

Conductor

Low energy electrons

Energized electrons

Load #2: Electrons lose the rest of their electrical potential energy. From here they must return to the source where they are to be energized again.

Conductor

Load #1: Flowing electorns give up some of their energy (acquired in the source) to do useful work. [Loads: heater, iron, motor, etc.]

Figure 2. Analysis of simple circuit.

EXERCISE 8.10

DIRECTIONS Here is a section from a textbook. You did an overview of this section at the beginning of this chapter. Read it carefully, and then take study notes on the important points on a separate sheet of paper.

Three Fundamental Groups of Construction Materials With few exceptions, construction materials are solid materials or harden into solid materials. Solid materials are grouped into three fundamental types: ceramics, metals, and organics.

The *ceramic* materials are rock or clay minerals, or are compounded from such minerals. Examples are sand, limestone, glass, brick, cement, gypsum, plaster, mortar, and mineral wool insulation. These are materials dug from the earth's crust with or without further processing and purification. Since they are extracted from the earth, they are relatively inexpensive as compared to metals or the organic materials. The ceramics have been used as building materials from time immemorial, and their virtues will ensure their use in the future: they are enduring, hard, and rigid. Their outstanding disadvantages are brittleness and their heavy weight.

Metals are extracted from natural ores, which of course are also ceramic materials. Such metallic ores are usually oxides or sulfides of metals. The metals are not as hard as the ceramic materials, and because they must be extracted from the ore by complex smelting processes, they are more expensive. Ceramic materials are brittle, and so are restricted to the carrying of compressive forces in buildings and structures. Metals are ductile and are used where tensile forces must be carried.

Ceramic materials do not corrode in the atmospheric conditions to which buildings are exposed; metals do. The corrosion process returns the metal to its original state as a mineral. When iron and steel rust, they oxidize to iron oxide, Fe_2O_3, which is the iron ore hematite. Aluminum oxidizes to Al_2O_3, which is the ore bauxite.

The *organic* materials are largely a development of the twentieth century, with the notable exception of wood and bitumens. These are the numerous and increasing synthetic materials based chemically upon carbon. The organics include wood, paper, asphalts, plastics, and rubbers.[11]

EXERCISE 8.11

DIRECTIONS   Take study notes on the following portion of a chapter.

BUILDING MATERIALS

> *There will be a shortage of standing room on earth before there is a shortage of granite. (J. A. S. Adams,* New Ways of Finding Minerals, *1959.)*

Building materials are the largest crop and, after fossil fuels, the second most valuable mineral commodity that we reap from the Earth. Because almost every known rock type and mineral contributes to the crop in some way, the origin of building materials embraces most of geology. We will concentrate mainly on uses and try to place this largest-volume mineral production into perspective with the other mineral products.

Although no classification is completely satisfactory, we will separate building materials into two groups: first, materials that are used as they come from the ground, without any treatment beyond physical shaping, such as cutting or crushing; second, the prepared materials that must be treated chemically, fired, melted, or otherwise altered before use so that they can be molded and set into new forms. The first group includes building stones, sand, gravel, and crushed stone for aggregate; the second includes clay for bricks, raw materials for cement, plaster, and asbestos.

Most building materials, unlike metals, have little intrinsic value; they are not scarce commodities and they are widely distributed, but when removed and processed to a useful form, they increase in value enormously. For example, the limestone and shale used to make cement may have intrinsic values of only $1 per ton or less in the ground, but after mining, crushing, firing, and conversion to a high-quality cement, the product is worth $20 or more per ton. The factors controlling location of production sites are most commonly such straightforward ones as local demand and transport costs; rarely are they problems of resources. . . .

Cement   The word cement refers to agents that bind particles together. Cement is rarely used alone; it is added to sand, gravel, crushed rock, oyster shells, or other aggregate as the binder needed to make concrete, a sort of "instant rock." As little as 15 percent of a concrete may be cement.

The forerunner of modern cement was discovered by the engineers of ancient Rome. They found that water added to a mixture of quicklime (CaO, obtained by heating—or calcining—limestone) and a natural, glassy volcanic ash from the town of Pozzuoli, near Naples, produced a series of reactions that caused the mixture to recrystallize and harden. The resulting mass was stable in air or water and it materially assisted the Romans in their remarkable engineering feats. Known as *pozzolan cement*, similar materials are still employed today, but on a decreasing scale. . . .

The "secret" was forgotten during the Dark Ages, and it was only rediscovered in 1756. John Smeaton, a British engineer engaged in designing and building the famous Eddystone Lighthouse, sought cementing materials to set and remain stable under water. He is said to have rediscovered the Roman cement formula through examination of an ancient Latin document. Natural cements soon became popular in Europe and subject to much experiment. In 1824 another Englishman, Joseph Aspidin, patented his formula for *portland cement*, so called because it resembled Portland stone, a limestone widely used in British buildings. It soon supplanted all other cements and is today the most common construction material in the world. . . .[12]

Choose one chapter from your reading this week. Take study notes on this chapter.

1. Do an overview of the chapter first. Use the title, headings, captions, italics, and boldface print.
2. Take study notes section by section.
3. Write down all the important points in the section (I, II, III, etc.).
4. Write down all the important supporting points (A, B, C, D). Indent these points beneath the main points.

QUICK PROGRESS TEST 3

DIRECTIONS   Here is a selection on the nature of matter. The questions that follow test your understanding of the material, and your ability to take notes on important points.

MATTER

All matter seems to be essentially electrical in nature, either negative or positive. This electrical nature was early illustrated by a simple experiment—a piece of fur and a piece of amber were rubbed together, and afterwards they could pick up light objects such as wool or feathers. But the material picked up by the fur was repelled by the amber. In the 16th century, William Gilbert, personal physician to Queen Elizabeth I, proposed that the power responsible for this phenomenon be called electricity, from the Greek word *elektron*, meaning amber.

We say that like electric charges repel each other and unlike charges attract each other. You have seen this principle in action in the poles of two adjacent magnets. The so-called north poles repel each other but are attracted by the south poles, and vice versa.

Electron, Proton, and Neutron   When we rub fur and amber together, particles are said to pass from the fur to the amber. The fur, then, has a deficiency of particles and is positively charged. Therefore, the particles that moved to the amber to cause the condition must be negatively charged. These particles are called *electrons.*

Atoms are built up in part of the electrons. But because electrons are negatively charged there must be some positively charged particles to attract them if they are to be built into an atom. Scientists believe that there is such a particle, which they call the *proton.* Many additional particles of subatomic size have since been identified, but the only other one of importance to us here is the *neutron*, a particle with no electric charge.

The Atomic Model   The electron, the proton, and the neutron gather together into what we call the atom. Our concept of the atom derives from a series of indirect observations which come from the physicist's laboratory. As a result of these observations, we now believe that an atom is composed of a cloud of electrons that revolve about a central core of protons or of protons plus neutrons. Repeated experiments show that every atom has the same number of electrons as it has protons. The positively charged protons form the nucleus of the atom, and around it orbit an equal number of electrons whose negative charges balance the positive charges of the protons in the core of the atom.

The neutrons are also found in the nucleus of the atom, but because they are electrically neutral they are not matched by the negatively charged electrons outside the nucleus. These electrons, which move very rapidly around the nucleus at speeds of hundreds of miles per second, remind us of planets swinging around a sun. . . .

Elements   An atom is the smallest unit of an element. Ninety-two elements are known to occur in nature, and a number of others have been made by man in the laboratory. Every element is a special combination of protons, neutrons, and electrons. Each element is identified by the number of protons in its nucleus and is designated by a name and a symbol.

Element Number 1 is a combination of one proton and one electron. Long before its atomic structure was known, this element was named hydrogen, or "waterformer" (from Greek roots *hydro* and *gen* meaning "water" and "to be born") because water forms when hydrogen burns in air. Its symbol is H. Hydrogen has first place in the list of elements because it has one proton in its nucleus.

Element Number 2 consists of two protons (plus two neutrons in the most common form) and two electrons. It was named helium, with the symbol He, from the Greek *helios,* "the sun," because it was first identified in the solar spectrum before it was isolated on the earth. Helium's place in the list of elements is Number 2, because it has two protons in its nucleus. . . .[13]

QUESTIONS

1. According to the author, all matter
   a. is composed of electrons, neutrons, and protons
   b. is essentially electrical in nature
   c. is made up of atoms
   d. all of the above
2. Atoms have been directly observed by physicists.   T   F

Quote from passage that proves answer: _____

3. List and define each of the subatomic particles given by the author.

_____

_____

_____

1. Dewey L. Yeager and Robert L. Gourley, *Introduction to Electron and Electro-Mechanical Devices.* Englewood Cliffs, N.J.: Prentice-Hall, Inc., 1976, p. 70.
2. Herbert E. Ellinger, *Automechanics.* Englewood Cliffs, N.J.: Prentice-Hall, Inc., 1972, p. 10.
3. Ellinger, *Automechanics,* pp. 3–4.
4. W. J. Patton, *Construction Materials.* Englewood Cliffs, N.J.: Prentice-Hall, Inc., 1976, pp. 3–4.
5. Patton, *Construction Materials,* pp. 4–5.
6. Willard J. Poppy and Leland L. Wilson, *Exploring the Physical Sciences,* 2d ed. Englewood Cliffs, N.J.: Prentice-Hall, Inc., 1973, pp. 244–45.
7. Yeager and Gourley, *Introduction to Electron and Electro-Mechanical Devices,* p. 67.
8. Patton, *Construction Materials,* pp. 3–4.
9. William Lee Stokes and Sheldon Judson, *Introduction to Geology: Physical and Historical.* Englewood Cliffs, N.J.: Prentice-Hall, Inc., 1968, pp. 58–59.
10. Dale Ewen et al., *Physics for Career Education.* Englewood Cliffs, N.J.: Prentice-Hall, Inc., 1971, pp. 247–48.
11. Patton, *Construction Materials,* pp. 3–4.
12. Brian J. Skinner, *Earth Resources,* 2d ed. Englewood Cliffs, N.J.: Reprinted by permission of Prentice-Hall, Inc., 1976, pp. 118, 122.
13. William Lee Stokes and Sheldon Judson, *Introduction to Geology.* Englewood Cliffs, N.J.: Prentice-Hall, Inc., 1968, pp. 14–15.

9

USING YOUR TEXTBOOK: STEP 2

COMBINING STUDY NOTES WITH UNDERLINING

No one takes notes on *every line* of a textbook. When you are reading a book, you need to work out a system to remember the information—but you are not likely to take notes on every word you read. Many people favor a combination of (1) marking their books with underlining and marginal notes and (2) then taking study notes.

This chapter will show you ways to combine these two techniques to help understand and remember technical materials.

UNDERLINING

Underlining is useful for drawing your attention to the most important points on the page and for distinguishing major categories.

Consider this passage, on which you took notes in the last chapter. If you read it first, and then went back and underlined the main ideas, it might look as follows:

Different construction methods are used among the manufacturers and their vehicle models. Separate body and frame construction has been used for the longest time. In this type of construction, the engine, drive line, and running gear are firmly fastened to the frame; then the body is mounted to the frame with insulators to minimize noise and vibration transfer.

A second type of construction is the <u>unitized body,</u> in which the frame is part of the body structure. Body panels add strength to the frame pieces that form part of the structure. The running gear and drive line are attached with large soft insulators to minimize noise and vibration. If the insulators are too soft they tend to give the vehicle a spongy ride, and if they are too hard they do not insulate properly. Careful insulator design and location will produce a vehicle that is satisfactory to drive and ride in.

<u>A third type of construction combines features from both</u> of the preceding types. It uses a <u>stub frame from the fire wall forward and a unitized body from the fire wall back.</u> The unitized portion is very rigid, while the stub frame provides an opportunity for good insulation. This construction method is generally applied to <u>larger body styles.</u>

Manufacturers select their construction method by deciding which type is most economical for them to build, while still providing the noise, vibration, and ride characteristics they want to have in their vehicle. The largest number of <u>standard-size vehicles use separate body and frame construction.</u> The majority of <u>small vehicles use unitized construction.</u>[1]

USING NUMBERS AND BOXES

You could make the listing pattern clearer by adding numbers, if you wished, and by putting boxes around each major subcategory.

Different construction methods are used among the manufacturers and their vehicle models. Separate body and frame construction has been used for the longest time. In this type of construction, the engine, drive line, and running gear are firmly fastened to the frame; then the body is mounted to the frame with insulators to minimize noise and vibration transfer.

A second type of construction is the unitized body, in which the frame is part of the body structure. Body panels add strength to the frame pieces that form part of the structure. The running gear and drive line are attached with large soft insulators to minimize noise and vibration. If the insulators are too soft they tend to give the vehicle a spongy ride, and if they are too hard they do not insulate properly. Careful insulator design and location will produce a vehicle that is satisfactory to drive and ride in.

A third type of construction combines features from both of the preceding types. It uses a stub frame from the fire wall forward and a unitized body from the fire wall back. The unitized portion is very rigid, while the stub frame provides an opportunity for good insulation. This construction method is generally applied to <u>larger body styles</u>.

Manufacturers select their construction method by deciding which type is most economical for them to build, while still providing the noise, vibration, and ride characteristics they want to have in their vehicle. The largest number of <u>standard-sized vehicles</u> use <u>separate body and frame construction</u>. The majority of <u>small</u> vehicles use <u>unitized construction</u>.[2]

Later in the semester, if you wanted to review this section of your book, and you looked over the underlining, it would help you to review. If you strung the phrases you had underlined together and said them to yourself, you would come out with something like "different construction methods: (1) separate body and frame, (2) unitized body, (3) combination method. The combination method is for larger bodies. The unitized is for small cars. The separate body and frame is for most standards."

USING MARGINAL NOTES

Note that it is not necessary to underline whole sentences. It is possible to string phrases together so that they make sense. Here is another example:

Wt.
vs.
mass
———→

The terms <u>weight and mass refer to different quantities.</u> │Weight│ is defined as <u>downward force due to the attraction of gravity</u>. This means that we do not weigh quite as much at the top of a mountain as we do in a low valley, because in the valley we are closer to the center of the earth, and the force of gravity is accordingly greater. The term│ mass │refers to the <u>amount of matter in a given entity</u>. Our mass is the same whether we are in New York City or in outer space.

In this example, the reader has underlined the main points and boxed the two main subtopics. There is also a note in the margin: "wt. vs. mass." Many readers use notes like this. When they review, they cover up the passage and see if they can recall the contents based on the marginal notes.

Underlining and marginal notes can be used with material that is not too dense. For instance, here is a passage in which underlining and marginal notes have been put to good use:

Limitations
of
Concrete

Concrete is extremely popular as a building material, primarily because of its durability and hardness. However, <u>concrete has certain limitations</u> as a construction material. It is somewhat │permeable;│① that is, it allows the penetration of a certain amount of fluid. It is subject to │expansion│② │and contraction.│ Also, it must be │reinforced│③ if its tensile strength is to be increased.

Here is a third example of underlining and marginal notes. In this case, the reader has made a simple review of the contents in the margin.

CARRYING

The abacus is a manual device for reckoning. The calculator is a mechanical device. The computer is an electronic device. Each of these devices has to take into account the operation of carrying; when 6 and 4 are added, we must "carry" one. How is this done in each device? With a bead-counting device such as the abacus or soroban, the person using the device personally "carries" the 1 to the next row of beads. The operation is manual. It depends entirely upon the speed and accuracy of the operator. With a mechanical device, however, the carry is automatic. When a column moves from 9 to 0, the column immediately to the left adds one. There is a device that automatically guarantees this. With the computer, the carry or adding of one to the next column is handled by electronic circuits.

Marginal notes:
① *Abacus — manual*
② *Calculator mechanical*
③ *Computer electronic*

LIMITATIONS OF UNDERLINING

In the three examples above, underlining is useful for indicating broad divisions and for later review. However, consider the underlining in the next two passages. What is wrong with it?

All five types of portland cement contain the same ingredients: iron, lime, alumina, and silica. The iron is obtained from iron ore. Lime comes from limestone, marl, oyster shells, and other calcareous materials. Alumina and silica are obtained from clay, shale, sand, and other argillaceous materials.

THREE FUNDAMENTAL GROUPS OF CONSTRUCTION MATERIALS

With few exceptions, construction materials are solid materials or harden into solid materials. Solid materials are grouped into three fundamental types: ceramics, metals, and organics.

The ceramic materials are rock or clay minerals, or are compounded from such minerals. Examples are sand, limestone, glass, brick, cement, gypsum, plaster, mortar, and mineral wool insulation. These are materials dug from the earth's crust with or without further processing and purification. Since they are extracted from the earth, they are relatively inexpensive as compared to metals or the organic materials. The ceramics have been used as building materials from time immemorial, and their virtues will ensure their use in the future: they are enduring, hard, and rigid. Their outstanding disadvantages are brittleness and their heavy weight.

Metals are extracted from natural ores, which of course are also ceramic materials. Such metallic ores are usually oxides or sulfides of
metals. The metals are not as hard as the ceramic materials. . . .[3]

In the first passage, almost every word has been underlined. But
there is no point in marking a passage for emphasis if you are going to
emphasize every word! In the second passage, not every word has been
marked, but the material is so complicated that merely underlining it
will not help you organize or remember it.

The second passage is organized in a long classification pattern.
There are many subdivisions, with details in each subdivision. As we
saw in Chapter 3, this pattern is typical in technical writing. To master
this sort of dense information, underlining is not enough. Taking notes
on the passage, by boiling down and organizing the information, will be
more helpful.

Groups of Construction Materials

I. Ceramics — Rock or Clay Minerals.

   A. Examples — sand, limestone, glass.

   B. Dug from earth's crust — with or without processing.

   C. Inexpensive and enduring — but brittle, heavy.

II. Metals — Extracted from Natural Ores.

   A. Usually oxides or sulfides.

   B. Not as hard as ceramics.

There are other types of passages in which underlining has only a
limited use. For instance, here is a passage organized as a description
of a process. How much of this passage could you underline?

> But electricity is not created at the flip of a switch. Electrical energy is
> the product of a number of energy conversions. For example, when
> coal is the fuel in use in the power plant, the chemical energy of the
> coal is converted to heat energy in the boiler when the water is heated
> to make steam. The steam moves the blades of the turbine, producing
> mechanical energy, and the mechanical energy of the turbine is con-
> verted to electrical energy in the generator.

Once you start underlining the elements in a causal chain or process, there is no end. You'll end up with most of the paragraph
marked:

> But electricity is not created at the flick of a switch. Electrical energy is
> the product of a number of energy conversions. For example, when
> coal is the fuel in use in the power plant, the chemical energy of the
> coal is converted to heat energy in the boiler when the water is heated

to make <u>steam.</u> The <u>steam</u> moves the <u>blades of the turbine,</u> producing <u>mechanical energy,</u> and the <u>mechanical energy</u> of the turbine is <u>converted</u> to <u>electrical energy in the generator.</u>

However, it is possible to handle causal chains by <u>combining</u> underlining and note-taking. Underline the main point, put a vertical mark down the side of the passage (meaning "to be reviewed"), and take notes on the casual chain.

Coal →
(Chem. energy)
steam →
(heat energy)
turbine →
turns
(mech. energy)
generator
& produces
elec.
energy.

But electricity is not created at the flick of a switch. <u>Electrical energy is the product of a number of energy conversions.</u> For example, when coal is the fuel in use in the power plant, the chemical energy of the coal is converted to heat energy in the boiler when the water is heated to make steam. Steam moves the blades of the turbine, producing mechanical energy, and the mechanical energy of the turbine is converted to electrical energy in the generator.

In this case, it is even possible to take simple notes right in the margin of the book.

Since technical writing includes so many dense passages in which information is classified, or procedures are described, we recommend you combine underlining and note-taking.

EXAMPLE: UNDERLINING, NOTES, AND DIAGRAM

Here is an example of a passage that a student has read, underlined and then used to take notes. In this case, since the material describes a process, the student has used a block diagram as part of the notes:

TEXTBOOK PASSAGE

In any transformation of one type of energy into another form, as we have learned, <u>energy cannot be destroyed, but it can be wasted</u>. By this is meant that energy can be dissipated and rendered incapable of being recaptured and utilized. . . .

In the <u>gasoline internal-combustion engine, the gasoline is not completely burned during the power stroke, and the heat developed goes into the gases themselves and into the engine.</u> In order to keep the engine from overheating, water is kept circulating through it and thus through a radiator, where the heat is transferred from the water to air, which is kept circulating by a fan. This removes about one-third of the heat generated by the combustion of the fuel. In the exhaust stroke the spent gases are expelled at a high temperature. This exhaust gas includes not only the products of the combustion but a certain amount of unburned gases. Another third of the energy of the gasoline is carried away through the exhaust and lost. This only leaves about 30 percent of the energy of the fuel to power the car.

All of these losses, great as they are, do not in any way contradict the law of conservation of energy. If it were possible to measure all the energy lost and add it to the amount delivered by the engine in the form of useful work, the sum would be found to be exactly equal to the chemical energy of the consumer fuel. No energy is created, nor is any destroyed.[4]

STUDENT NOTES ON PASSAGE

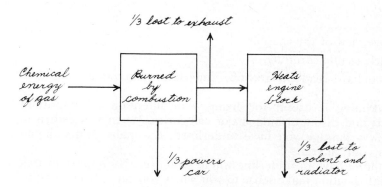

COMMON MARKINGS AND SYMBOLS

There are many symbols you can use when you take notes in your book. Most students develop their own style and their own types of abbreviations. However, here are some common markings that are used:

Main point
Main division

Concrete and cement are not identical. Cement is an adhesive. . . . Concrete is a kind of "instant stone."

* !!
Impt. ⟶ Important

Weight and mass are not identical: *Impt!* ⟵
Weight is the. . . .

① ② ③

There are three types of rock:① igneous ② sedimentary, and③. . .

Used in margin to mark more than two lines of type.

To develop an understanding of voltage drop, consider the analogy of. . . .

LOOKING AHEAD By the time you finish this chapter, you should be able to:

1. Underline the main points and major subpoints in a passage.
2. Take marginal notes that could be used to review materials.
3. Combine underlining and note-taking in a system for studying technical materials.

SUMMARY

1. Do an overview of the chapter.
2. Read each section carefully.
3. After you have read the section, underline main points and divisions.
   a. Underlining is useful for fixing your attention on important points and distinguishing major categories. When you return to review a passage you have underlined, the main points should "jump out" at you.
   b. You don't have to underline whole sentences. It's important that the information make sense to you when you say it over to yourself, not that it be marked "in complete sentences."
   c. Write numbers (1, 2, 3) into the text to indicate divisions. Underline main points, and box key words in subpoints.
   d. Use marginal notes to summarize important points.
4. Then take notes on the entire section.

EXERCISE 9.1

DIRECTIONS   Underline the phrases or sentences that best sum up the main point of the passage.

EXAMPLE   We often interchange the terms "concrete" and "cement." However, concrete and cement are not identical. Concrete is an artificial stone made up of cement, water, and some type of stone aggregate. Cement is the substance that, in combination with water, makes up an adhesive that binds together the stone aggregate.

1   In a negative feedback system, the controller is actuated by the existence of error. Such a system will strive to eliminate all error, regardless of the source. For instance, there are many possible causes for malfunction in an elevator. A system with negative feedback control will attempt to compensate for whatever errors are detected. Errors caused

by aging of system components will be handled. Errors caused by random external influences will also be handled.

2   Water cannot go through a pipe unless pressure is applied to it. In the same way, current cannot flow through a conductor unless there is a force driving it. Electromotive force is the push that drives the current through a conductor.

3   Nuclear energy offers many advantages as a source of electrical energy. However, nuclear energy has many serious limitations that must first be handled. It produces radioactive materials that remain very dangerous for thousands of years. As yet, no satisfactory method has been found for disposing of these materials. Also, nuclear energy creates a certain amount of heat pollution. This is because the production of nuclear energy requires a great deal of water for cooling purposes. This water becomes very hot and when it is returned to the local river, it heats up the water.

EXERCISE 9.2

DIRECTIONS   Read each passage through. Then underline the phrases or sentences that sum up the main point. Then box and number the subpoints.

EXAMPLE   Nuclear energy offers many advantages as a source of electrical energy. However, <u>nuclear energy has many serious limitations that must first be handled.</u> As yet there is no foolproof way to guarantee that the extremely serious consequences of radioactivity will not ensue. Also, nuclear energy creates a certain amount of heat pollution. This is because the production of nuclear energy requires a great deal of water for cooling purposes. This water becomes very hot and when it is returned to the local river, it heats up the water.

1   Rocks have been used as a building material for millennia. Scientists classify rocks in three major categories: igneous, sedimentary, and metamorphic. Ingenous rock is formed when magma, the plastic material that lies beneath the earth's crust, wells up to the earth's surface, and then cools. Sedimentary rock results from the breakdown of primary rock. Metamorphic rock is formed from igneous or sedimentary rock as a result of heat or chemical energy.

2   Wood is a building material whose use extends from antiquity. Wood is classified into two major categories: deciduous woods and conifers. The decidous or hardwoods are categorized on the basis of their broad leaf and the fact that their seeds are usually in a seed case. The conifers or softwoods are distinguished by a needlelike leaf and the fact that their seeds are in the form of cones.

THE HYDROSPHERE

3   The Earth is like a four-ring circus with acts peculiar to each ring going on simultaneously. Solid rocks and sediments are made, destroyed, and moved around in the *lithosphere;* water permeates the rocks, fills basins, evaporates, condenses, and flows in channels—this realm is called the *hydrosphere;* gases surrounding our planet compose the *atmosphere;* and all of life in whatever environment it finds itself is called the *biosphere.* Unlike the rings of a circus, the four Earth "spheres" are not isolated from each other. One influences the other and at times the boundaries are not easily discerned.[5]

EXERCISE 9.3

DIRECTIONS   Here is a section from a physics text. Read it through. Then underline the main points.

MECHANICAL ENERGY

A quantity very basic to the understanding of physical phenomena is energy. This quantity is rather difficult to define precisely, but most of us have a concept of what it is. We are well aware that our existence here on Earth depends on the energy received from the Sun. It is stored in the foods we eat to stay alive, in the coal and gas we burn to keep us warm, and in the gasoline our engines consume to help us commute from one place to another. We depend on electrical energy to furnish us with light at night and to operate all the appliances we have in our modern homes. What is this thing called energy that is so varied, but yet so very essential to each of us? What do we mean when we say that a person is very "energetic"? At first glance there seems to be nothing in common among all these energies, but upon further study we see that any form of energy is capable of doing something useful. Therefore, we define energy as ability to do work. . . . Not all forms of energy are easily converted to work, but all forms through suitable transformations can do work. The word energy was derived from the Greek *en,* meaning "in," and *ergon,* meaning "work."

WORK

In everyday usage, the word work is used when referring to almost any kind of useful activity that makes us tired. In mechanics, however, it is understood in a more restricted sense: there it means the effect that is accomplished when a force is exerted upon some object and moves it a certain distance. If there is no motion, there is no work. A boy who sits down quietly with a book to study does no mechanical work. A less studious boy who goes outdoors and plays a game of tennis does work. The first boy may have accomplished a much more useful result; he may have conceived a new idea that will bring him fame and fortune as well as help all of mankind. But he has exerted no mechanical force, nor moved an object; therefore, he has done no work. The other boy has probably accomplished something useful too in terms of health, but that in itself does not constitute work. The essential difference is that he has exerted forces and moved objects. He has exerted forces upon the racket, the ball, and upon his own body, and made them move. He has done work. . . .

POWER

A certain amount of work might be done in a second, in a week, or in a month. How fast the work is done is very important. This is particularly true for machines in this age of automation. They are used to run factories, to drive dynamos for generating our electricity, to power our automobiles, trains, airplanes, and for many other purposes. The value of a machine depends on how much work it can do per hour or per second. A diesel engine must be able to exert a large force on a long train to accelerate it and move it at a high speed. A large force acting over a great distance each minute means that many joules of work per minute are being done. . . .

The rate at which work is done is called power:

$$Power = \frac{\text{work}}{\text{time}}$$

EXERCISE 9.4

DIRECTIONS   Combine the two methods: (1) Underline the main point. (2) Take study notes on a separate sheet of paper.

The base of a number system is the number of digits that can be used in the system. In the binary system, there are two digits available, 0 and 1. This is a base-2 system. In the octal system, there are eight digits available, 0–7. This is a base-8 system. In the decimal system, there are ten digits available, 0–9. This is a base-10 system. In the hexadecimal system, there are 16 digits available. It is a base-16 system.

EXERCISE 9.5

DIRECTIONS   Read the following selection. Then underline main points and make marginal notes.

PERMANENT MAGNETISM

Undoubtedly at some time or other each of you has seen and even used a permanent magnet. But have you ever stopped to think what magnetism is? A magnet can lift certain things; it has ability to do work. But this is the definition of energy. Magnetism, then, must be a form of energy. However, we know that energy is not created but is merely transformed from one type of energy to another. What is the origin of this energy we call magnetism? To answer this question let us first consider a mechanical analogy.

A pile driver when raised to the top of its lift has energy due to its elevated position—potential energy. When released it will fall, but in falling it is losing elevation. It must also be losing potential energy. This energy is not lost, because as the pile driver falls it gains speed. The potential energy is converted to energy of motion. In mechanics this energy is called *kinetic energy.* The lower the pile driver falls, the lower its potential energy; but it is moving faster, and so the greater its kinetic energy.

Electron theory of magnetism.   The electrical picture is very similar. A stationary charge has energy due to the position of its electrons. In Chapter 1 we called this energy a dielectric or electrostatic field and said it was a form of potential energy. If this charged body is made to move, some of this potential energy is converted to energy of motion, called magnetic energy. In other words, magnetism is energy due to motion of a charged body. . . . [6]

EXERCISE 9.6

DIRECTIONS   In cases where the passage describes how a machine works, your own illustrations are an excellent way to "take study notes." Read the following passage. Underline when possible. After you have finished, cover up the two figures. Then draw the two figures based upon their descriptions in the passage.

Let's first consider the rotor or armature of the dc machine. The armature is made of a soft steel cylinder mounted on a shaft. The cylinder is constructed with evenly spaced slots in which the armature coils are placed. A schematic diagram of the cutaway end view of a typical armature is shown in Fig. 1(a). The ends of the armature coils are soldered to a commutator, which is also affixed to the armature shaft. The commutator is a smaller cylinder made of copper bars that are insulated from each other with thin sheets of mica. The ends of the armature windings are soldered to these individual copper bars.

External connection to the commutator is made through brushes. Brushes are usually made of carbon or graphite blocks positioned loosely in brush holders. The brushes must be free to move slightly in order to follow the irregularities of the commutator. Springs hold the brushes against the commutator to insure continuously maintained contact. Figure 1(b) shows a greatly simplified representation of a dc machine armature that contains one winding. . . . [7]

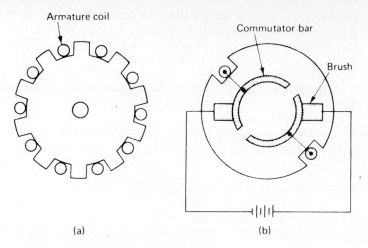

Figure 1. DC armature construction.

EXERCISE 9.7

DIRECTIONS Read the selection below on number systems. Then (1) under-line important points, (2) take study notes on the selection. The notes have been started for you.

FOUR NUMBER SYSTEMS

The base of a number system is the number of digits that can be used in the system. In the binary or base-2 system, there are two digits avail-able: 0 and 1. In the octal or base-8 system, there are eight digits avail-able, 0 through 7. In the decimal or base-10 system, there are ten digits available, 0 through 9. In the hexadecimal or base-16 system, there are 16 digits available.

All four of these systems—binary, octal, decimal and hexadecimal—are *positional* number systems. This means that the value of the digit is determined by its *position* or *place*. Let us say that the digit in question is "6". "6" by itself means one thing; "6" in "61" means another. The dif-ference doesn't have to do with the 6, which is the same in both cases. The difference has to do with the *position* of the number.

Let us start with the decimal system, since that is the one we are most familiar with in our everyday lives. In the decimal system, the po-sitional values of the digits are based on 10.

The number in the first position to the left of the decimal point can be taken at its face value: 1 = 1, 2 = 2, 3 = 3. The number in the sec-ond position to the left of the decimal point represents not itself, but a power of 10, that is, the number of 10s or *10*s. A 2 in the second or ten column is not taken at face value. It represents 2 tens. Therefore, any number in the ten position is multiplied by 10^1 to get its actual value. The third position to the left of the decimal point also represents a power of 10; that is, 100, or 10^2. A 2 in the 100 column represents 2 one-hundreds. Any number in the 100 column is multiplied by 100 or 10^2.

Using this information, we might express the number 457 as follows:

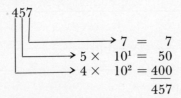

$$
\begin{aligned}
7 &= 7 \\
5 \times 10^1 &= 50 \\
4 \times 10^2 &= \underline{400} \\
&\ 457
\end{aligned}
$$

To indicate the base in which 457 occurs, we may write the number as $(457)_{10}$, meaning this number is an expression of base 10.

STUDENT NOTES

Number Systems

I. Based on the <u>number of digits</u> that can be used.
  A. Binary — base 2   2 digits   0 – 1
  B. Octal — base 8   8 digits   0 – 7
  C. _____
  D. _____

II. Decimal System
  A. Number to left of decimal has its face value. 1.

EXERCISE 9.8

DIRECTIONS   Read the selection below on ancestors of electronic computers. Then (1) underline important points, (2) take study notes on the selection. As a model, the study notes have been started for you. Continue them on a separate sheet of paper.

ANCESTORS OF ELECTRONIC COMPUTERS

Many of us have the notion of great technological "discoveries" that occur at distinct, drama-filled moments in time; "Eureka!" exclaims the scientist, as all is revealed in one blinding flash of revelation.

Actually, this is not the way men and women have accumulated most of their technical knowledge. Our knowledge is socially acquired; that is, it is the result of one small piece of information built on to another and handed down from one person to the next. Gradually the knowledge builds to such a point that it is possible for certain individuals to "see" a way to put the information together to invent something. It is at such moments that famed individual discoveries are made; but it is important to realize how much the individual discoveries are bound by the accumulated knowledge of the time.

The history of electronic computers is a good example of the way that knowledge builds socially over centuries.

Computers are distinguished for the speed and accuracy of their operation. These two qualities were not suddenly realized in the 1940s; they were the product of a long historical development in which the goals of speed and accuracy in computation were approached repeatedly, using the technology available to the experimenters at the time.

Electronic computers owe some of their earlier development to adding machines. One of the earliest adding machines that we know of is the abacus, a computing device that uses beads for counting. The beads are strung in groups of ten; the counting is completely manual. Therefore, the speed of counting depends on the speed of the operator. Another way to express it is to say that the speed and accuracy of the abacus is *limited* by the operator's speed and accuracy.

In contrast, the early computing machines of Pascal (1623–1662) and Leibniz (1646–1716) were not completely manual. These machines employed a mechanical device for certain processes. This meant that the speed and accuracy of the particular process would not be completely limited by the speed and accuracy of the operator.

Pascal's device, which added and subtracted, became the prototype for other early calculators. Pascal employed a device called the decimal counting wheel. This is a wheel with ten notches; each notch represents a digit 0–9 in the decimal or base-10 system. Let us say that we want to add the sum of 45 and 11, using Pascal's machine. In this case, the first number we enter is 45. We move the first wheel five notches. The index shows that we have entered the number 5. Then we move to the left and use the next wheel. We move this second wheel four notches.

The index shows the number 4. Then, when we want to add 11 to this number, we turn each wheel one notch. In this way we store the number 56.

Like Pascal and other scientists who were interested in using technology to compute, Gotfried Wilhelm Leibniz was searching for ways to develop a counting machine that would spare people the tedium of hour after hour in the "labor of calculation." Leibniz developed a machine that could automatically multiply and divide as well as subtract and add. The latter operations were made possible by a device invented by Leibniz, the Leibniz wheel.

Charles Babbage (1791–1871), a third great figure in the development of the computer, was also searching for a way out of the tedium and attendant error involved in extensive mathematical calculation. As a young man, Babbage was engaged in the calculation of tables of logarithms; he found the work very monotonous. He applied for a grant from the British Treasury and began to develop an engine for the automatic calculation of tables. He did not complete this machine, nor the second machine he attempted later in life, the Analytical Engine. However, the latter machine was a milestone in the history of the computer.

The data or information fed into Babbage's engine was entered by means of cards on which holes had been punched.* The cards were fed into the engine. One part of Babbage's engine was called the mill; this was where the operations of addition, subtraction, multiplication, and division on the data occurred. The other half of the machine was called the store; this was where the variables on each particular operation were stored. Today we refer to the store as the memory.

STUDENT NOTES

Ancestors of electronic computers

I. Speed and accuracy products of long, historical development.
   a. Abacus — earliest, used beads. But was done by hand and therefore limited by person's accuracy.
B. Pascal's device —

EXERCISE 9.9

DIRECTIONS   Read the passage below on number systems. Then (1) underline important points, (2) take study notes on the selection. The study notes have been started for you. Continue them on a separate sheet of paper.

*This was a technique developed by Joseph Marie Jacquard for use with looms in which the weaving pattern, as well as directions for repetition (iteration), were punched on the cards.

NUMBER SYSTEMS

In the binary system there are two digits, 0 and 1. The positional values are powers of two. The procedure that we discussed for the decimal system would be followed for the binary system, except that we would be operating in terms of powers of two instead of powers of ten. The number to the left of the decimal would be taken at face value. The second position to the left would *not* be taken at face value. It would represent the first power of 2, that is, the number of "2s" or "2^1s". The third position to the left represents the second power of 2; that is, it represents the number of 4s or 2^2s. Any number in this column is multiplied by 2^2 or 4.

Using this information, we can express the binary number 1010 in the decimal number system as follows:

$$
\begin{array}{llll}
1 & 0 & 1 & 0
\end{array}
$$

$$
\begin{aligned}
0 &= 0 \\
1 \times 2^1 &= 2 \\
0 \times 2^2 &= 0 \\
1 \times 2^3 &= \underline{8} \\
&\ 10
\end{aligned}
$$

To indicate the base in which 1010 occurs, we may write it as $(1010)_2$, meaning: this number is an expression of the base-2 system.

Using the rule that a system's base is the number of digits available, we can say that the octal or base-8 system has eight digits available. An octal number can be expressed as follows: the first column to the left of the decimal is taken at face value; the second column to the left of the decimal is an expression of 8^1, or the number of 8^1s in this position. The third column to the left of the decimal is an expression of how many 8^2s are in the column. Any number in this column is multiplied by 8^2 or 64.

Using this information, we might express the octal number $(762)_8$ as follows:

$$
\begin{array}{lll}
7 & 6 & 2
\end{array}
$$

$$
\begin{aligned}
2 &= 2 \\
6 \times 8^1 &= 48 \\
7 \times 8^2 &= \underline{448} \\
&\ 498
\end{aligned}
$$

There is one final system we will consider, as it has particular use in the study of computers. This is the hexadecimal system. As its name implies (*hexa*, six; *decimal*, ten) there are 16 digits available for use in this system, making it a base-16 system. This presents no problem for the first ten digits, which can be numbered 0 through 9, but there is a difficulty after 9. For example, the number "10" in the hexadecimal system $(10)_{16}$ does not stand for ten. It represents $0 + 1 \times 16^1$ or 16. Similarly, "11" is read as "17" in hexidecimal:

10
└──→0   = 0
└──→1×16^1 = 16
                    ───
                     16

11
└──→ 1   = 1
└──→ 1×16^1 = 16
                    ───
                     17

The problem is that there is no way to represent numbers 10 through 15 using the 10 digits 0 through 9. To handle this difficulty, letters are used to represent the final 6 digits in this system. Therefore, the hexadecimal digits are: 0,1,2,3,4,5,6,7,8,9,A,B,C,D,E,F.

STUDENT NOTES

Number Systems

I. Binary System — 0/1. Positional values of 2.
A.   X.) Taken at face value. 1 = 1   0 = 0.
B. XX., Number of 2¹. Multiply number by (2).
C. XXX., Number of 2². Multiply number by (4).

EXERCISE 9.10

DIRECTIONS   Here is a long section taken directly from a chapter on current and voltage. Do an overview first. Then read the section, underline the important points, and take study notes. Don't forget to use the illustration on electric potential difference. Add your own version to the study notes.

POTENTIAL DIFFERENCE

We have noted that electric current does not flow in the conductors of our basic electric circuit until we add a device, such as a battery, which can impart energy to the free electrons in the conductors in such a manner that they flow along the length of the conductor. We say that the battery is the source of an **electron-moving force** or **electromotive**

force, usually abbreviated to **emf** (ee-em-eff). We must now investigate the nature of electromotive force and determine a suitable means of expressing its magnitude numerically.

Since we are more familiar with the effects of gravitational force than we are with the effects of electric force, we can consider first of all the operation of the hydroelectric generating station shown in simplified cross section in Fig. 1. Water from above a waterfall is diverted so that it flows through a "waterwheel" or turbine and is then discharged into the river below the waterfall. In falling 100 meters, the water loses some of its potential energy. In accordance with the law of conservation of energy, the potential energy lost by the water is converted into mechanical energy by the turbine and is then converted into electric energy by the electric generator or **dynamo.**

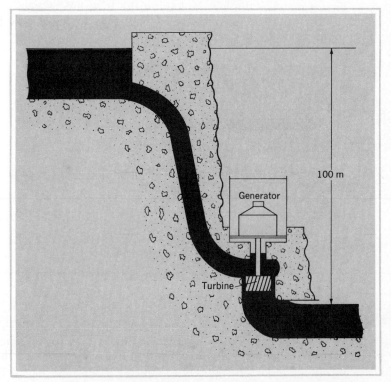

Figure 1. Simplified cross section of a hydroelectric generating station.

Since objects at the surface of the Earth are 6400 kilometers away from the center of gravity of the Earth, the difference in gravitational force acting on a cubic meter of water above and below the generating station shown in Fig. 1 is negligible. But there is an appreciable difference in the potential energy of a cubic meter of water above and below the station, as we would discover if we had to carry or pump a cubic meter of water from the river below the station 100 meters uphill against the force of gravity to the top of the escarpment. The "force" which operates the hydroelectric generating station is not simply gravitational force. Rather, it is the potential energy difference between a unit quantity of water above and below the generating station. The law of conservation of energy requires the potential energy difference, or simply **potential difference,** between a unit quantity of water above and below the generating station to be equal to the energy expended in raising the unit quantity of water the 100 meters against the force of gravity.

We can now return to the electric circuit described earlier in which we connected an electric conductor between the terminals of a battery. This circuit is shown again in Fig. 2. In this case, we have turned the battery on its side so that the terminology we shall use in the electric circuit matches the terminology of the hydraulic system of Fig. 1. Since the battery is the source of emf in Fig. 2, we must now find out what happens inside the battery.

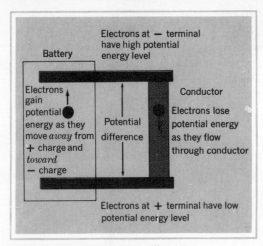

Figure 2. Electric potential difference.

We noted earlier that free electrons in the conductor flow away from the negative terminal of the battery and toward the positive terminal. To maintain the negative and positive charges at the two battery terminals, *inside* the battery, an equivalent number of electrons must be removed from the positive terminal and added to the negative terminal. Thus, inside the battery, electrons must move *away* from the positive terminal and *toward* the negative terminal. In other words, electrons must move *against* the electric forces acting on them, just as water moves against gravitational force when it is pumped uphill. To accomplish this, the electrons must acquire potential energy at the expense of the chemical energy stored by the battery. Consequently, an electron arriving at the (−) terminal is at a higher potential energy level than it was when it left the (+) terminal of the battery. There is an electric **potential** energy **difference** between free electrons at the negative and positive terminals of the battery, with electrons at the negative terminal being at a higher potential than those at the positive terminal.

Under the influence of gravitational force, the water in the hydro-electric generating system of Fig. 1 always tend to fall to a lower potential energy level. Similarly, electrons at the negative terminal of a source of emf tend to "fall" to a lower potential energy level. They can do this via the external conductor connected between the battery terminals. In flowing from the (−) terminal to the (+) terminal in the external circuit, electrons lose as much potential energy as they gained in being moved from the (+) terminal to the (−) terminal inside the battery. This energy "lost" in the external circuit is converted into light, heat, or some other useful form of energy, depending on the nature of the **load** component in the electric circuit.

The electromotive "force" generated by a source of emf is, therefore, a **potential difference** between a unit quantity of charge carriers at its two terminals. When electric current flows in an electric circuit, the charge carriers experience a **potential rise** within the source of emf and an equivalent **potential fall** or **potential drop** in the external circuit. Electromotive force represents the amount of work done in moving electric charges from a lower to a higher potential.[9]

SPRINGBOARD 9

Choose one chapter from your reading this week.

   1. Do an overview of the chapter first.
   2. Read each section.
   3. After you finish each section, go back and underline important points.
   a. Use numbers to indicate lists.
   b. Use marginal notation to summarize important points.
   c. After you have finished underlining, the main points should "jump out" at you.
   4. Take notes on the entire chapter.

NOTES

1. Herbert E. Ellinger, *Automechanics,* 1st ed. Englewood Cliffs, N.J.: Prentice-Hall, Inc., 1972, p. 10.
2. Ellinger, *Automechanics,* pp. 3–4.
3. W. J. Patton, *Construction Materials.* Englewood Cliffs, N.J.: Prentice-Hall, Inc., 1976, p. 3.
4. E. J. Cable, et al., *The Physical Sciences,* 5th ed. Englewood Cliffs, N.J.: Prentice-Hall, Inc., 1969, pp. 124, 128.
5. Karl K. Turekian, *Oceans,* 2d ed. Englewood Cliffs, N.J.: Prentice-Hall, Inc., 1976, p. 7.
6. Cable et al., *The Physical Sciences,* pp. 36–38.

7. J. J. DeFrance, *Electrical Fundamentals*. Englewood Cliffs, N.J.: Prentice-Hall, Inc., 1969, pp. 162–63.
8. Dewey A. Yeager and Robert L. Gourley, *Introduction to Electron and Electro-Mechanical Devices*, Englewood Cliffs, N.J.: Prentice-Hall, Inc., 1976, p. 70.
9. Herbert W. Jackson, *Introduction to Electric Circuits*, 4th ed. Englewood Cliffs, N.J.: Prentice-Hall, Inc., 1976, pp. 28–31.

10

USING YOUR TEXTBOOK: STEP 3

"To write or not to write" is the question when you are taking notes on your reading.

Selecting what is important, and what is not, is a complicated business; it is a skill you will acquire gradually, with practice.

Outlining and abbreviation are two ways to reduce your notes; both skills can help you to focus in on and simplify the job of note-taking.

OUTLINING

Have you ever tried to solve a gear-train problem where there was a first driver, a second driver, a third and fourth driver? Technical writing can be like a gear train, with wheels within wheels within wheels.

When the material you are studying gets complicated, with many divisions and subdivisions of main points, you may want to use three-level and four-level outlining. It is essentially the same as the informal study notes you have learned, only there is opportunity for more subdivisions.

The form for an outline appears on the next page.

Title

I. _____

   A. _____

   B. _____

      1. _____

      2. _____

         a. _____

         b. _____

II. _____

   A. _____

   B. _____

      1. _____

      2. _____

         a. _____

         b. _____

The outline is more "formal" than study notes; that is, many conventions have developed in regard to its form. Here are some of the conventions that people follow when they outline:

1. Major categories or ideas are indicated by Roman numerals, beginning with I.

2. Subcategories are indicated by capital letters, beginning with A.

3. Details supporting the subcategories are indicated by numbers, beginning with 1.

4. Further supporting details are indicated by lower-case letters, beginning with a.

5. Indentation is used at each level.

6. Capitalization is used for the first letter of the first word of each item.

7. Shortened language is used. While it is possible to transfer entire sentences word-for-word from your text while you are outlining, it is more useful to condense the information as you write it down. The intellectual effort involved in "thinking through" information as you shorten it is helpful in mastering and retaining the information.

It isn't necessary to start worrying about whether you have put the Roman numerals before the A's, and the numbers before the small a's. That's not the point of outlining. The important thing is to drop to a new level and indent each time you begin a new group of supporting points. The new level and indentation are important because they show the relationship of major points to subordinate points.

There are many abbreviations that can help to simplify the job of note-taking. The trick is to use the abbreviations and still be able to understand the notes when you return to them later. Many students have had the unpleasant experience of working on notes for hours, using many abbreviations and understanding them perfectly. Then, when they returned to their notes to review for a test, they couldn't figure out what they had written!

To avoid this, you will have to be systematic; that is, you will have to develop a set of abbreviations that you use consistently, and not switch from one notation to another.

Here are some general suggestions for using abbreviations to reduce the amount of notes you take.

Use cause-effect notation when possible.   Cause-effect notation is particularly useful in taking notes on science passages, since cause-effect relationships are the core of science. Here is an example of a paragraph with cause-effect notes taken beside it. The cause-effect notation allows you to be both clear and brief.

Electrical energy is the product of a number of energy conversions. For example, when coal is the fuel in use in the power plant, the chemical energy of the coal is converted to heat energy in the boiler when the water is heated to make steam. The steam moves the blades of the turbine, producing mechanical energy, and the mechanical energy of the turbine is converted to electrical energy in the generator.

Electrical energy the product of energy conversions:
Chem. energy (coal) →
heat energy (steam) →
mech. energy (turbine turns) →
generator produces elec. energy.

Use numerals instead of spelling out numbers.   Instead of spelling out *one, two, three, first, second,* use 1, 2, 3, 1st, 2nd, and so on.

All five basic types of portland cement contain the same four basic ingredients: iron, lime, alumina, and silica.

5 basic types portland cement have 4 ingred.—iron, lime, alumina, silica.

Remove connecting words and use dashes instead.   For instance, use dashes to connect terms and their definitions. Omit all the words in between.

The fluid that is used within the battery is called an electrolyte.

Electrolyte —fluid within battery.

Mechanical weathering is called disintegration.

Mechanical weathering—disintegration.

Chemical weathering is called decomposition.

Chemical weathering—decomposition.

When you say that an engine is efficient, you are saying that you are obtaining the highest possible output for a given input.

Efficiency—highest output for given input.

You can use dashes to develop a phrase-outline instead of a whole-sentence outline. Here is an example from an earlier chapter, which is outlined in sentences and in phrases.

I. Radiation is a method of heat transfer by which electromagnetic waves emitted by warm substances are absorbed by the objects on which they fall.

I. Radiation—electromagnetic waves emitted by warm substance, absorbed by objects.

  A. The heat of a bonfire reaching people standing nearby is one example. The heat of the sun reaching earth is another example.

A. Heat of bonfire, to people, heat of sun to earth— radiation.

  B. Note that no medium is required for heat transfer by radiation. The heat travels as well in a vacuum as in the atmosphere.

B. No medium required— travels in vacuum.

Develop a system of abbreviations for words that you use. You can substitute & for *and,* ex. or e.g. to signal examples, fr. for *from.* It's possible to use abbreviations that you learn in your other classes: Fe for *iron,* H_2O for *water* (see Table 10.1). Note that there are many ways to abbreviate the same words. For instance, the sentence "Iron is obtained from iron ore," might be shortened in any one of the following ways:

1. Iron — fr. iron ore.
2. Iron ore ⟶ iron.
3. Iron ore ⟶ Fe.

COMBINING OUTLINING AND ABBREVIATION

If you substitute abbreviations and dashes for lengthy writings out of sentences, you will find that your notes begin to boil down to essentials. Here is an example of a paragraph you looked at earlier. First the original paragraph is given, then notes on the paragraph where all of the items are written out. Finally, there is an abbreviated version of the paragraph.

ORIGINAL   All five of the basic types of portland cement contain the same ingredients: iron, lime, alumina, and silica. The iron is obtained from iron ore. Lime comes from limestone, marl, oyster shell, and other calcareous materials. Alumina and silica are obtained from clay, shale, sand, and other argillaceous materials.

NOTES   I. Five basic types of portland cement contain same ingredients: iron, lime, alumina, and silica.
A. Iron is obtained from iron ore.
B. Lime comes from limestone, marl, oyster shell, and other calcareous materials.
C. Alumina and silica are obtained from clay, shale, sand, and other argillaceous materials.

ABBREVIATED
NOTES

I. 5 basic types portland cement have same 4 ingred.— Fe, lime, alumina, silica.

A. Iron — fr. iron ore.
B. Lime — fr. limestone, marl, oyster, etc.
C. Alumina } clay, shale, sand, etc.
   Silica }

Table 10.1. Common Abbreviations and Symbols

Abbreviation or Symbol	Meaning	Abbreviation or Symbol	Meaning
$>$	greater than	X^2	X squared
$<$	less than	X^3	X cubed
$\geq$	greater than or equal to	°	degrees, as in 90°
$\leq$	less than or equal to	e.g.	for example, such as, like, for
$\pm$	plus or minus		instance, as in the following
$=$	equals	i.e.	that is, in other words
$\neq$	does not equal	&, +	and
/	per (as in 4/100)	$\therefore$	therefore $\therefore$
$\simeq$	is approximately	$\rightarrow$	yields, results in, produces,
$\equiv$	is equivalent to		has the consequence of
$\propto$	is proportional to	fr.	from

Table 10.1 Continued

Abbreviation or Symbol	Meaning	Abbreviation or Symbol	Meaning
α	alpha	cm	centimeter
β	beta	d-a	digital-analog
γ	gamma	dB	decibel
δ	delta	dc	direct current
ϵ	epsilon	G	giga-
η	eta	GHz	gigahertz
σ	theta	hp	horsepower
μ	mu	Hz	hertz
π	pi	ic	integrated circuit
Σ, σ	sigma	k	kilo
τ	tau	kV	kilovolt
ϕ	phi	kW	kilowatt
ω	omega	m	milli-
tan	tangent	M	mega-
cot	cotangent	ms	millisecond
sec	secant	mm	millimeter
cosec	cosecant	μ	micro
sin	sine	μm	micrometer
cos	cosine	V	volt
A	ampere	VA	voltampere
ac	alternating current	W	watt
a-d	analog-digital		

LOOKING AHEAD   By the end of this chapter you should be able to:

1. Take three- and four-level notes on technical information.
2. Use common abbreviation and punctuation to simplify outlining and note-taking.

SUMMARY

1. An outline is a formal way to show the relationship of major points to minor points.
2. Major categories are indicated by Roman numerals; successive categories are indicated by A, B, C, then 1, 2, 3, then a, b, c.
3. Indentation is used at all levels except for the first (I). The first letters of first words are usually capitalized.
4. Abbreviation is desirable in outlining.
5. Be systematic in abbreviations. Don't change abbreviations from one day to the next.
6. Master a set of abbreviations to use on terms encountered in your books.

EXERCISE 10.1

DIRECTIONS   Abbreviate each of the following sentences:

EXAMPLE   Concrete and cement are not identical.

Concrete and cement — not identical.

1. All five types of portland cement contain the same basic ingredients: iron, lime, alumina and silica.

2. The iron is obtained from iron ore. _____

3. Alumina and silica are obtained from clay, shale, sand, and other argillaceous materials. _____

4. Concrete is an artificial stone made up of cement, water, and some type of aggregate. _____

5. Cement is a substance that combines with water to make up an adhesive that binds together the stone aggregate. _____

EXERCISE 10.2

DIRECTIONS: Abbreviate each of the following sentences:

1. Scientists classify rocks in three major categories: igneous, sedimentary, and metamorphic.

2. Igneous rock is formed when magma, the plastic material that lies beneath the earth's crust, wells up to the earth's surface and then cools.

3. Metamorphic stone is formed from igneous or sedimentary rock as a result of heat or chemical energy.

4. The deciduous or hardwoods are categorized on the basis of their broad leaf and the fact that their seeds are usually in a seed case.

5. The conifers or softwoods are distinguished by a needlelike leaf and the fact that the seeds are in the form of cones.

---

6. When a rock crumbles, the smaller pieces of it may be of the same chemical composition as the original rock. This is referred to as physical change.

---

7. If minerals in the rock interact with carbon dioxide to form new minerals, a chemical change occurs.

EXERCISE 10.3

DIRECTIONS   Make a simple outline using the information in each list. Use only one major category (I). Remember to (1) indent for sub-categories, (2) capitalize first letters of first words in each item.

EXAMPLE   chemical energy. forms of energy. coal. turbine. oil. wheel. mechanical energy.

> I. Forms of energy
>   A. Chemical energy
>   1. Coal
>   2. Oil
>   B. Mechanical energy
>   1. Turbine
>   2. Wheel

1. English system. two systems of measurement. metric system. grams. kilometers. pounds. feet. miles.

2. sociology. economics. natural sciences. chemistry. physics. biology. social sciences. anthropology. two sciences.

3. expanded brain. biological inheritance. opposable thumb. laws. morals. humanities. cultural inheritance. two inheritances.

EXERCISE 10.4

DIRECTIONS   Outline this passage on a separate sheet of paper. Use only one
major category.

Weathering is a special term meaning "rock decay" or "fragmentation."
There are two kinds of weathering: mechanical weathering and chemical weathering.

Mechanical weathering is called disintegration. In mechanical weathering the rock breaks into smaller particles that are the same as the larger rock. There is no real change in the actual composition of the rock; the particles are merely smaller.

Chemical weathering is called decomposition. In chemical weathering, the actual composition of the constituent minerals in the rocks changes.

EXERCISE 10.5

DIRECTIONS   Outline this passage. Use only one major category.

Erosion is the transporting of weathered materials downhill. It may occur in two ways. One way is through an agent of transportation. A second way is through gravity in the form of landslides or slow creep.

Agents of transportation vary. Streams are a primary agent. They transport large amounts of sand, gravel, and boulders. When the stream is the agent, it deposits its fragments in different places according to their sizes. The largest boulders are deposited in the upper reaches of the stream. Medium particles such as gravel will be carried further downstream. Silt and clay will travel the furthest; they may move out of the stream when it floods, or even be carried out to sea. The wind is a second major agent of erosion. In deserts the wind carries along sand, gravel, silt, and clay. Ice is the third agent.

EXERCISE 10.6

DIRECTIONS   Outline this passage. Use only one major category.

Weathering may occur by either mechanical or chemical means. The mechanical agents include heat and cold. Heat during the day and cold at night result in expansion and contraction of the constituent materials in rocks. Eventually this may lead to fragmentation. Ice is a second mechanical agent. It expands in the cracks of rocks, exerting tremendous pressure on the surrounding walls. This eventually leads to fragmentation. The prying work of rootlets is another agent of fragmentation. Many animals also contribute to rock decay. Burrowing animals dig tunnels. Worms pass particles of the soil through their bodies.

The main chemical agent of weathering is oxidation. As a result of oxidation, rocks that contain iron disintegrate after prolonged contact with moist air. Carbonation, the process by which minerals in the rock combine with carbon dioxide present in the air, also causes rock decay. Hydration is the third chemical agent.

EXERCISE 10.7

DIRECTIONS   Outline the following passage.

THE THREE ROCK
FAMILIES

Igneous rocks, the ancestors of all other rocks, take their name from the Latin *ignis,* "fire." These "fire-formed" rocks were once a hot, molten, liquidlike mass known as a **magma,** which subsequently cooled into firm, hard rock. Thus, the lava flowing across the earth's surface from an erupting volcano soon cools and hardens into an igneous rock. But there are other igneous rocks now exposed at the surface that actually cooled some distance beneath the surface. We see such rocks today only because erosion has stripped away the rocks that covered them during their formation.

Most **sedimentary** rocks (from the Latin *sedimentum,* "settling") are made up of particles derived from the breakdown of preexisting rocks. Usually these particles are transported by water, wind, or ice to new locations where they are deposited in new arrangements. For example, waves beating against a rocky shore may provide the sand grains and pebbles for a nearby beach. If these beach deposits were to be hardened, we would have sedimentary rock. One of the most characteristic features of sedimentary rocks is the layering of the deposits that make them up.

Metamorphic rocks compose the third large family of rocks. Metamorphic, meaning "changed form," refers to the fact that the original rock has been changed from its primary form to a new one. Earth pressures, heat, and chemically active fluids beneath the surface may all be involved in changing an originally sedimentary rock into a new metamorphic rock.[1]

EXERCISE 10.8

DIRECTIONS   Outline the following passage. Don't forget to use the illustration
of the rock cycle. Add your own version to your study notes.

THE ROCK CYCLE

We have suggested that there are definite relationships among sedimentary, igneous and metamorphic rocks. With time and changing conditions, any one of these rock types may be changed into some other form. These relationships form a cycle, as shown in Figure 1. This is simply a way of tracing out the various paths that earth materials follow. The outer circle represents the complete cycle; the arrows within the circle represent shortcuts in the system that can be, and often are, taken. Notice that the igneous rocks are shown as having formed from a magma, and as providing one link in a continuous chain. From these parent rocks, through a variety of processes, all other rocks can be derived.

First, weathering attacks the solid rock, which either has been formed by the cooling of a lava flow at the surface, or is an igneous rock that was formed deep beneath the earth's surface and then was exposed by erosion. The products of weathering are the materials that will eventually go into the creation of new rocks—sedimentary, metamorphic, and even igneous. Landslides, wind, running water, and glacier ice all help to move the materials from one place to another. In the ideal cycle, this material seeks the ocean floors, where layers of soft mud, sand, and gravel are consolidated into sedimentary rocks. If the cycle continues without interruption, these new rocks may in turn be deeply buried and subjected to heat, to pressures caused by overlying rocks, and to forces developed by earth movements. The sedimentary rocks may then change in response to these new conditions and become metamorphic rocks. If these metamorphic rocks undergo continued and increased heat and pressure, they may eventually lose their identity

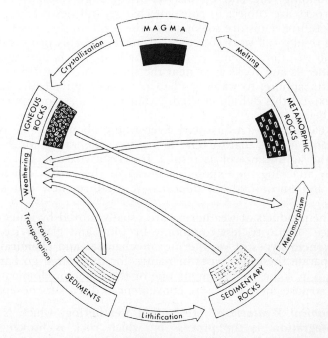

Figure 1. The rock cycle, shown diagramatically. If uninterrupted, the cycle will continue completely around the outer margin of the diagram from magma through igneous rocks, sediments, sedimentary rocks, metamorphic rocks, and back again to magma. The cycle may be interrupted, however, at various points along its course and follow the path of one of the arrows crossing through the interior of the diagram.

and melt into a magma. When this magma cools, we have an igneous rock again, and we have come full cycle.

But notice, too, that the complete rock cycle may be interrupted. An igneous rock, for example, may never be exposed at the surface and hence may never be converted to sediments by weathering. Instead, it may be subjected to pressure and heat and converted directly into a metamorphic rock without passing through the intermediate sedimentary stage. Other interruptions may take place if sediments, or sedimentary rocks, or metamorphic rocks are attacked by weathering before they continue to the next stage in the outer, complete cycle.[2]

EXERCISE 10.9

DIRECTIONS   Outline the following selection.

WEATHERING

Shattered rock on a mountain slope, the crumbling foundations of an old building, the blurred inscription of a gravestone—all remind us that rocks are subject to constant change and destruction. Changes of temperature, moisture soaking into the ground, the ceaseless activity of living things—all work to alter rock material. This process of alteration we call weathering, and we can define it as the changes that take place in minerals and rocks at or near the surface of the earth in response to the atmosphere, to water, and to plant and animal life. Later on, we will extend this definition slightly, but it will serve our purpose for the time being.

Weathering leaves its mark everywhere about us. The process is so common, in fact, that we tend to overlook the way in which it functions and the significance of its results. It plays a vital role in the rock cycle, for by attacking the exposed material of the earth's crust—both solid rock and unconsolidated deposits—it produces new material for new rocks.

The products of weathering are usually moved by water and the influence of gravity, less commonly by wind and glacier ice. There are two general types of weathering: **mechanical** and **chemical.** It is hard to separate these two types in nature for they often go hand in hand, though in some environments one or the other predominates. Still, for our purposes here it is more convenient to discuss them separately.

Mechanical Weathering   Mechanical weathering, which is also called **disintegration,** is the process by which rock is broken down into smaller and smaller fragments as the result of the energy developed by physical forces. For example, when water freezes in a fractured rock, enough energy may develop to pry off pieces of rock. Or a boulder moved by gravity down a rocky slope may be shattered into smaller fragments. Note that in mechanical weathering the size of the material changes from large to small, but the composition remains unchanged.

Expansion and Contraction Resulting from Heat. Changes in temperature, if they are rapid enough and great enough, may bring about the mechanical weathering of rock. For instance, in areas where bare rock is exposed at the surface, unprotected by a cloak of soil, forest or brush fires can generate enough heat to break up the rock. The rapid and violent heating of the exterior zone of the rock causes it to expand and if the expansion is great enough, flakes and larger fragments of rock are split off. Lightning often starts such forest fires, and in rare instances, may even shatter exposed rock by means of a direct strike.

Variations in temperature from day to night and from winter to summer cause expansion and contraction of rock material. Occasionally these changes are known to cause mechanical failure of rock. But it still seems unlikely that temperature changes are great enough to cause extensive mechanical weathering. Theoretically, such changes in temperature should cause disintegration. For instance, we know that the different minerals which form a granite expand and contract at different rates as they react to rising and falling temperatures. We would expect, then, that even minor expansion and contraction of adjacent minerals would, over long periods of time, weaken the bonds between mineral grains, and that it would be thus possible for disintegration to occur along these boundaries. But evidence from the laboratory to support these speculations is inconclusive. In one laboratory experiment, coarse-grained granite was subjected to temperatures ranging from 58°F to 256°F every 15 minutes. This alternate heating and cooling was carried on long enough to simulate 244 years of daily heating and cooling. Yet the granite showed no signs of disintegration. Perhaps experiments extended over longer periods of time would produce observable results. In any event, we are still uncertain of the mechanical effect of daily or seasonal temperature changes. If these fluctuations do bring about the disintegration of rock, they must do so very slowly.

Frost Action. Frost is much more effective than heat in producing mechanical weathering. When water freezes, its volume increases about 9 percent. So when water that trickles down into the cracks, crevices, and pores of a rock expands as it passes from the liquid to the solid state, it sets up pressures that are directed outward from the inside of the rock. And these pressures are great enough to dislodge fragments from the rock's surface. In fact, by the time the temperature has fallen to about −7.6°F, the resulting pressures may be as great as 30,000 pounds per square inch, equivalent to the pressure produced by a 15-ton granite block. This temperature is not unusually low and is experienced several times a year even in temperate latitudes.

Under actual conditions, however, pressures like this are probably never produced by frost action, at least close to the earth's surface. For an internal pressure of 30,000 pounds per square inch to build up, a rock crevice would have to be completely filled with water and completely sealed off, and the containing block would have to be strong enough to withstand the pressures at least up to that point. But most crevices contain some air in addition to water and are open either to the surface or to other crevices. Furthermore, no rock can withstand a pressure of 30,000 pounds per square inch directed from within toward the outside.

And yet frost action is responsible for a great deal of mechanical weathering. Water that soaks into the crevices and pores of a rock usually starts to freeze at its upper surface, where it is in contact with the cooling air. This means that in time the water below is confined by an ice plug. Then, as the freezing continues, the trapped water expands, and pressure is exerted outward. Rock may be subjected to this action several times a year. In high mountains, for example, the temperature may move back and forth across the freezing line almost daily.

A second type of mechanical weathering produced by freezing water is **frost-heaving.** This action usually occurs in fine-grained, unconsolidated deposits rather than in solid rock. Much of the water that falls as rain or snow soaks into the ground, where it freezes during the winter months. If conditions are right, more and more ice accumulates in the zone of freezing as water is added from the atmosphere above and drawn upward from the unfrozen ground below, much as a blotter soaks up moisture. In time, lensshaped masses of ice are built up, and the soil above them is heaved upward. Frost-heaving of this sort is common on poorly constructed roads. And lawns and gardens are often soft and spongy in the springtime as a result of the heaving up of the soil during the winter.

Certain conditions must exist before either type of frost action can take place: (1) there must be an adequate supply of moisture; (2) the moisture must be able to enter the rock or soil; and (3) temperatures must move back and forth across the freezing line. As we would expect, frost action is most pronounced in high mountains and in moist regions where temperatures fluctuate across the freezing line, either daily or seasonally.[3]

EXERCISE 10.10

DIRECTIONS   Outline the following passage.

TIME IN GEOLOGY

The importance of time in geologic processes has been touched upon in connection with almost every topic discussed in previous chapters. It has been suggested and inferred repeatedly that lengthy spans of time seem to have been necessary to bring the earth to its present condition. We should now devote our attention specifically to the subject of time and its measurement as applied to geology.

Absolute and Relative Time   We may think of geologic time in two ways: relative and absolute. *Relative time* relates to whether one event in earth history came *before or after* another event, but disregards years. *Absolute time* measures whether a geologic event took place a *few thou-*

sand years ago, a *billion years* ago, or at some date even further back in earth history.

Relative and absolute time in earth history have their counterparts in human history. In tracing the history of the earth, we may want to know whether some occurrence, such as volcanic eruption, preceded or followed another, such as a rise in sea level, and how these two events are related in time to a third event, perhaps a mountain-building episode. In human history, too, we try to establish relative positions in time. Thus, in studying American history it is important to know that the Revolution preceded the War Between the States, and that the Canadian-American boundary was fixed some time between these two events.

Sometimes, of course, events in both earth history and human history can be established only in relative terms. But our record becomes increasingly precise as we fit more and more events into an actual chronological calendar. If we did not know the date of the U.S.-Canadian boundary treaty—only that it was signed between the two wars—we could place it between 1783 and 1861, but we could be no more precise than that. Recorded history, of course, provides us with the actual date, 1846.

Naturally, we would like to be able to date geologic events with precision. But so far this has been impossible, and the accuracy achieved in determining the dates of human history, at least written human history, will probably never be achieved in geology. Still, we can determine approximate dates for many geologic events. Even though they may lack the precision possible in recent human history, they are probably of the correct order of magnitude. For instance, we can say that the dinosaurs became extinct about 63 million years ago, and that about 11,000 years ago the last continental glacier began to recede from New England and the area bordering the Great Lakes.

Years and Seasons   The rotation and revolution of the earth provide us with our most important and useful measures of time—the year and the day. Commencing with crude observations of the changing seasons and positions of the heavenly bodies, man has become quite accurate in fixing the length of the year as 365 days, 5 hours, 49 minutes, and 12 seconds. Although such measures of the week, hour, minute, or second (defined as $1/31,556,925.9$ of the year) are accepted standards of time measurement, they are purely artificial fractional measures invented by man. Obviously, if the length of the year should change or vary, so would the second and all of its multiples. It is now proposed to adopt a new standard for defining the second—9,192,631,770 cycles of vibration of the cesium atom. This atomic standard is being checked against the astronomic standard with the hope of discovering whether there are actual variations in either. The lengths of the year and the day are accepted as basic to time measurement, but the geologist is interested to know how long these familiar cycles have been in effect.

Evidence for our regular yearly journey around the sun exists in the form of seasonal effects. Because the axis of the earth is inclined to the plane along which it travels, characteristic changes of light, temperature, and precipitation are repeated with the seasons. These effects exercise a profound influence on the food supply and growth patterns of plants and animals and, locally at least, on the erosion, transportation, and deposition of sediments. Seasonal effects are recorded in living and nonliving materials in many ways and have thereby become permanently recorded in the earth's crust.

Growth Rings in Plants and Animals   The best-known seasonal records preserved in living organisms are **tree rings.** The width and spacing of the rings depend on temperature, light, and moisture variations that are largely of a seasonal nature. Each ring consists of two parts: the so-called "summer wood," which has small cells with thick walls, and the "spring wood," which has larger cells with thinner walls. The study of tree rings, called **dendrochronology,** has made significant contributions to the dating of individual archaeological sites, especially in the arid portions of the American Southwest where wood is easily preserved. A continuous chronology going back to 1550 B.C. has been pieced together for that region, and many important ruins have been dated by pieces of structural wood.

An even longer sequence of rings exists in the individual trunks of the sequoia trees of California. Studies of the annual rings prove that some of them are over 3,000 years old. The sequoia trees have long been regarded as the oldest living things on earth, but this claim has been challenged by a less spectacular tree, the bristlecone pine, which is found in various drier parts of California, Nevada, and Utah. The oldest tree of this species so far dated is at least 4,800 years old.

Animals also respond to seasonal changes, usually by variations in growth rates corresponding with variations in the favorability of growth conditions. Shells of clams and other aquatic organisms show growth "rings" much like those of trees. Fish scales reveal their age by similar marks. Less well-known examples are layering in the spines and otoliths (ear bones) of fish, in coral growths, in the horns of mammals, and in the limb bones of certain reptiles.

How Old Is the Earth?   Granting that the earth has been making a yearly circuit of the sun for many, many years, we are led to ask just how many such journeys it may have made—or, in other words, how old it is. Until fairly recent times, the origin and age of the earth were not considered to be subjects for serious inquiry. Interpretations of Hebrew scripture, basis of the Christian faith of the Western world, were considered to be the final and sufficient word on the subject. In 1654, Archbishop James Usher concluded from scriptural analysis that the earth had been created in 4004 B.C. This was printed as a marginal date in several editions of the Bible and was quite generally believed by most Christians. A few years later, a learned Biblical scholar, Dr. John Lightfoot of Cambridge, felt that he could be even more specific, and wrote that "Heaven and earth, center and circumference, were made in the same instance of time, and clouds full of water, and man was created by the Trinity on the 26th of October 4004 B.C. at 9 o'clock in the morning." The idea of a 6,000-year-old earth was entirely satisfactory as long as there were no reasons for believing otherwise. It is interesting to note, however, that ancient Hindu thinkers had placed the age of the earth at almost 2 billion years.

As the spirit of scientific inquiry began to assert itself, the age of the earth became a subject for serious consideration. Facts were few and meaningful observations were just beginning to be undertaken. Yet to some thinkers every natural feature of the landscape gave evidence of great antiquity. The cutting of valleys, the advance and retreat of glaciers, the destruction of coasts by erosion and their restoration by deposition, all seemed to demand long time periods. But quantitative data were needed, and in the 18th and 19th centuries a few preliminary attempts were made to actually measure and evaluate certain properties of the earth in order to establish its age.

Among the natural phenomena that seemed to offer clues in the search were (1) the saltiness of the ocean, (2) the internal heat of the earth, and (3) the rate of deposition of sediments.

It was assumed in the first case that the original ocean was fresh and that salt had been added at approximately the current rate ever since rivers commenced to run. Therefore, if we divide the amount of sodium now in the ocean by the amount brought in annually, we have the age of the ocean. The method gives answers of 90 to 100 million years.

It was assumed in the second method that the earth must have cooled from an originally molten condition. Since the approximate rate of cooling and the present temperature can be measured, the entire period of cooling may be calculated. This gives a span of 20 to 40 million years. As an incidental argument, it was contended that no known source of heat could have supported the sun's output for much longer than a 20-million-year period, and that the earth could not be older than the sun.

Finally, with regard to deposition of sediments, it was reasoned that if we determine how many feet of sediment have been laid down and how long it takes a foot to accumulate under average conditions, we may by simple division arrive at an estimate of how long erosion and deposition have been going on. Latest figures show that the cumulative maximum thickness of rock laid down since abundant fossils appeared is at least 450,000 feet or about 80 miles. Although rates of deposition vary from time to time and place to place, an average of one foot in 1,000 years may not be far wrong. At this rate, the fossil-bearing sedimentary rocks would have taken 450 million years to accumulate.

Although these earlier hypotheses were well conceived and the supporting calculations were mathematically correct, they involved so many unknowns and gave such varied results that no one now has much confidence in any of them. It is likely that the seas have always been about as salty as they now are, and we know from the presence of thick salt beds that much salt has been returned to the lands from the seas. It is also known that the earth contains its own heat-producing radioactive elements, which would totally confuse any calculations based on gradual cooling from an original molten state. The heat of the sun is now known to be provided by nuclear reactions and not by ordinary combustion as once was supposed. Finally, the rates of formation of a foot of sediment range from thousands of years for limy ooze to a few hours for river-laid sand, so that it seems impossible to arrive at reliable rates of deposition. Aside from indicating that periods longer than 6,000 years are needed, these methods still failed to provide a reliable estimate of the age of the earth.[4]

SPRINGBOARD 10

Choose one chapter from your reading this week.

1. Do an overview of the chapter first.
2. Read each section, underlining important points.
3. Outline the information in the chapter,
   a. Use Roman numberals (I, II, III) for major categories; A, B, C for the next level; 1, 2, 3 for the next level; a, b, c for the next level.
   b. When possible, abbreviate your notes. Use the cause-effect arrow, & for *and,* e.g. instead of *for example.*

QUICK PROGRESS TEST 4

DIRECTIONS   After you read this selection from a geology text, underline important points and then take notes on the information. Don't forget to use the illustration—include your own version of it in your study notes.

RUNNING WATER

Of all the agents at work leveling the earth's surface, running water is most important. Year after year, the streams of the earth move staggering amounts of debris and dissolved materials through their valleys to the great settling basins, the oceans.

"All the rivers run into the sea, yet the sea is not full: unto the place from whence the rivers come, thither they return again," reads *Ecclesiastes* 1:7. And thither they shall return, for nearly all the water that runs off the slopes of the land in thin sheets, and then travels on in rills, streams and rivers, is derived from the oceans. There is only one exception: Volcanic eruptions apparently bring water to the surface from deep beneath the earth. But once it has reached the surface, the water also follows the general pattern of water movement from sea to land and back again to the sea, a pattern that we call the *hydrologic cycle.*

Precipitation and Stream Flow   Once water has fallen on the land as precipitation, it follows one of the many paths that make up the hydrologic cycle. By far the greatest part is evaporated back to the air directly or is taken up by the plants and transpired (breathed back) by them to the atmosphere. A smaller amount follows the path of *runoff*, the water that flows off the land. And the smallest amount of precipitation soaks into the ground through *infiltration*. . . .

Bearing in mind the ways in which water proceeds through the hydrologic cycle, we can express the amount of runoff by the following generalized formula:

Runoff = Precipitation − (Infiltration + Evaporation and Transpiration)[5]

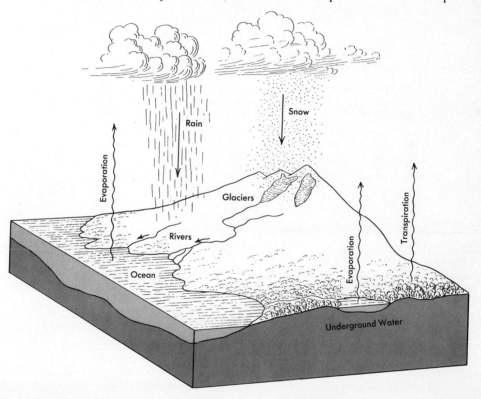

Figure 1. In the hydrologic cycle water evaporated into the atmosphere reaches the land as rain or snow. Here it may be temporarily stored in glaciers, lakes, or the underground before returning by the rivers to the sea. Or some may be transpired or evaporated directly back into the atmosphere before reaching the sea.

NOTES

1. William Lee Stokes and Sheldon Judson, *Introduction to Geology.* Englewood Cliffs, N.J.: Prentice-Hall, Inc., 1968, p. 33.
2. Stokes and Judson, *Introduction to Geology*, pp. 33–34.
3. Stokes and Judson, *Introduction to Geology*, pp. 55–59.
4. Stokes and Judson, *Introduction to Geology*, pp. 244–51.

III

ON YOUR OWN

Building Technical Vocabulary Skills
General Study Techniques

11
BUILDING TECHNICAL VOCABULARY SKILLS

Can you understand this sentence?

"The octal number system has a radix of 8. . . ."

To understand it, you have to know what an "octal number system" is, and what the word "radix" means.

What about this sentence?

"When the anode of the semiconductor diode is positive in relation to its cathode, the diode is conductive. . . ."

Unless you know the meanings of "anode," "semiconductor," "diode," "cathode," and "conductive," you will not be able to understand this sentence.

We talked about this in Chapter 1, "Definitions of Terms." One hallmark of the language of science is a highly specialized terminology. To understand the language, you must understand the terms.

However, these highly specialized terms are easier to acquire than a general vocabulary is—for several reasons.

PRECISION OF SCIENTIFIC VOCABULARY

The vocabulary of science is precise and consistent. No term will be vague in meaning, or have a meaning that is not clear. This is very different from the way in which words are used in our everyday lives.

translate it? The word is not precise. Maybe the author meant "content"; there is a Spanish word for that. Or maybe the author meant "pleased." There is also a Spanish word for that. There are many ways to translate the word "happy."

The language of science is entirely different from this. In science, there is an almost one-for-one match when you are translating from one language to another. This is an amazing fact; such a thing is impossible with our everyday language. It shows how precise the language of science is.

You can depend on this precision when you are acquiring technical vocabulary. You will find it in all the language used in science. There is a reason for this consistency: scientists want to make sure that experiments carried out in one place can be done in exactly the same way in another place. "Inertia" has to mean the same in Boston as it does in San Francisco. If you want to make sure other people will be able to replicate what you are doing, your language has to be accurate and uniform. Otherwise there will be many mistakes.

GREEK AND LATIN BASIS OF SCIENTIFIC VOCABULARY

Most technical vocabulary is based directly on Latin and Greek words. For example, the word "malleable" is taken directly from the Latin word *malleus,* meaning hammer, and *abilis,* able. As scientific knowledge grew, people deliberately went to Greek and Latin roots to build the new vocabulary they needed for the new sciences.

You may have once tried to memorize some Greek and Latin roots, then decided they were not very helpful, since they rarely showed up in the words you were learning, or showed up in such different forms that you did not recognize them.

This is not the case for the Greek and Latin roots in science, since they are the basis for the language. The roots will open the way to understanding many related words.

Table 10.1 lists a number of useful Greek and Latin roots and affixes, and Table 10.2 lists some useful prefixes.

Table 10.1 Useful Greek and Latin Roots and Affixes

Root	Meaning	Example
ante	before	antechamber
bene, bonus	well, good	benign
calx	lime	calcareous
circum	around	circumnavigate
contra	against	contradictory
di, bi, duo	twice, two	duo, duplicate
dia	through	diagonal
hepta, septem	seven	September
hex, sex	sixth	hexagon, sextet
hyper	beyond, above, over	hyperactive
hypo	below	hypoactive
inter	between	interaction

Table 10.1 (Continued)

Root	Meaning	Example
intra	inside	intravenous
macro	long, large	macroscopic
meter	measure	dynamometer
micro	small	microscope
mono	one	monotone
neo	new	neodymium
octo	eight	octagon
penta	five	pentagonal
plumbo	lead	plumber
poly	many	polymorphous
proto	first in time, original	prototype
quadr, tetra	four	quadrangle
retro	backwards	retroactive
rheos	current	rheostat
rota	wheel	rotary
sub	below	substructure
super, supra	above	superstructure
technē	builder, carpenter	technology
tele	far off, over a distance	telecast
trans	through	transparent
tri, ter	three	triangle

Table 10.2. Useful International System Prefixes

Prefix	Meaning
micro	millionth
milli	thousandth
centi	hundredth
deci	tenth
deka	ten
hecto	hundred
kilo	thousand
mega	million
giga	billion

HOW TO USE AN ETYMOLOGY

The etymology of a technical word will help to fix its meaning in your mind. The etymology of a word—its history—gives you a sense of where the word comes from and builds up your knowledge of roots. The etymology of each word is given in the dictionary after the entry word and pronunciation. Usually there are boldface brackets around it.

Here is an example of a typical etymology:

az·ure (azh′ər) *adj.* [ME. *asur* < OFr. *azur* (with omission of initial *l-*, as if *l'azur*) < Ar. *lāzaward* < Per. *lāzhuward*, lapis lazuli] of or like the color of a clear sky; sky-blue —*n.* **1.** sky blue or any similar blue color **2.** [Poet.] the blue sky

Many students ignore the etymology because they have trouble with the abbreviations. Here is how the etymology of the word *azure* would read: in Middle English the word is found in the form *asur*, and that word is derived from the Old French *azur*, and that word derives from the Arabic *lazaward*. This in turn is derived from the Persian *lazhuward*, meaning lapis lazuli.

The meanings of all abbreviations used in a dictionary are given at the front of the dictionary in a table. Here are some of the most common abbreviations used in etymologies:

Gk	Greek	ME	Middle English
M Gk	Middle Greek	Fr	French
L Gk	Late Greek	G	German
L	Latin	fr	from
LL	Late Latin	lit.	literally
<	derived from	see prec.	see preceding entry

If the root *azure* occurs in other words, the etymology will not be given again. Instead, there will be a cross-reference to the first etymology. It is usually printed in small capitals.

USING THE DICTIONARY

In mastering technical vocabulary, because of its precision and its direct relationship to Greek and Latin, the dictionary is probably your best aid. You will need a dictionary on the collegiate level, at least, as simpler dictionaries have very little etymological information. Your textbooks will also provide definitions, either within the chapters or in a glossary. For more inclusive information you can also consult a technical dictionary, which will provide complete definitions of terms within your field.

If you are using a regular dictionary, you will soon realize that both general and technical meanings for words are given. You will need to read past the general meanings until you find the technical definition. Here is an example of an entry that gives both general and scientific definitions:

> **a·mor·phous** (ə môr′fəs) *adj.* [ModL. *amorphus* < Gr. *amorphos* < *a-*, without + *morphē*, form] **1.** without definite form; shapeless **2.** of no definite type; anomalous **3.** unorganized; vague **4.** *Biol.* without definite or specialized structure, as some lower forms of life **5.** *Chem. & Mineralogy* lacking a definite crystalline form; not crystalline

In this case, meanings within biology, chemistry, and mineralogy are given after the general definitions.

If you use a technical dictionary, the entry will concentrate on the meaning of the word within the field; the general meanings will be given little or no attention.

The dictionary is particularly important in developing technical vocabulary. Usually we get the meanings of many words from their context or setting, using other words in the sentence as "clues." But as technical terminology is so specific in meaning, a general "sense" is not enough. Regular and technical dictionaries are necessary. In addition, many words have specific technical meanings that can't be derived from their ordinary everyday meanings. Words such as "force" and "weight" have special, technical meanings. Your ordinary understanding of these words will not be helpful; in fact, it will usually be misleading.

PRONOUNCING NEW WORDS

Saying new words out loud is one of the best ways to fix them in your mind. The pronunciation spelling given in the dictionary can help you when you set out to acquire new vocabulary.

Many students do not know how to use the pronunciation spelling given in the dictionary. It is usually given in parentheses immediately after the boldface entry word.

duc.tile (dukt′l)

A full key to pronunciation appears at the beginning of all dictionaries. Figure 11.1 is the key taken from the *Collins' Second College Edition of the Webster's New World Dictionary.*[3]

B. *Key to Pronunciation*

An abbreviated form of this key appears at the bottom of every alternate page of the vocabulary.

Symbol	Key Words	Symbol	Key Words
a	asp, fat, parrot	b	bed, fable, dub
ā	ape, date, play	d	dip, beadle, had
ä	ah, car, father	f	fall, after, off
		g	get, haggle, dog
e	elf, ten, berry	h	he, ahead, hotel
ē	even, meet, money	j	joy, agile, badge
		k	kill, tackle, bake
i	is, hit, mirror	l	let, yellow, ball
ī	ice, bite, high	m	met, camel, trim
		n	not, flannel, ton
ō	open, tone, go	p	put, apple, tap
ô	all, horn, law	r	red, port, dear
o͞o	ooze, tool, crew	s	sell, castle, pass
oo	look, pull, moor	t	top, cattle, hat
yo͞o	use, cute, few	v	vat, hovel, have
yoo	united, cure, globule	w	will, always, swear
oi	oil, point, toy	y	yet, onion, yard
ou	out, crowd, plow	z	zebra, dazzle, haze
u	up, cut, color	ch	chin, catcher, arch
ᵾr	urn, fur, deter	sh	she, cushion, dash
		th	thin, nothing, truth
ə	a in ago	*th*	then, father, lathe
	e in agent	zh	azure, leisure
	i in sanity	ŋ	ring, anger, drink
	o in comply	′	[see explanatory note
	u in focus		below and also *For-*
ər	perhaps, murder		*eign sounds* below]

The qualities of most of the symbols above can be readily understood from the key words in which they are shown, and a speaker of any dialect of American English will automatically read his own pronunciation into any symbol shown here. A few explanatory notes on some of the more complex of these symbols follow.

Figure 11.1

A shortened form of this key appears at the bottom of every alternate page in the dictionary. You can refer to it as you try to pronounce new words. Pronunciation spelling is valuable in two ways:

1. When you use it to sound out a word that looks unfamiliar, you may find that you have already heard it in class or in the laboratory.

2. You can use the symbols when you take notes on new words. Then you can practice saying the new words, using the symbols to guide you.

For instance, let's say you come across the word "pico." To remember the word, do the following: Write it down on a 3 × 5 card. Look it up in the dictionary. Write down the word, derivations, and pronunciation on the front of the card. Then write a definition and examples on the back.

| Front | Back |

Some of the symbols used in pronunciation spelling are probably unfamiliar to you:

1. ā, ē, ı, ō: This means that the vowel is pronounced with the same sound it has in the alphabet.

ā / ape, date, play / āp, dāt, plā.
ē / even, money / ē'-vən, mun'-ē.
ı / ice, bite, high / ıs, bıt, hı.
ō / open, tone, go / o'-pən tōn, gō.

2. ə: You may find this symbol baffling. This is a *shwa*, and it is used to represent the sound of unaccented vowels; this sound is pronounced "uh" and is the same as the following:

a, ago, ə -gō'
e, agent, ā́-jənt
ī, sanity, sań-ə-tē
o, comply, kəm-plī'
u, focus, fṓ-kəs

If you write out new words on 3 × 5 cards and include pronunciation spelling, it will greatly aid you in remembering them.

<table>
<tr><td>

bias — bī´-as

fr. slope, slant

</td><td>

*fixed voltage
applied to
circuit to control
mode of operation.*

</td></tr>
</table>

Note that there are two kinds of accent marks: a strong stress is indicated by a dark stroke ('); a weak stress is shown by a lighter stroke (').

SUMMARY

There are many systems for acquiring vocabulary words. We would suggest that for technical vocabulary you:

1. Use the dictionary. A precise understanding of terms is fundamental.
2. Write new words out in pronunciation spelling if you have trouble saying them. It's easy to practice saying them when they are broken down in this way.
3. Write out the root when you think it is useful. This is one of the best ways to help keep a new word in mind. Also, it may help you with another new word that shares the same root.
4. Keep a file of 3 × 5 cards of new words. Write the pronunciation and etymology on the front. Write the technical definition on the back. Test yourself by trying to say the definition before looking at it.

EXERCISE 11.1

DIRECTIONS The following words have been written in pronunciation spelling. Write out the regular spelling for each word.

EXAMPLE: pə ten´ shē äm´ ə ter   *potentiometer*

1. chōk

2. hēt

3. skē mat´ ik

4. ak´ sēz

5. tork _____

6. ī´ən _____

7. so´lə noid _____

8. dɪ nə mo _____

9. boi´ən sē _____

DIRECTIONS   Write out the following words in pronunciation spelling. Use the key, Fig. 11.1.

EXAMPLE   diode ___dī´ōd___

1. machine_____

2. potential energy_____

3. rheostat_____

4. nickle _____

5. axis _____

6. axes _____

7. electrode _____

8. pressure _____

9. heat _____

10. choke _____

11. dynamo_____

DIRECTIONS   Write out the following words in pronunciation spelling.

1. benzene_____

2. convection_____

3. radiation _____

4. formula _____

5. bimetalic _____

6. niobium _____

7. chassis _____

EXERCISE 11.4

DIRECTIONS   Upon which Latin or Greek roots are the following words based? Give both the root and the meaning. Use either a collegiate or an unabridged dictionary.

EXAMPLES: pyrostat *pyro, fire + stat, stationary*
commutator *commute, to change*

1. acute _____

2. contradict _____

3. hypothesis _____

4. machine _____

5. technology _____

6. rotary _____

7. thermal _____

8. carbon _____

9. ferrite _____

10. plumb, as in plumb line _____

11. rheostat _____

12. hypothermal _____

EXERCISE 11.5

DIRECTIONS   What is the meaning of each of these combining forms? Give two words using each root.

EXAMPLE: circum *around; circumspect, circumnavigate*

1. contra _____

2. hyper _____

3. macro _____

4. kilo _____

5. proto _____

6. retro _____

7. trans _____

DIRECTIONS   Look up each of the italicized words in a collegiate or unabridged dictionary. Answer the questions about each word.

1. For whom is the electric unit the *ampere* named?_____

2. What is *malleable* iron? _____

3. What is the root of the word *torque*? _____

4. What does a *torque wrench* do? _____

5. What are the roots of the word *dynamometer*? _____

6. What is the root of the word *igneous*?_____

7. What is the root of the word *ductile*?_____

8. What is a *pseudoscience*?_____

9. What does the word *sidereal* mean? _____

10. How much is a *milliampere*? _____

DIRECTIONS   All the units of measurement listed below are derived from
names of scientists. Look up each of the units in a collegiate,
unabridged, or technical dictionary. After whom is each of
these units named?

EXAMPLE: ampere *André Marie Ampère, French physicist and mathematician*

1. coulomb _____

2. hertz _____

3. joule _____

4. ohm _____

5. gauss _____

Prefixes

deci	1/10	10^{-1}	kilo	1,000	10^3
centi	1/100	10^{-2}	mega	1,000,000	10^6
milli	1/1,000	10^{-3}			
micro	1/1,000,000	10^{-6}			

DIRECTIONS   Write out the answer to each question in words.

EXAMPLE   How much is a milliamp? *one-thousandth of an amp.*

1. How much is a decimeter?_____

        a centimeter? _____

        a millimeter?_____

2. How much is a centigram? _____

        a milligram?_____

        a microgram? _____

3. Write out the word that could stand for
    one-thousandth of an ampere

    _____

    one-millionth of an ampere

    _____

    one-thousand volts _____

    one million volts _____

EXERCISE 11.9

DIRECTIONS   Here are two excerpts from a textbook. As you read them, underline the key terms. Afterward, write out each term on a 3 × 5
card. Look up each word and determine its origin and pronunciation. Write down the pronunciation on the front of the card.
Write the meaning on the back. Then check yourself by pronouncing the words, using the front of the cards, and reciting the
meanings before checking the back of the cards.

A systematic examination of all known rock types shows that two principal kinds predominate. The first are *igneous rocks,* formed by the cooling
and crystallization of liquids from deep in the crust or upper part of
the mantle, called *magmas.* The second are *sedimentary rocks,* formed by
compaction and cementation of sediment derived from the continuous
erosion of the continents by water, atmosphere, ice, and wind. Most of
the sediments are deposited in the sea along the margins of continents.
As the marginal piles of sediment grow larger and are buried deeper,
increasing pressure and rising temperature produce physical and
chemical changes in them. The resulting *metamorphic rocks,* however,
generally show whether they were originally sedimentary or igneous

rocks. When a sedimentary pile becomes thick enough, material near the bottom may melt to form magma. The newly formed magma, being less dense than the rocks from which it was derived, will tend to rise up, intruding its parents, and as it cools and crystallizes it will form a new igneous rock. Thus, there seems to be a sequential process in rocks, whereby igneous rocks become sediments, sediments become sedimentary rocks, then metamorphic rocks, and eventually igneous rocks again. The sequence is slow — hundreds of millions of years are necessary — and the details are complicated. As weathering and erosion occur, some substances are dissolved and removed in solution while others are transported as suspended particles.[4]

EVAPORATION AND TRANSPIRATION

Water will *evaporate* from any wetted surface. A significantly large fraction of the rainfall that falls on land is returned to the atmosphere in this fashion. In addition, water is assimilated by root systems of growing plants and is later *transpired* from the leaf surfaces by a process essentially identical to evaporation. The two effects, evaporation and transpiration, cannot be individually discriminated for their effectiveness in returning rainfall to the atmosphere, but their sum contribution can be evaluated and is usually called the *evapotranspiration* factor. The fraction of rain falling on the United States that is returned to the atmosphere by evapotranspiration, for example, is 70 percent; for the world as a whole, approximately 62 percent (see Fig. 1). In arid countries such as Australia the fraction is larger, and in less arid areas such as the United Kingdom it is lower. Water returned to the atmosphere by evapotranspiration is unavailable to man, except in the sense that useful plants may be grown in the place of useless ones. It cannot be trapped and redistributed for industrial or other purposes.

In regions of low rainfall, plant cover will develop to a point where all precipitation is used in evapotranspiration and none remains for stream flow. Seasonal rainfalls provide a qualifier for this statement because streams will flow even in the most arid areas during periods of maximum rainfall. In general, if the potential evapotranspiration — that which would result from the maximum plant cover a region could support under ideal circumstances — should exceed the precipitation, overland stream flow ceases. Conversely, if evapotranspiration is less than precipitation, runoff is generated.

The amount by which precipitation exceeds evapotranspiration is the perennial yield of stream flow water, and this is the usable fraction of rain and snowfall. Across the entire United States the water yield amounts to 30 percent of the total rainfall, or approximately 1.77×10^{15} liters per year. But when we consider the distribution of water deficiencies and surpluses we find that essentially the entire eastern half of the United States, together with a small region in the Pacific northwest, enjoys water surplus, while most of the country to west of the Mississippi is water-deficient and arid.[5]

SPRINGBOARD 11

Choose one chapter from your reading this week.

1. As you read the chapter, underline words that you do not know.
2. Pick out ten of these words.
3. Write each word down on a 3 × 5 card. Look it up in the dictionary. If you have trouble pronouncing it, write down the pronunciation spelling. Include derivations on the front of the card when you think it will be useful to you.
4. Flip the card over. Write the definition on the back.
5. Then review the word by saying the definition to yourself.

NOTES

1. From *Webster's New World Dictionary,* Second College Edition. William Collins & World Publishing Company, Inc., and Prentice-Hall, Inc.
2. From *Webster's New World Dictionary,* Second College Edition.
3. From *Webster's New World Dictionary,* Second College Edition.
4. Brian J. Skinner, *Earth Resources,* 2d ed. Englewood Cliffs, N.J.: Prentice-Hall, Inc., 1976, pp. 16–17.
5. Skinner, *Earth Resources,* pp. 129, 131.

12

GENERAL STUDY TECHNIQUES

How do you get the information you need to do well in a technical class?

1. First and foremost there is your textbook. We've covered ten ways to get the most out of it. The study notes you take on your textbooks provide a review of the course.

2. The vocabulary building you do on your own will be very helpful. A clear-cut, precise definition for all of the terms you use in technical classes is fundamental.

3. Laboratory and "hands-on" classes help bring home the reality behind the theory. In these courses the emphasis is on doing; they involve you in an actual process—whether it is wiring a circuit or building a relay, operating a turret lathe or reading an n-c tape, verifying Ohm's law or learning how to conduct a Brinell Hardness Test.

Another major source of information is the notes you take on the instructor's lectures. Students get a large part of the information they need from listening to, taking notes on, and then studying the information presented in classroom lectures.

Taking notes is a complicated skill that combines listening and writing. You have to strike a balance between listening to understand, and writing to remember. However, note-taking is worth the effort. It will be a major source of information when the time comes to review for tests; you will also discover that in struggling to write down lecture information in an organized way, you have taken the first step in mastering the information.

This chapter will give some general suggestions for taking notes on technical lectures and preparing for tests. All of the other chapters had practice exercises; this one doesn't. After you finish reading it, you're on your own. Your practice will be real classroom lectures — and real tests!

TAKING NOTES ON A TECHNICAL LECTURE

Your goal should be to take down the most important parts of what the instructor is saying. Usually, the material that is covered in the lectures appears in one form or another on the tests. You may think to yourself, "That's in the book. I don't have to write it down. I can read it at home in my textbook." However, you probably will not be going home to look at your textbook for many hours. You may go to another lecture or lab, or you may go off and work an eight-hour day at your job. By the time you look at your textbook, the information in the lecture, which seemed so clear at the time, will have faded away. You will forget which points were emphasized, and in what way.

It is not necessary to write down everything the instructor says. The trick is to focus in on the most important points and write them down. As you learn how to do this, you will find that your ability to retain lecture information increases. This is not surprising if you consider how much effort taking notes requires. For instance, contrast the difference between taking notes on a lecture and using a tape recorder. If you tape the lecture, you will surely get every single word. However, as a listener you have been idle — all you've done is press a "start" lever. When you take notes, you are selecting and organizing main points, boiling down the information. By the time you've finished doing this kind of work, you have taken the first step in making the information your own.

Guidelines for Note-Taking

1. *When possible, read the assignment first.* If the subject is completely new to you, you may not understand much of it before you have heard the lecture or done some work in the laboratory. However, if you try to read through the material before the lecture, you will break the ice. You'll have some familiarity with the new terms; it will be easier to capture the flow of the speaker's ideas. After the lecture read the chapter carefully, taking notes, and do the practice problems.

2. *Listen first, write second.* Some students start writing the moment the instructor starts talking. Don't do this. In a technical lecture it is very important to listen before you begin to write; try to get a notion of

what the instructor is talking about before you start moving your pencil. Otherwise you may end up with pages of notes and no understanding of the main points that were made.

3. *Use a two-column system.* Leave 2 inches on the left-hand side of your notebook page blank as you take notes, using simple outlining form. Use Roman numerals for the most important points, and indent supporting points beneath them.

When you go over your notes, use the empty space on the left-hand side as a "recall" column. Write in this column key words or questions that will help you "recall" the contents of the lecture. Then cover up your lecture notes and try to recite from memory, using the recall column for clues.

Samples of two-column notes are shown in Figs. 12.1 and 12.2.

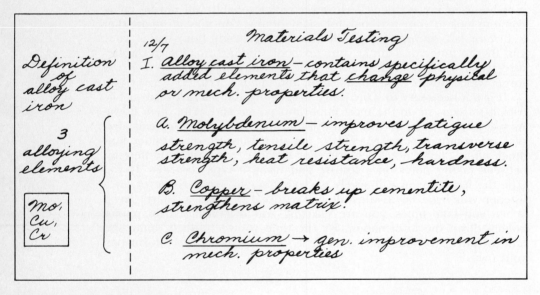

Figure 12.1. Two-column notes.

4. *Take down all diagrams, circuits, or other illustrations from the board or from overhead projections.* Technical lectures rely heavily on illustrations in the same way that technical textbooks do.

If the problems the instructor is going over involve illustrations of phase diagrams or circuits, copy them down. To review for tests later on, you will want to re-do these problems, and you'll probably need the illustrations.

Be sure to label all of the drawing that you take down. Make the connection between the illustrations and the point clear. This sort of thing seems obvious while you're in class; but by the time you start to review your notes later, you may have forgotten the connection. For instance, Fig. 12.3 shows some lecture notes taken by a student; the illustrations have also been taken down, but the connection between the illustrations and the notes is not clear.

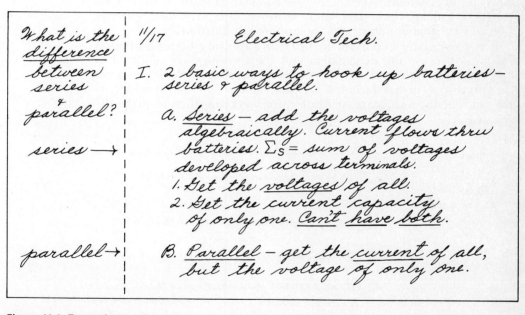

What is the difference between series & parallel?

series →

parallel →

11/17   Electrical Tech.

I. 2 basic ways to hook up batteries — series & parallel.

  a. Series — add the voltages algebraically. Current flows thru batteries. Σ_S = sum of voltages developed across terminals.
  1. Get the voltages of all.
  2. Get the current capacity of only one. Can't have both.

  B. Parallel — get the current of all, but the voltage of only one.

Figure 12.2. Two-column notes.

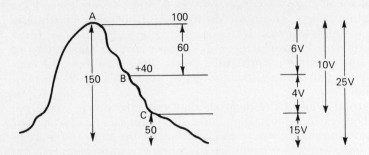

I. Voltage (potential difference = difference in energy levels between 2 charges)

There are reasons why it is difficult to get down both the illustration and the point. Usually the instructor puts the illustration on the board, or on an overhead projector, and then explains it. If you're busy looking at the illustration and copying it down, you will tend to skip writing down the explanation. After all, it seems clear enough while the instructor is talking. Two days later, however, you may find that you have no idea what the illustration is supposed to illustrate.

It is particularly important to work on capturing both illustrations and ideas because the explanation and the drawings are designed to work together. Figure 12.4 is an example from a set of classroom notes where the student has included an explanation with the drawing. As you can see, the two parts of the lecture work together to make the idea clearer.

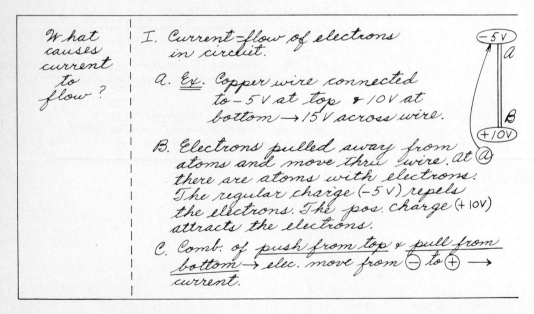

Figure 12.4. Notes explaining a drawing.

238

5. *Afterward, read over your lecture notes.* Fill in the recall column. Use it to review the information in the lecture. Underline parts of the lecture you still have trouble remembering. Work out all of the problems on your own; then check the solution with your notes.

6. *Then reread the assigned textbook chapter.* Go over it carefully, taking notes on the main points.

TEST-TAKING

Your textbook and lecture notes are the two main sources to use when you prepare for tests.

Go over lecture notes first. The classroom notes you have taken are based on material preselected by the teacher from the entire range of materials in your textbook.

Do a thorough job when you review them. Make sure you can do all the demonstration problems, and that you can recite important points using the "recall" column. If you still have difficulty, underline crucial points in a different color, add clues to the recall column, and go through the information again.

After you have reviewed the lecture notes, look over the underlining and marginal notation in your textbook. Mentally review the contents of the chapter, using only the underlinings and the clues you've written in the margin. Then go over the textbook notes you've taken. Read them through, and review each section in your mind until you are comfortable with all the points. Afterward, go over all the problems done in class or given on quizzes. Re-do homework problems in which you made mistakes the first time through. Final examinations include the same sort of problems as those done throughout the semester.

It is a good idea to practice "working against the clock." Do an extra set of problems in a short amount of time; this will prepare you for the pressure of taking real tests in timed conditions.

Many tests in the social sciences and humanities include long "essay" questions. This type of question is unusual in technical tests. Usually you are required to solve problems, provide short answers and choose multiple-choice items. You may also be asked to write out two or three paragraphs in answer to specific questions. No matter which type of test it is, be sure to bring your pocket computer with you—and don't forget a spare battery. Pocket computers are famous for fading away just as you are about to solve a problem.

Time I know one teacher who does not time tests. "Take as long as you want," are the instructions. However, this is very unusual. Tests are usually *timed,* and test-takers gradually develop strategies to help them use the time wisely.

Here are some strategies that students have said are effective:

1. Scan the test before beginning. Estimate how long it will take.
2. Begin working. Go as quickly as possible.
3. Watch the clock. If the test is long, make up a mental schedule and check regularly to make sure you're keeping up with it.

4. Skip items that are unfamiliar. Mark them with a light question mark and return after finishing all the items that you know.

5. Use the time at the end to answer items that you skipped, and to check through the test for errors.

Double check One student worked out an entire problem carefully and correctly on scrap paper, and then forgot to mark the answer on the actual test paper. About an hour after he left, he realized his mistake, and was very upset. "And I knew the answer," he exclaimed. "How could I have been so careless?"

It's easy to make careless mistakes on tests; most people are nervous to begin with when they go in to take a test. It is common under such conditions to accidentally skip questions, forget to write down answers, confuse the nature of questions, or write down the opposite of what one intended to write.

To avoid problems of this type, follow these rules:

1. Read the directions carefully. Go back and check again to make sure you are following them correctly. In your nervousness, you may misunderstand them. Nerves play strange tricks on us when we're taking tests. If you are not clear about the directions, ask the instructor.

2. Read each item carefully. Make sure you understand what you are being asked to do. It's easy to go astray here. Always double check each question.

3. Check each of your answers carefully. Did you follow the directions? Did you perform the right operation? Did you write down what you meant to write down? Did you put the answer in the right place?

Multiple-choice tests In a test like this, you are often in a race with time. Look over the test first and get a general idea of what you are expected to do. Then go through the questions answering the ones you know. Don't sit staring at a particular item, waiting for the answer to come to you. After you have completed all the items you are reasonably certain of, go back to the ones that confuse you. For each of these, eliminate as many of the choices as you can, and then make a guess.

Short-answer Tests In this type of test you are required to fill in a blank with a few words, or write out one or two sentences. Often you are required to give definitions. If you know the item, fill it in. If you don't, skip it and go on to the next item. If you have time at the end of the test, you can go back and "ponder" the items you don't know.

Computer-scored tests More and more schools, especially those in technical fields, are switching to computer-scored tests. They have many advantages. For instance, if the test involves circuit problems, the computer can assign different values to each circuit. This means that each student solves a different set of problems. The computer can also score the answers.

If this is the case, you will put your answers on a pressure-sensitive card that can be scored at a terminal.

Open-book Tests   Usually when an instructor says the test will be open-book, you may open up the book to use the tables of information included in the appendices. You can mark these tables off before the test so that your book will easily fall open to them during the examination. However, often you are not allowed to use the rest of your book. It's important to clear this up before the test; often the expression "open book" does not mean the book is as open as it sounds.

SUMMARY

1. When you take notes on a technical lecture, you have to strike a balance between listening to understand and writing to remember.

2. Listen first, write second. Usually the speaker will make a point, give examples, and then make the point again. Listen before you write; you can take advantage of a certain amount of natural repetition to keep up with the flow of the speaker's ideas.

3. Use a two-column method; leave space for a "recall column."

4. Take down all diagrams, circuits, or other illustrations. Label all illustrations, so that the connection between the illustration and the idea is clear.

5. Afterwards, fill in the recall column with key words, phrases, or questions. Work out problems done in class on your own and check the solutions with your notes.

6. Use your lecture notes, textbook notes, homework problems, and quizzes to prepare for examinations.

7. Don't linger over test items that you do not know. Go on to the items that you are reasonably sure you can answer correctly. If you have time later, you can go back and ponder the items you don't know.